Criminology Interactive

Companion Text

Robert Mutchnick

Indiana University of Pennsylvania

Prentice Hall

Boston Columbus Indianapolis New York San Francisco Upper Saddle River

Amsterdam Cape Town Dubai London Madrid Milan Munich Paris Montreal Toronto

Delhi Mezico City Sao Paolo Sydney Hong Kong Seoul Singapore Taipei Tokyo

Editor in Chief: Vernon Anthony
Acquisitions Editor: Tim Peyton
Editorial Assistant: Lynda Cramer
Director of Marketing: David Gesell
Senior Marketing Manager: Adam Kloza
Senior Marketing Coordinator: Alicia Wozniak
Senior Managing Editor: JoEllen Gohr
Project Manager: Jessica H. Sykes
Senior Operations Supervisor: Pat Tonneman
Operations Specialist: Laura Weaver

Senior Art Director: Diane Ernsberger
Text Designer/Composition/Full-Service
   Project Manager: Naomi Sysak
Cover Art: Jeff Vanik
Cover Designer: Diane Lorenzo
Lead Media Project Manager: Karen Bretz
Printer/Binder: Bind-Rite Graphics/Robbinsville
Cover Printer: Coral Graphics
Text Font: Times Roman

10 9 8 7 6 5 4 3 2

Prentice Hall
is an imprint of

www.pearsonhighered.com

ISBN 10: 0-13-505723-X
ISBN 13: 978-0-13-505723-0

Contents

Chapter 2 ▪ The Classical Perspective

Chapter 3 ■ The Biological Perspective   35

Chapter 7 ■ Sociological Theories III: Social Conflict   **125**

Chapter 10 ■ Crimes Against Persons   203

Criminology Interactive: A User's Guide

CRIMINOLOGY INTERACTIVE: THE FIRST "HYBRID" TEXTBOOK

This companion text is designed to be used with *Criminology Interactive* online. Together, the *Criminology Interactive* online media (designed to encourage active learning) and this printed companion text (designed to make it easy to review key concepts) make up a "hybrid" learning system. Like hybrid cars, which utilize both gas and electricity to deliver an efficient driving experience, *Criminology Interactive* uses both interactive multimedia materials and a concise printed text to deliver an efficient (and engaging) learning experience.

HOW TO USE THE *CRIMINOLOGY INTERACTIVE* TEXT

Whereas *Criminology Interactive* online is designed to deliver an active and engaging learning experience, this companion text is designed to be used for reviewing key ideas and concepts when you are not online. Using this text, you can quickly find and review just the information you need. Features of the companion text include:

- *A concise and straightforward presentation of all key concepts in an outline format.* Instead of overwhelming you with too much text, this book includes just the facts and ideas that you need to know in order to succeed in this course.

- *A logical and easy-to-use organization.* All topics are presented in numbered modules. In addition to the Table of Contents, a Chapter Outline is included at the start of each chapter. These features make it easy to quickly find the material you are looking for.

- *"Key Ideas" and "Key Terms" at the beginning of each chapter.* These lists quickly summarize the important ideas and vocabulary that you will need to know in order to understand the concepts presented in each chapter.

- *Definitions of key terms in the margin next to where the term first appears, as well as in a comprehensive glossary at the end of the book.* Having key terms defined both when you first read them and again in a glossary at the back of the book makes reviewing key term definitions efficient and easy.

- *Icons throughout the text, which let you know when a video clip related to what you are reading about is available online.* After you've read about a topic, you can watch a video explanation online. This will help reinforce your understanding of what you have read.

- *Chapter Summaries and Review Questions.* These features will help you make sure that you have learned what you were supposed to in the chapter.

- *A list of application and review materials related to each chapter that are available online*. There are many resources available online to help you apply and review what you have read in the book. There is a handy list of these resources at the end of each chapter.

HOW TO USE *CRIMINOLOGY INTERACTIVE* ONLINE (WWW.PRENHALL.COM/CI)

The online companion to this printed text is a complete multimedia introduction to criminology. To access *Criminology Interactive* online, you will need to register at www.prenhall.com/ci with the access code that was included with this book. The access code is printed on the inside cover of this book.

At *Criminology Interactive* online you will navigate through a three-dimensional environment and enter virtual rooms where you will learn about various crime theories and types of crime. Each room includes a variety of multimedia resources:

- Brief lecture videos that introduce you to key ideas and concepts

- Crime scenario videos and case files that allow you to apply crime theories

- Quizzes and vocabulary review games to assess your understanding of the material

- Links to related Web sites to help you with online research for class assignments and papers

The purpose of the *Criminology Interactive* online is to provide you with an engaging introduction to criminology that encourages active learning by:

- *Presenting* key concepts

- Letting you *apply* key concepts

- Allowing you to *review* key concepts

Chapter 1

Criminology and Crime Theory

CHAPTER OUTLINE

KEY IDEAS

➤ Criminology is an academic discipline and a science. As a discipline, it seeks to educate. As a science, it relies on the scientific method as a way to analyze crime.

➤ Important to criminology is the way that crime is perceived. The consensus view looks at crime in terms of the consensus of morality in society. The conflict view holds that society is made up of diverse entities, and the definition of crime is determined by those of power or wealth.

➤ Criminology and criminal justice are related fields, but there are important differences. Criminology seeks to identify the origin of crime. Criminal justice focuses on the laws and policies that enforce the law.

➤ Criminologists study criminal behavior in an attempt to determine what causes crime.

➤ Also related to criminology are penology, the study of corrections and techniques of crime control, and victimology, which focuses on crime from the victim's point of view.

➤ A theory is a series of interrelated propositions that attempts to explain, predict, and control a series of events.

➤ Specialized definitions of theories include Talcott Parsons's definition that a theory is a logically interdependent generalized concept of empirical reference that can explain all behavior. Robert King Merton developed a similar definition of theory, but with the qualification that theory should be much more limited in scope.

➤ Deductive reasoning is an approach to developing theory that moves from given statements toward a set of conclusions. Inductive reasoning starts with an observation and then moves to patterns in the phenomenon observed.

➤ Theories help researchers by providing a framework for scientific inquiry. The process begins with a hypothesis that is then tested using various research methods.

➤ A conceptual scheme, which is used to build a theory, relies on descriptive comments, which label phenomena and operative concepts that distinguish the properties of a concept.

➤ Propositions are part of a deductive system that provides the grounds for prediction through the use of the scientific method.

KEY TERMS

conceptual scheme
conflict perspective
consensus perspective
criminal behavior
criminal justice
criminalization
criminology
deductive reasoning
deviant behavior
etiology
hypothesis
inductive reasoning
penology
propositions
research methods
scientific method
theory
victimology

1.0   Criminology and crime theory

1.1   **Criminology**

CRIMINOLOGY

An interdisciplinary profession built around the scientific study of crime and criminal behavior, including their form, causes, legal aspects, and control.

CRIMINAL BEHAVIOR

Behavior that violates the laws that society has mandated.

CRIMINAL JUSTICE

The scientific study of crime, the criminal law, and components of the criminal justice system, including the police, courts, and corrections.

SCIENTIFIC METHOD

A methodology that relies on observable, empirical, and measurable evidence to prove a hypothesis.

1.1.1   An academic discipline and science that addresses a wide range of questions/problems relating to crime, including the:

- Causes of **criminal behavior**
- Development of criminal law
- Methods of crime control
- Functioning of the **criminal justice** system

1.1.2   Criminology as an academic discipline

- An area of knowledge and study with specific programs and courses of study devoted to:
  - ❖ Disseminating this knowledge
  - ❖ Preparing individuals for careers in areas relating to crime and crime control

1.1.3   Criminology as a science

- Pursues knowledge about crime and its control through the **scientific method**
- Scientific method
  - ❖ The use of systematic techniques of observation to produce objective and verifiable information
  - ❖ How is the scientific method different from casual observation?
    - ◆ The collection of information is based on a plan
    - ◆ The plan specifies who/what will be observed and how many observations will occur.
    - ◆ The plan specifies the purpose of the observation.
    - ◆ The plan is adhered to as closely as possible to keep the process as objective as possible.
- The data is verified and determined to be valid.
- Criminologists use a wide range of specific scientific techniques for collecting data.

1.1.4   Criminology as an interdisciplinary science

- A variety of different disciplines based on common interests and concerns over crime control have come together to study and explain crime.
- The interdisciplinary nature of criminology is expressed in its various theories.

■ Some fields contributing to criminology include:

- ❖ Psychology
- ❖ Sociology
- ❖ Economics
- ❖ History
- ❖ Political science
- ❖ Anthropology
- ❖ Biology
- ❖ Chemistry

1.2 Perspectives on crime

1.2.1 The perspective on crime is an important consideration. It influences:

■ Data collection

■ Theories adopted

■ Policies supported/promoted

1.2.2 Different views of crime

■ **Consensus** vs. **conflict perspective**

- ❖ Consensus perspective (Siegel, 2007) is the most common view in criminology.
  - ◆ Society has consensus about values and beliefs.
  - ◆ These beliefs become the basis for criminal law.
  - ◆ Criminal law determines/defines crime.
  - ◆ Crimes are behaviors that violate criminal law.
  - ◆ Summary of consensus view
    - ❏ Crime is defined in terms of morality.
    - ❏ Criminal law protects society from disorder and decay.
- ❖ Conflict perspective
  - ◆ Society is made up of diverse groups with differing needs, beliefs, and morals.
  - ◆ The variations among groups sometimes create conflict.
  - ◆ Some groups accumulate more political power and use the law and the criminal justice system to maintain/advance their economic and social positions.
  - ◆ The powerful transform their beliefs into law and use the criminal justice system to enforce adherence to those beliefs.

CONSENSUS PERSPECTIVE

An analytical perspective on social organization, which holds that most members of society agree as to what is right and what is wrong, and that the various elements of society work together in unison toward a common and shared vision of the greater good.

CONFLICT PERSPECTIVE

A view based on the assumption that society is composed of diverse groups and that disagreement is common among people over laws and differences.

- ◆ Summary of conflict view
  - ❑ The definition of crime is determined by wealth/power.
  - ❑ Those in power use the law and criminal justice system to impose their beliefs on others.
  - ❑ Law and the criminal justice system are used to maintain/expand power/wealth.
- ■ Bierne and Messerschmidt (2000) present a different scheme for conceptualizing crime.
  - ❖ Crime can be viewed as:
    - ◆ A social problem
    - ◆ A legal category
    - ◆ Sociological definitions can include:
      - ❑ Violation of conduct norms
      - ❑ Social harm
      - ❑ Violation of human rights
      - ❑ A form of deviance
  - ◆ Bierne and Messerschmidt's conceptualization has some overlap with the consensus and conflict approaches.

1.3   Describing the discipline

     1.3.1   Criminology distinguished from criminal justice

- ■ Criminology and criminal justice are linked.
  - ❖ The concern over the crime problem in the 1960s created the rise of criminology as a separate discipline.
  - ❖ The Law Enforcement Assistance Administration (President's Commission on Law Enforcement and the Administration of Justice, 1967) provided:
    - ◆ Funding for research
    - ◆ Seed money to establish academic programs
    - ◆ Monies to support the purchase of equipment and to hire more personnel
  - ❖ Today, there are many academic programs in criminology/criminal justice.
    - ◆ These academic programs provide:
      - ❑ Research support for the criminal justice system
      - ❑ Education for individuals seeking careers in the criminal justice system
- ■ Important differences between criminology and criminal justice
  - ❖ Criminal justice
    - ◆ Agencies of social control that implement and enforce the law, and deal with those who violate the law

◆ Criminal justice researchers focus on:

   ❑ How agencies function

   ❑ Issues relating to crime control

❖ Criminology

   ◆ Is an academic discipline that has crime/criminal behavior as its subject matter

   ◆ Seeks to explain the **etiology** of crime and criminal behavior and the extent and nature of crime in society.

ETIOLOGY

The branch of knowledge that studies the cause or origin of various phenomena.

1.4   Distinctions between crime and deviance

1.4.1   **Deviant behavior**

■ Behavior that violates social norms

■ Behavior that deviates from standards of expected conduct

DEVIANCE or DEVIANT BEHAVIOR

Behavior that violates social norms.

1.4.2   Crime vs. deviance

■ Not all crimes are deviant or unusual acts.

■ Not all deviant acts are violations of the criminal law.

1.4.3   How behaviors come to be seen as crimes

■ Distinctions between crime and deviance lead criminologists to study the processes by which behaviors come to be seen as crime.

   ❖ This process is referred to as **criminalization**.

   ❖ There is great interest in how this process occurs, especially for behaviors that are not necessarily deviant and behaviors whose status changes from deviant to criminal.

CRIMINALIZATION

The process by which behavior is classified a crime.

1.5   What criminologists do

1.5.1   Study crime and criminal behavior

■ Both are often categorized as subfields of study.

1.5.2   Construct theories

■ Theories attempt to answer the question, "Why do people commit criminal acts?"

■ These theories reflect the personal beliefs, experiences, values, etc., of the criminologists who propose them.

1.5.3   Sociology of law

■ Considers how social forces shape the law and how the law shapes society

■ Creates a context for criminologists to debate and study the criminalization of behavior

1.5.4   Criminal behavior systems

- The study of or research on specific types of criminal behavior, including violent crime, theft, organized crime, etc., or even more specialized crimes, such as domestic violence, theft by computer, and gambling.

1.5.5   Criminal statistics

- Measures the amount, trends, and changes in criminal activity

- Addresses a variety of questions:
  - ❖   How much crime occurs annually?
  - ❖   Where do crimes occur?
  - ❖   Who commits most crimes?

- Reliable and valid measures of criminal behavior must be achieved, as they are crucial to criminological research and policy.

PENOLOGY

The study of the techniques of crime control, the punishment of criminals, and the management of prisons.

1.5.6   **Penology**

- The study of corrections and techniques of crime control

- Overlaps with criminal justice

- Considers research and policy-making on:
  - ❖   Rehabilitation and treatment programs
  - ❖   Capital punishment
  - ❖   Mandatory sentencing

VICTIMOLOGY

The study of victims and their contributory role, if any, in crime causation.

1.5.7   **Victimology**

- Proposes that the study of crime is not complete unless the victim's role is considered

- Four basic areas of victimology:
  - ❖   Victim surveys that measure the extent and nature of crime
  - ❖   Assessing risk
  - ❖   Examining what precipitated the crime for the victim
  - ❖   Designing services for crime victims

1.6   Criminology as a science

1.6.1   Ultimate goal of all science is to:

- Create a better understanding of the world.

- Help solve problems.

- Improve the human condition.

1.6.2   To accomplish these goals, a science must:

- Describe phenomena.

- Identify/explain causal relationships.

1.6.3   **Theory** plays a key role in the pursuit and satisfaction of these goals.

For more on theory, visit Criminology Interactive online > Introduction to Theory > What Is Theory?: What Is Theory?

1.7   What is theory, and what does it do?

1.7.1   Definitions from various theorists

- Talcott Parsons (1949)

    ❖ A theory is a logically interdependent and generalized concept of empirical reference.

    ❖ Parsons believed that a single grand theory could be developed that would explain all behavior.

- Robert King Merton (1947)

    ❖ Theory is a set of logically interconnected concepts that are limited in scope.

    ❖ Merton did not believe it was possible to have a single theory that could explain all behavior.

- Jonathan Turner (1974)

    ❖ Theory is the means by which science realizes its three main goals:

        ◆ Clarify and organize events

        ◆ Explain and predict

        ◆ Demonstrate understanding

    ❖ Turner defines theory in terms of what it intends to accomplish rather than what comprises it.

- John Braithwaite (1953)

    ❖ Theory is an explanation of phenomenon through the use of a **deductive reasoning** system.

For more on theory, visit Criminology Interactive online > Introduction to Theory > What Is Theory?: Definition of Theory.

1.7.2   Deductive vs. **inductive reasoning**

- Deductive reasoning starts with a theory and then moves to the development of an **hypothesis**, which leads to observations, and finally to the confirmation, rejection, or modification of the original theory.

THEORY

A series of interrelated propositions that attempt to describe, explain, predict, and ultimately control some class of events. A theory gains explanatory power from inherent logical consistency, and is "tested" by how well it describes and predicts reality.

DEDUCTIVE REASONING

Reasoning that moves from given statements toward conclusions.

INDUCTIVE REASONING

Reasoning moves from an observation to arrive at a hypothesis, and then a theory.

HYPOTHESIS

(1) An explanation that accounts for a set of facts, which can be tested by further investigation. (2) Something that is taken to be true for the purpose of argument or investigation.

- Inductive reasoning starts with an observation, after which the researcher looks for patterns.
  - ❖ These patterns lead to the development of a tentative hypothesis, and eventually to the development of a general theory.
- When comparing the two approaches, deductive reasoning is considered to be more narrow and top-down, while inductive reasoning is considered to be more open and bottom-up.

1.8   Link between theory and research

   1.8.1   Theories are symbolic guides to observation, interpretation, and explanation of a specific phenomenon.

   1.8.2   Theories help researchers

- Provides a framework for asking questions
  - ❖ Specific questions that are derived from theory are called hypotheses.
    - ◆ Definition of hypothesis
      - ❏ An explanation for a set of facts that can be tested and measured
      - ❏ A hypothesis is a prediction about what causes something to happen.
- Research is done to test hypotheses/theories.
  - ❖ Theories are neither facts nor truths.
    - ◆ Theories are potential explanations.
    - ◆ Research is done to find out how true they are.
  - ❖ Data are collected to see if what the theory predicted actually exists.
- The specific ways that data are collected are the **research methods**.
- Theory impacts research and research impacts theory.
  - ❖ If the data are consistent with the hypothesis, the theory is supported.
  - ❖ If the data are not consistent with the hypothesis, then the theory may need to be modified.

RESEARCH METHODS
The various methods that structure and offer logic to data gathering.

   For more on theory, visit Criminology Interactive online > Introduction to Theory > What Is Theory?: Hypothesis.

1.9   General characteristics of a theory

   1.9.1   Theories are built from concepts.

- Generally, concepts denote or point to a phenomenon.

- Concepts isolate features of the world that are important to the theory at hand. Example:
  - ❖ Notions of atoms, protons, neutrons and the like are concepts.

- Familiar criminological concepts can include:
  - ❖ Group
  - ❖ Norm
  - ❖ Role
  - ❖ Status
  - ❖ Crime
  - ❖ Criminal
  - ❖ Offender

 For more on concepts, visit Criminology Interactive online > Introduction to Theory > What Is Theory?: Introduction to Concepts.

1.9.2   **Conceptual scheme** (a set of concepts)

- When used to build a theory, two general types of concepts can be distinguished:
  - ❖ Descriptive concepts
    - ◆ Demonstrate what the theory is about
    - ◆ Label phenomena and allow us to distinguish properties
    - ◆ Examples of descriptive concepts:
      - ❏ Individualism
      - ❏ Suicide
      - ❏ Protestantism
      - ❏ Dog
      - ❏ Cat
      - ❏ Group
      - ❏ Social class
    - ◆ Dog is an example of a descriptive concept because one is able to describe characteristics that describe the concept of "dog."
      - ❏ Four legs
      - ❏ Tail
      - ❏ Snout
      - ❏ Hair/fur
      - ❏ Barks
  - ❖ Operative concepts
    - ◆ Properties of nature
    - ◆ This form of variable allows us to distinguish properties.
    - ◆ These types of concepts are variables.

CONCEPTUAL SCHEME

A set of concepts used to build a theory.

- ◆ Examples of operative concepts:
  - ❏ Suicide rate
  - ❏ Incidence of Protestantism
  - ❏ Dogs
  - ❏ Cats
  - ❏ Groups
  - ❏ Social classes
- ◆ Dog*s* is an operative concept because it allows us to categorize different types of dogs into a single category, "dogs."
  - ❏ Collie
  - ❏ Setter
  - ❏ Poodle
  - ❏ German Shepherd

- A conceptual scheme alone is insufficient to constitute a theory.

For more on variables, visit Criminology Interactive online > Introduction to Theory > What Is Theory?: Variables.

1.9.3   Statements

- Concepts are organized into groups of statements.
  - ❖ Existence statements:
    - ◆ Indicate when and where in the world instances of a particular concept can be found
  - ❖ Relational statements:
    - ◆ State how the relationships between or among concepts can be predicted and explained
    - ◆ Consider concepts, denoting variable properties of phenomena, and help researchers make conjectures about how one variable may be caused by another
    - ◆ Types of relational statements
      - ❏ Associational relational statements
        - • Statements that stop short of proclaiming that variations in one phenomenon cause variations in another
      - ❏ Causal relational statements
        - • One set of variable properties denoted by one concept is seen as causing the occurrence of other variable properties denoted by another concept.

For more on statements, visit Criminology Interactive online > Introduction to Theory > What Is Theory?: Statements.

1.9.4   **Propositions**

- Propositions state a relationship between at least two properties.

- Propositions form a deductive system.
    - ❖ A deductive system also provides grounds for prediction.

- Contingent propositions
    - ❖ Some of the propositions of a scientific theory must be contingent in the sense that experience is relevant to their truth or to that of propositions derived from them.

- Noncontingent propositions
    - ❖ Propositions of this type are noncontingent in that experience is irrelevant to their truth.

- Higher-order propositions
    - ❖ More general propositions are called "higher-order" propositions.

- Lower-order propositions
    - ❖ Less general propositions are called "lower-order" or "empirical" propositions.

1.9.5   Power of a theory

- A wide variety of empirical propositions may be derived from a few higher-order propositions under different given conditions.

1.9.6   Completeness of a theory

- George Casper Homans
    - ❖ Claimed that theories could never be complete
    - ❖ The most general propositions in the theory, as formulated, may themselves be explainable by another, still more general set of propositions.
    - ❖ Some of the lower-order propositions in a theory are often themselves explainable by deductive systems, though the theorist for one reason or another may not want to explain them.

For more on what makes a good theory, visit Criminology Interactive online > Introduction to Theory > What Is Theory?: What Is Good Theory?

For more on how theory affects research and policy, visit Criminology Interactive online > Introduction to Theory > What Is Theory?: Theory, Research, and Policy.

PROPOSITION

A statement that indicates a relationship between at least two properties.

CHAPTER SUMMARY

➤ Criminology is an academic discipline and a science that offers a systematic way to understand crime and criminal behavior. As an academic discipline, its purpose is to educate others about crime and its origins. As a scientific discipline, it encompasses other disciplines in both behavioral and social science. As a science, criminology also employs the scientific method to pursue knowledge of crime, its control, and its origin through systematic methods of observation.

➤ There are two major views on the cause of crime: The consensus perspective claims that a society is a cohesive unit and its members have the same beliefs in terms of norms of behavior and morality. These beliefs become the basis for criminal law. Criminal behavior, then, violates the legal requirements of that society. The conflict view, on the other hand, sees society as groups of diverse people with social values that conflict with one another. That conflict leads to crime. Those with wealth and power within the society, it follows, determine the nature of crime.

➤ Criminology and criminal justice are linked. While criminology attempts to understand the origin of crime and its extent in society, criminal justice is concerned with implementing and enforcing the law. As such, criminal justice focuses on how various agencies control crime. Important to any understanding of criminology and criminal behavior is an understanding of the relationship between crime and deviance.

➤ Deviance is any behavior that violates the norms and expectations of a society or community as a whole. Criminal behavior, on the other hand, violates the laws of society. The process by which behavior becomes a crime is called criminalization, and is a primary concern of criminology.

➤ Criminologists study crime and criminal behavior in all of its many facets. Using scientific research methods, they construct theories about the causes of crime. That research may involve studies of legal and judicial issues, specific types of criminal behavior, criminal statistics, correctional systems, and victims of crime. Penology, the study of corrections and techniques of crime control, and victimology, which focuses on crime from the victim's point of view, are two specialized areas of interest in criminology.

➤ The ultimate goal of all science, including criminology, is to create a better understanding of the world, to help solve problems, and to improve the human condition. In order to do this, science must describe phenomena and explain causal relationships. Theory helps to satisfy these goals.

➤ There are several specialized definitions of theory. Talcott Parsons considers theory to be a logically interdependent generalized concept of empirical reference. Parsons asserted that a single grand theory could be developed to explain all behavior. Robert King Merton considered theory to be a set of logically interconnected concepts that were more limited in scope. Jonathan Turner suggested that theory has three goals: to clarify and organize, to explain and predict, and to demonstrate understanding. John Braithwaite claimed theory was an explanation of phenomenon using a deductive system.

➤ Deductive and inductive reasoning are two approaches to developing theory. Deductive reasoning moves from the more general to the specific, starting with a theory and then developing a hypothesis, which leads to observations. Finally, this process leads to confirming or disproving the theory. Inductive reasoning starts with an observation, after which the researcher looks for patterns in the phenomenon observed. This leads to a tentative hypothesis, and eventually to a more general theory.

➤ Theories help researchers by providing a framework for inquiry. The specific questions that are derived from theory are called hypotheses, and these hypotheses need to be tested. Theories in and of themselves are not facts, but provide potential explanations. Research is then done to determine how true the theory is. The research method is a specific way that data are collected. Research affects theory and theory impacts research. Data that is consistent with the hypothesis shows that the theory is supported. If the hypothesis is not supported, the theory must undergo modification.

➤ Theories are built from concepts that denote or point to a phenomenon. A conceptual scheme is a set of concepts that is used to build a theory. Descriptive concepts label phenomena. Operative concepts distinguish the properties of a concept. Both descriptive concepts and operative concepts help define and demonstrate a theory.

➤ Concepts are organized into groups of statements. Existence statements show where and when a particular concept can be found. Relational statements show how one variable in a concept affects another.

➤ Propositions form a deductive system that provides grounds for prediction through the use of the scientific method. Contingent propositions rely on experience to determine whether they are true or false. Non-contingent propositions consider experience irrelevant. Higher-order propositions are more general, while less general propositions are called "lower-order" or empirical.

STUDY QUESTIONS

1. What are the differences between the consensus and the conflict perspective?
2. What are the distinctions between criminology and criminal justice?
3. How is deviant behavior different from criminal behavior?
4. What is the goal of a criminologist?
5. What does penology study?
6. Victimology focuses on crime from whose point of view?
7. What is the primary difference between Talcott Parsons's definition of theory and Robert Merton's definition of theory?
8. What are the differences between deductive and inductive reasoning?
9. What is a hypothesis? What role does a hypothesis play in a theory?
10. What are concepts? How do descriptive concepts differ from operative concepts?

ONLINE@CRIMINOLOGY INTERACTIVE

Build a Theory

Chapter 2

The Classical
Perspective

CHAPTER OUTLINE

KEY IDEAS

➤ The classical perspective, first developed in the eighteenth century, is based on five major principles: rationality, hedonism, punishment, human rights, and due process.

➤ Fundamental to the classical perspective is the notion that human beings have free will and their actions are the result of their own choices.

➤ Cesare Beccaria, a major theorist of the Classical School, based his ideas on Rousseau's *Social Contract*. Beccaria published *Essays on Crimes and Punishments*, which laid the foundation for punishment as a deterrent and set forth the notion that guilt had to be proven.

➤ Jeremy Bentham developed the notion of hedonistic principle, which suggested that human beings make decisions based on whether their decision would cause more pain than pleasure.

➤ In the nineteenth century, neoclassicism emerged, which contended that free will is limited and that individuals make decisions about their behavior based on a set of available options.

➤ The routine activities theory was proposed in 1979 by Lawrence Cohen and Marcus Felson as a variation of the classical perspective.

KEY TERMS

capable guardian
capital punishment
classical perspective
deterrence
hedonistic calculus
neoclassical perspective
Panopticon House
rationality
routine activities theory
social contract
utilitarianism

2.0   Classical perspective

2.1   Major principles

2.1.1   **Rationality**

- Human beings have free will, which means that the actions they undertake are the result of their choice.

2.1.2   Hedonism

- Pleasure and pain, or reward and punishment, determine human behavior.

- **Hedonistic calculus**
  - ❖ Concept originated by Jeremy Bentham
  - ❖ Criminal weighs in his or her mind the possible pain of punishment against any pleasures thought to be derived from committing the crime before deciding to commit it.
  - ❖ Fear of punishment is part of the hedonistic calculus.
    - ◆ If the potential gain is greater, the individual chooses crime.
    - ◆ If the potential punishment (pain) is greater, the individual controls behavior.

2.1.3   Punishment

- Criminal punishment is a deterrent to unlawful behavior, and **deterrence** is the best justification for punishment.

- Punishment is an effective deterrent if it is appropriately severe, swift, and certain.

2.1.4   Human rights

- Society is made possible by individuals cooperating together.
  - ❖ Society should provide its citizens respect for their rights in the face of government action and for their autonomy, as long as this autonomy can be secured without angering others or negatively affecting the greater good.

2.1.5   Due process

- An accused should be presumed innocent until proved otherwise.

- An accused should not be subject to punishment before guilt is lawfully established.

For more an introduction to the Classical School, visit the Criminology Interactive online > Classical School > Theory Explained: Basic Principles.

2.2   Classical School

2.2.1   Cesare Beccaria (1738–1794)

MAJOR IMPACT: Cesare Beccaria, an Italian who was trained in Catholic schools and earned a doctor of laws degree at 18, developed early ideas on laws and the justice system based on the notion of free will and derived, in part, from Jean-Jacques Rousseau's the *Social Contract* (1762).

SELECTED PUBLICATION: *Essays on Crimes and Punishments* (1764)

■ The naturalists

  ❖ A group of philosophers who claimed that society was ordered, and that this order was not determined by religion or an allegiance to God.

■ Based ideas, in part, on the *Social Contract* (1762), written by Jean-Jacques Rousseau. **The social contract** contends that:

  ❖ An individual is bound to society only by his consent, and society is then responsible to the individual, as well as the reverse.

  ❖ Each individual surrenders only enough freedom to the state to make society viable.

  ❖ The only natural form of society is the family.

    ◆ Children are only bound to the family as long as there is need; the father is only responsible to care for the family for the same length of time.

      ❑ If the family stays together after dependence is no longer needed, they are doing so voluntarily.

  ❖ According to Rousseau, the social contract provides the solution to the following problem:

    ◆ "to find a form of association which will defend and protect with the whole common force the person and goods each associate, and in which each, while uniting himself with all, may still obey himself alone, and remain free as before" (1762, Book 1, Chapter 7)

  ❖ The social contract created the basis for the establishment of the state.

    ◆ Those governed must consent to be governed.

    ◆ This, in turn, creates the position of sovereignty.

SOCIAL CONTRACT

The Enlightenment concept that human beings abandon their natural state of individual freedom to join together and form a society. Although individuals surrender some freedoms to society as a whole in the process of forming a social contract, government, once formed, is obligated to assume responsibilities toward its citizens and to provide for their protection and welfare.

- In *Essays on Crimes and Punishments* (1764), Beccaria offered his observations on laws and the justice system.

  - ❖ Legitimate punishment must come from the law that represents the wishes of the people.

  - ❖ Laws must be made by a legislative body to ensure their impartiality.

    - ◆ The person who makes the law should not also enforce the law. If a sovereign exists, magistrates, not the sovereign, should enforce the law.

    - ◆ The magistrate, an independent third party, is charged with determining the truth.

    - ◆ Magistrates do not interpret the law; they are only responsible for its application.

    - ◆ Punishments must be appropriate to the offense and no greater than necessary to preserve the peace and security of society.

    - ◆ Punishments for the same offense must be the same for all regardless of the offender's station in life.

- Proof of guilt

  - ❖ Beccaria identifies two types of guilt:

    - ◆ Perfect guilt

      - ❏ In this type of guilt, there is no possibility of innocence.

      - ❏ Perfect guilt is most closely associated with today's concept of "proof beyond a reasonable doubt."

      - ❏ In most cases, there is no perfect guilt.

    - ◆ Imperfect guilt

      - ❏ Many types of imperfect proofs are necessary to constitute a "perfect" proof.

        - • Many pieces of evidence when taken collectively are able to acceptably establish guilt.

        - • When taken individually, each piece of evidence is not in and of itself sufficient to establish guilt.

      - ❏ Imperfect guilt is most closely associated with today's concept of "probable cause."

- The jury

  - ❖ Beccaria called for a panel of peers.

  - ❖ When a crime involves two citizens, Beccaria proposed that the jury be equally divided between the peers of both the defendant and the victim.

  - ❖ Defendants should have the right to reject a potential juror if they suspect he is not impartial.

- Witnesses
  - ❖ Credibility of a witness was an important factor for Beccaria.
  - ❖ Number of witnesses each side used could potentially influence the outcome of the trial.
    - ◆ If the number of witnesses the prosecution and defense present are equal, it would be difficult, if not impossible, for a magistrate to determine guilt.
    - ◆ Therefore, if a magistrate is to make a judgment, one side needs to have one more witness than the other side.

- Secret accusations and torture
  - ❖ Torture is an inappropriate measure to be taken against suspected criminals.
    - ◆ A person who is suspected of a crime is not a criminal until he has been convicted in a court.
    - ◆ Torture could compel a weak, but innocent individual to confess to a crime he did not commit, while a strong but guilty person might be able to withstand the torture and thereby be set free.
      - ❏ If the accused person who is actually innocent is able to withstand the torture and is set free, he has then suffered punishment he did not deserve.

- Torture is inappropriate because it relies on pain and suffering to determine the truth rather than evidence.

- Interrogations
  - ❖ Individuals who refuse to answer questions, according to Beccaria, should be punished, a punishment that is fixed by law.
  - ❖ If the individual is guilty beyond a reasonable doubt, then no additional punishment for refusing to answer questions is needed.
  - ❖ In the same way that confessions are not necessary when there is proof beyond a reasonable doubt, interrogations are useless for those whose guilt is established by other forms of evidence.
  - ❖ Beccaria expected individuals to deny their guilt. In fact, claiming innocence was in the best interest of the individual given the procedures used by the justice system.

- Oaths were useless because they did not compel individuals to tell the truth.

- Right to appeal
  - ❖ Individuals should have the right to present new evidence that would support their contention of innocence.
  - ❖ While a defendant should be allowed to present his defense, it should be brief so that the punishment can be prompt if the person is found to be guilty.

- Promptness of punishment
  - ❖ The more promptly and closely punishment follows the commission of a crime, the more just and useful it will be. (Beccaria, 1963, p. 55)
  - ❖ "When the length of time that passes between the punishment and the misdeed is less, so much stronger and more lasting in the human mind is the association of these two ideas, crime and punishment." (Beccaria, 1963, p. 56)

- Mildness of punishments
  - ❖ For Beccaria, the only appropriate punishment is that which is necessary to prevent new or additional crime and deter others from committing similar acts.
  - ❖ Individuals (criminals) sometimes commit additional crimes to try to avoid punishment for the first crime, because the punishment is so severe.

- Certainty of punishment
  - ❖ Certainty of punishment is more important than the intensity of the punishment.
  - ❖ An actual punishment, even if it is mild, will make a stronger and more lasting impression than the threat of a stronger punishment.
  - ❖ The more immediately after a behavior the punishment occurs, the greater its impact.
  - ❖ The greater the probability of the punishment occurring is, the greater the impact it will have.
  - ❖ If a person believes that he is not likely to be punished or that he can talk his way out of the punishment, then the fear of the occurrence of punishment is not sufficient to deter him from committing the crime.
  - ❖ The inevitability of punishment is a necessity if the system is designed to deter individuals from engaging in criminal activity.
  - ❖ "The right to inflict punishment is a right not of an individual, but of all citizens, of their sovereign. An individual can renounce his own portion of right, but cannot annul that of others." (Beccaria, 1963, p. 58)

- Death penalty
  - ❖ Beccaria opposed the death penalty, and instead proposed life imprisonment.
  - ❖ Beccaria could permit the death penalty if it is the only way of keeping other individuals from committing crimes.

- Classification of crime
  - According to Beccaria, there are three types of crimes:
    - Those that threaten security of the state
      - These are considered the most serious because they threaten the existence of the state. These include high treason.
    - Those that injure citizens or their property such as murder, robbery, burglary, and aggravated assault
    - Those that are contrary to the social order, such as rabble rousing or inciting disorder
  - Beccaria also singled out specific crimes, including:
    - Injuries to honor
      - Acts that cause injury to honor should be punished with disgrace.
    - Theft
      - Fines should be the appropriate punishment and should be used to make restitution to the victim.
    - Smuggling
      - Considered a crime of the second magnitude
      - Beccaria adopted this position on smuggling because those who engage in this crime do not realize the damage that can result from the act since the consequences are remote.

- The measure of crimes
  - The actions of an individual are of utmost importance.
  - What is the actual degree of injury or harm that is done to society by the criminal act?
    - Intent was not Beccaria's concern; only whether or not the person committed the act.

- Beccaria believed the punishment should fit the crime.
  - Individuals should be punished based on the degree of injury they caused.
  - Purpose of punishment should be deterrence.
    - Punishment should be imposed to prevent offenders from committing additional crimes.
    - Types of deterrence
      - General
        - Focus is on preventing others from committing crimes.
        - Individual who committed a crime is punished in a public setting to discourage others from engaging in illegal behavior.

◻ Specific

- Focus is on the individual offender.
- Intent is to prevent the individual from committing another crime.

❖ Only the legislature can specify a punishment.

❖ The law must apply equally to all citizens, and no defenses for criminal acts are permitted.

❖ The court determines the guilt or innocence.

❖ Judges are instruments of the law.

❖ The law is structured, and theoretically impartial.

❖ The person who chooses to do wrong deserves to be punished.

For more on Cesare Beccaria, visit Criminology Interactive online > Classical School > Theory Explained: Cesare Beccaria.

2.2.2   Jeremy Bentham (1748–1832)

MAJOR IMPACT: Jeremy Bentham, a British philosopher who was trained in law, introduced the notion of the hedonistic principle. It contended that individuals make decisions about their behavior based on whether the incident would cause more pleasure than pain, and vice versa. Bentham also introduced utilitarianism, the philosophy that society should be based on the greatest good for the greatest number.

SELECTED PUBLICATION: *Introduction to the Principles of Morals and Legislation* (written in 1780, not published until 1789)

■ Hedonism

❖ Pain of crime commission must outweigh pleasure derived from criminal activity.

❖ Considers human beings as fundamentally rational, and that criminals will weigh in their minds the pain of punishment against any pleasures

❖ Seeking pleasures while avoiding pains are the ends sought.

- If it is a consideration of a single person, the "value of a pleasure or pain considered by itself will be greater or less, according to the four following circumstances:" (Bentham, 1789, Chapter IV, Section II)

  ◻ Its intensity
  ◻ Its duration
  ◻ Its certainty or uncertainty
  ◻ Its propinquity or remoteness

- ◆ If it is a consideration of a number of persons "with reference to each to whom to the value of a pleasure or a pain is considered, it will be greater or less, according to seven circumstances:" (Bentham, 1789, Chapter IV, Section IV)
  - ❏ Its intensity
  - ❏ Its duration
  - ❏ Its certainty or uncertainty
  - ❏ Its propinquity or remoteness
  - ❏ Its fecundity
  - ❏ Its purity
  - ❏ Its extent, the number of persons to whom it extends, (in other words), who are affected by it (Bentham, 1789, Chapter IV, Section IV)

- ❖ The pleasures to which human nature is susceptible include:
  - ◆ Sense
  - ◆ Wealth
  - ◆ Skill
  - ◆ Amity
  - ◆ Good name
  - ◆ Power
  - ◆ Piety
  - ◆ Benevolence
  - ◆ Malevolence
  - ◆ Memory
  - ◆ Imagination
  - ◆ Expectation
  - ◆ Dependent on association
  - ◆ Relief

- ❖ The pains to which human nature is susceptible include:
  - ◆ Privation
  - ◆ The senses
  - ◆ Awkwardness
  - ◆ Enmity
  - ◆ An ill name
  - ◆ Piety
  - ◆ Benevolence
  - ◆ Malevolence
  - ◆ Memory

- ◆ Imagination
- ◆ Expectation
- ◆ Dependent on association
- ❖ The pleasures of sense include:
  - ◆ The taste of palate, including whatever pleasures are experienced in satisfying the appetites of hunger and thirst
  - ◆ Intoxication
  - ◆ The organ of smelling
  - ◆ The touch
  - ◆ Simple pleasures of the ear; independent of association
  - ◆ Simple pleasures of the eye; independent of association
  - ◆ The sexual sense
  - ◆ Health, or the internal pleasurable feeling or flow of spirits (as it is called), which accompanies a state of full health and vigor, especially at times of moderate bodily exertion
  - ◆ Novelty, or the pleasures derived from the gratification of the appetite of curiosity, by the application of new objects to any of the senses
- ❖ Bentham holds that when punishment is to be considered for an act, four articles need to be considered (Bentham, 1789, Chapter VII, Section VI):
  - ◆ The act itself, which is done
  - ◆ The circumstances in which it is done
  - ◆ The intentionality that may have accompanied it
  - ◆ The consciousness, unconsciousness, or false consciousness that may have accompanied it

- **Utilitarianism**
  - ❖ The greatest good for the greatest number
- Bentham distinguished between 11 different types of punishment:
  - ❖ **Capital punishment**, or death
  - ❖ Afflictive punishment, which includes whipping and starvation
  - ❖ Indelible punishment, which includes branding, amputation, and mutilation
  - ❖ Ignominious punishment, or public punishment involving use of stocks or pillory
  - ❖ Penitential punishment, whereby the offender might be censured by his community
  - ❖ Chronic punishment, such as banishment, exile, or imprisonment

UTILITARIANISM

The belief first proposed by Jeremy Bentham, that behavior holds value to any individual undertaking it according to the amount of pleasure or pain that it can be expected to produce for that person.

CAPITAL PUNISHMENT

The killing of a person by judicial process for retribution and incapacitation.

❖ Restrictive punishment, such as license revocation or administrative sanction

❖ Compulsive punishment, which requires an offender to perform a certain action to make restitution

❖ Pecuniary punishment, which involves use of fines

❖ Quasi-pecuniary punishment, in which the offender is denied services that would otherwise be available to him

❖ Characteristic punishment, such as mandating that prison uniforms be worn by incarcerated offenders

■ **Panopticon House**

❖ Bentham suggested a specific design for a prison that consisted of a circular building with cells along the circumference.

❖ Each cell would be clearly visible from a central location staffed by guards.

❖ Prisons should be constructed near or within cities so they may serve as examples of what would happen to people who commit crimes.

❖ Prisons should be managed by contractors who could profit from the labor of prisoners.

❖ While a Panopticon was never built in England, a modified version was built in France, and three prisons modeled after the Panopticon were constructed in the United States.

For more on Jeremy Bentham, visit the Criminology Interactive online > Classical School > Theory Explained: Jeremy Bentham.

2.2.3   Neoclassical perspective

■ Flourished during the nineteenth century and focused on the notion of free will

❖ People choose behaviors from available options.

■ Viewed penalties that resulted from classical doctrine as too severe and all-encompassing for humanitarian spirit of the time

■ Emphasized the need for an individual reaction to offenders

■ Called for criminal codes to permit more judicial discretion, although only under objective circumstances

■ The intent of the offender was not considered.

■ Children under 7 years of age were exempt from the law because they were thought to be unable to understand the difference between right and wrong.

PANOPTICON HOUSE
A prison designed by Jeremy Bentham, which was to be a circular building with cells along the circumference, each clearly visible from a central location staffed by guards.

NEOCLASSICAL PERSPECTIVE
A contemporary version of classical criminology, which emphasizes deterrence and retribution with reduced emphasis on rehabilitation.

- Mental disease or insanity could be a reason to exempt a suspect from conviction.

- Doctrine of free will could no longer stand alone as an explanation for criminal behavior.

For more on the neoclassical perspective, visit Criminology Interactive online > Classical School > Theory Explained: Neoclassical School.

2.3 Routine activities theory

2.3.1 Lawrence Cohen and Marcus Felson

MAJOR IMPACT: Cohen and Felson developed the routine activities theory based on a rational choice model, with individuals making decisions using some conscious thought process prior to engaging in criminal activity.

PUBLICATION: "Social Change and Crime Rate Trends: A Routine Activity Approach," *American Sociological Review* (Vol. 44, No. 4:588)

- Human beings engage in movements that occur repetitively over time.
    - ❖ Daily life is a predictable pattern of events.
    - ❖ This regular pattern of activity is necessary to meet family, work, and play obligations.

- Routine activities "include formalized work, as well as the provision of standard food, shelter, sexual outlet, leisure, social interaction, learning, and child-rearing." (Cohen and Felson, 1979, p. 593)

- While patterned activities can become efficient in accomplishing tasks, they can also have dysfunctional and problematic qualities that engage people in dangerous and criminal situations.

2.3.2 Elements of routine activities theory

- Routine activities theory indicates that three elements need to occur for a crime to take place.
    - ❖ Motivated offenders
    - ❖ Suitable targets
    - ❖ Absence of **capable guardians**

- Motivated offender
    - ❖ The individual must be motivated enough to commit the crime.
    - ❖ For an individual to be a motivated offender, two things are necessary:
        - ◆ An interest in breaking the law
            - ❐ While a person may have the skills necessary to commit the crime, he may not be motivated to engage in criminal activity.

CAPABLE GUARDIAN

A person, who if present, could prevent the occurrence of the crime.

- ◆ The ability to break the law
    - ❑ Certain crimes may require a level of knowledge or capability that not all individuals have:
        - • Education
        - • Training
        - • Technique

- ■ Suitable targets
    - ❖ There are different categories of targets: people, objects, and places.
    - ❖ The suitability of a target has been explained by the acronym VIVA, which stands for:
        - ◆ Value
            - ❑ Dependent on the assessment of the individual considering the criminal act, not on the actual economic value assigned by society
        - ◆ Inertia
            - ❑ Dependent on the actual size of the target
        - ◆ Visibility
            - ❑ The potential offender knows the location of the target he is interested in.
        - ◆ Accessibility
            - ❑ Involves two elements:
                - • Getting to the target
                - • Escaping from the target
    - ❖ The suitability of a target can change based on the location of the person or object.
        - ◆ Target access may change by reducing escape routes or adding alarms or other security devices.

- ■ Absence of capable guardians
    - ❖ Capable guardians can include:
        - ◆ Friends
        - ◆ Neighbors
        - ◆ Co-workers
        - ◆ Police/security officers
        - ◆ Electronic equipment such as alarms and closed-circuit television cameras

- ■ Convergence
    - ❖ Three factors must all occur for the individual to commit the crime: a motivated offender, a suitable target, and the absence of capable guardians.
    - ❖ If there is a lack of any of these elements, the crime will not occur.

ROUTINE ACTIVITIES THEORY
A brand of rational choice theory, which suggests that lifestyles contribute significantly to both the volume and type of crime found in any society.

❖ The convergence of the requirements is based on the routine activities in which people engage.

◆ Routine activities are the everyday activities such as school, work, and home.

❖ **Routine activities theory** is considered very useful in explaining both employee theft and corporate crimes.

CHAPTER SUMMARY

➤ The classical perspective, which was developed in the eighteenth century, is based on five major principles. Rationality held that all human beings have free will and choose how they behave. From this overarching view, the classical perspective developed views on issues of punishment, human rights, and due process. The hedonistic calculus proposes that an individual weighs his choices based on the possibility of punishment or pain. If the potential gain is greater than the punishment, the criminal chooses to commit the crime. Punishment, then, is a deterrent to unlawful behaviors if it is swift, appropriate, and certain. This perspective takes a strong position on human rights, claiming that society has an obligation to its citizens to respect their rights and their autonomy as long as this does not interfere with the greater good. Finally, the classical perspective contends that an individual has the right to due process—presumed innocent until proven guilty.

➤ One of the major theorists of the classical school, Cesare Beccaria, based his ideas on Jean-Jacques Rousseau's *Social Contract*, which contended that the individual was bound to society by his consent and therefore society was responsible to the individual, as well as the reverse. For the classicist, this meant that only the state could punish the individual. Punishment, according to Beccaria, was an effective deterrent if it was prompt, certain, inevitable, and of appropriate severity to fit the crime. Becarria was fundamentally opposed to the death penalty on the grounds that the state does not have the right to take lives, and that capital punishment is not a useful or necessary form of punishment. Beccaria also described how proof of guilt should be achieved: through a jury of peers with evidence presented, and ultimately, a right of appeal. Beccaria condemned torture and secret accusations as a way to prove guilt.

➤ Jeremy Bentham also made major contributions to the classical perspective. It was Bentham who developed the concept of "hedonistic calculus," which suggested that when human beings make choices, they calculate whether the pleasure derived from a criminal choice outweighs the pain of the ensuing punishment. Bentham further refined this notion by identifying when and how human beings weighed pleasure, and identified 12 pains and 14 pleasures. Bentham is probably best known for his development of and advocacy for utilitarianism, a philosophy that argues that any decision or policy should represent the greatest good for the greatest number of people.

➤ During the nineteenth century, the notion of free will was re-examined by the neoclassicists. While the classicists believed that people made choices based on unlimited options, the neoclassical perspective believed in limited free will; that is, people choose their behavior from a number of available options. Like the classicists, the intent to commit a crime is not relevant to the judgment of the crime itself. The neoclassicists also were the first to recognize mental disease as a defense in a crime, and developed the standard that for an individual to be proven guilty, he would have to know the quality of the act as well as the difference between what is right and wrong.

➤ The routine activities theory proposed by Lawrence Cohen and Marcus Felson in 1979 is an application of the classical perspective of criminology that considers routine activities, or lifestyle issues, as a factor in crime. The routine activities theory suggests that three things need to occur for a crime to take place: a motivated offender, suitable target, and the absence of a capable guardian.

STUDY QUESTIONS

1. What is free will? How does it help define the classical perspective?
2. Which elements of the *Social Contract* did Beccaria use to develop his theories of justice and punishment?
3. What is the premise of the "hedonistic calculus"?
4. How is the neoclassicists's view of free will different from that of the classicists?
5. What are the elements that characterize the routine activities theory?

ONLINE@CRIMINOLOGY INTERACTIVE

Theory in Action

Case File #1: Crack Dealer—John
Case File #2: Joy Rider—Peter

Review

Vocabulary Shootout
Essay Questions
Section Test

Readings and Research

Web Links

Chapter 3

The Biological Perspective

CHAPTER OUTLINE

KEY IDEAS

➤ The biological perspective focuses on biological forces, particularly the brain, to explain human behavior.

➤ One of the early theories of the biological perspective attempted to link physical features and deviant behavior.

➤ An important biological theory, the Positivist School rejected free will and focused entirely on heredity and physical feature to explain human behavior.

➤ The work of Charles Darwin on evolutionary theory strongly influenced positivism.

➤ Theorists in the twentieth century specifically looked at body types to explain temperaments and personalities.

➤ Early biological theorist studied families in an attempt to confirm that criminal behavior ran in families.

➤ Twin studies and adoption studies have also been used to explain the role of genetics.

➤ Neurophysiology, or the study of the nervous system, has also been used to explain human behavior.

KEY TERMS

atavism
constitutional theory
criminaloid
cycloid personality
dyplastic personality
ectomorph
endomorph
eugenic criminology
mesomorph
neuroendocrinology
neurophysiology
phrenology
positivism
schizoid personality
sociobiology
somatyping

3.0   Biological perspective

3.1   Major principles

    3.1.1   The brain is the controlling factor in human behavior, and is where the personality resides.

    3.1.2   Human behavior, including criminal tendencies are, for the most part, predetermined andgenetically based.

    3.1.3   The factors that determine human behavior can be passed on from generation to generation.

    3.1.4   Some human behaviors are the result of biological factors that have been inherited from more primitive developmental stages in the evolutionary process.

For more on the major principles of the biological perspective, visit the Criminology Interactive online > Biological Theories > Theory Explained: Basic Principles.

PHRENOLOGY

The belief that the characteristics of the brain are mirrored in bumps in the skull.

3.2   **Phrenology** uses physical features of the skull to explain specific forms of behavior.

    3.2.1   Franz Joseph Gall (1758–1828)

        MAJOR IMPACT: Through research of human heads and head casts of both criminal and mainstream individuals, Gall founded the school of phrenology, a perspective that claimed that the shape of the human skull affected personality and caused criminal behavior.

    ■ Compared the heads and head casts of individuals who had not been institutionalized to those of criminals, and discovered distinctively different features among criminals.

    ■ Gall's approach offered four controlling ideas:
        ❖ The brain is the organ of the mind.
        ❖ The shape of a person's skull follows the shape of the brain underneath and indicates personality.
        ❖ Different characteristics of personality emanate from different zones in the brain.
        ❖ The personality characteristics that are associated with well-developed areas of the brain will become more prominent. Personality traits in areas that are less developed are less prominent.

    ■ Gall was one of the first Western writers to propose various locations of personality traits in the brain.
        ❖ Conventional thought before Gall was that aspects of personality resided in the organs of the body.
        ❖ Gall proposed a model that divided the brain into 26 areas or zones.

- Gall was the first to identify the gray matter of the brain with active tissue, and the white matter of the brain with conducting tissue.

3.2.2 Johann Gaspar Spurzheim (1776–1853)

MAJOR IMPACT: Spurzheim expanded Gall's research and brought phrenology to America.

- Spurzheim was Gall's student, as well as his assistant, secretary, and confidant.
  - Increased number of zones of the brain to 35
  - Identified the areas of the brain with labels such as:
    - Friendliness
    - Benevolence
    - Aggressiveness
- Spurzheim brought phrenology to America through a series of publications.
- Phrenology's prominence in America extended into the twentieth century when it was used to classify newly admitted prisoners.

3.2.3 Phrenology's link to criminal behavior

- By the early nineteenth century, phrenology expanded to include the notion that abnormalities in the human mind could be linked to criminal behavior.
- These theories, which included the work of Sigmund Freud (1856–1939), were called psychological theories, and are the subject of the next chapter.

For more on phrenology, visit the Criminology Interactive online > Biological Theories > Theory Explained: Phrenology.

3.3 Positivist School

3.3.1 Major principles

- Determinism
  - Behavior is determined by both internal and external factors.
    - The factors are beyond the control of the individual.
- Constitutional approach to crime
  - Structure of physical characteristics, or an individual's constitution, determines that person's behavior.
- Emphasized philosophy of individualized, scientific treatment of criminals based on findings of physical and social sciences
- Represented the rise of the scientific approach as the primary way of studying behavior

POSITIVISM

A philosophy with several varieties, the first being a product of eighteenth-century Enlightenment philosophy, with its emphasis on the importance of reason and experience.

3.3.2   Roots of **positivism**

■ August Comte (1798–1857)

MAJOR IMPACT: Comte, a prominent figure in early applications of the scientific method and often called the founder of sociology, developed the term positivism to describe how societies come to terms with the larger world around them.

SELECTED PUBLICATION: *System of Positive Polity* (1851)

❖ Positivism

◆ Proposed that societies pass through stages of how they understand the world

❏ Final stage is called the positive stage

• In this stage, people adopt a scientific view of the world.

❖ In *System of Positive Polity*, Comte proposed the use of scientific method in the study of society.

❖ Holds that social phenomena are observable, explainable, and measurable in quantitative terms

For more on positivism, visit the Criminology Interactive online > Biological Theories > Theory Explained: The Positivist School.

3.3.3   Charles Darwin (1809–1882)

MAJOR IMPACT: A strong influence during the positivist period, Charles Darwin was a naturalist who is credited with developing the evolutionary theory, the notion that human beings and other living organisms are the end products of evolution that is determined by such rules as "natural selection" and "survival of the fittest." Darwin was also instrumental in disseminating and promoting the scientific method.

SELECTED PUBLICATIONS: *On the Origin of Species by Means of Natural Section or the Preservation of Favored Races in the Struggle of Life* (1859), *The Descent of Man and Selection in Relation to Sex* (1871)

■ *On the Origins of Species* (1859)

❖ Many high-ranking Christian officials condemned this book since it went against the traditional view of the creation of man and earth.

❖ These attacks did not affect the popularity of this book.

❖ The book directly led to the increasing acceptance of science in the study of all human activities.

- *The Descent of Man* (1871)
  - ❖ In the introduction to the text, Darwin states:
    - ◆ "The sole object of this work is to consider firstly, whether man, like every other species, is descended from some pre-existing form; secondly, the manner of his development; and thirdly, the value of the differences between the so-called races of man."

3.3.4 Cesare Lombroso (1835–1909)

MAJOR IMPACT: Born in Verona, Italy, Cesare Lombroso is regarded as the father of modern criminology, and used the scientific method to study deceased offenders to offer a physical explanation for criminal behavior.

SELECTED PUBLICATIONS: *L'Uomo delinquente* (1876), *The Female Offender* (1893)

- Italian, trained as a medical doctor, and served as army prison physician

- The most prominent figure in early biological criminology

- Rejected notion of free will developed by classicists, and focused instead on the biological causes of crime

- Identified what he believed to be biological and genetic differences between criminals and noncriminals
  - ❖ Believed serious offenders were "born criminals" and that they inherited criminal traits
  - ❖ Criminals inherited physical characteristics that determined their behavior.

- Studied cadavers of executed offenders and deceased criminals.
  - ❖ A well-known criminal named Vilella provided Lombroso with many of his findings.
  - ❖ Upon examination of Vilella's brain, Lombroso identified a number of features of as being similar to those found in lower primates.
  - ❖ Lombroso conducted autopsies on 65 more executed offenders and examined 832 living prison inmates, and compared his measurements to those of 390 soldiers.
  - ❖ Cataloged body features that characterized criminal behavior
  - ❖ **Atavism**
    - ◆ Lombroso adapted a term Darwin used, **atavism**, to suggest that criminality was primitive behavior that had somehow survived the evolutionary process.

ATAVISM

Subhuman or primitive trait used by Lombroso to describe the characteristics of criminals. The term "atavism" is derived from the Latin term *atavus*, which means "ancestor."

♦ He used the term atavistic stigmata to describe the inherited physical features that he claimed characterized criminal behavior. These included exceptionally long arms, fleshy pouches in the cheek, eyes that were either very close or far apart, a crooked nose, and so on.

   ❐ Lombroso believed criminals had simply not evolved as far as noncriminals.

♦ **Criminaloid**

   ❐ An individual who is motivated by environment as well as by physical make-up to commit criminal acts

   ❐ Also called "occasional criminals"

   ❐ Exhibited some degree of atavism

   ❐ Differed from "born criminals" in degree, not kind of atavism

❖ Lombroso wrote the *The Female Offender* in 1893.

   ♦ Contended that women have far less anatomical variations than men

   ♦ At the same time, criminal behavior among women was also based in atavism

   ♦ Developed masculinity hypothesis: women who displayed masculine features and behavior were more apt to be criminals

CRIMINALOID

A term used by Cesare Lombroso to describe occasional criminals who were pulled into criminality primarily by environmental influences.

For more on Cesare Lombroso, visit Criminology Interactive online > Biological Theories > Theory Explained: Cesare Lombroso.

3.3.5   Raffaele Garofalo (1851–1934)

MAJOR IMPACT: Garofalo, born in Naples, Italy, and a student of Lombroso, looked at pain thresholds as well as physical features to offer an expanded view of Lombroso's typologies.

SELECTED PUBLICATION: *Criminology* (1885)

▪ Agreed with Lombroso that a criminal is abnormal since he lacked the degree of "sentiments and certain repugnance" held by others in society

▪ Garofalo noted some physical differences between criminals and noncriminals, but was cautious in his analysis since he did not think there was enough scientific evidence to support the theories.

▪ He did not agree with the classification of criminals used by Lombroso.

   ❖ Created his own classification system of criminals based on the moral inferiority of criminal types

- Two crime typologies
  - ❖ Property crime
  - ❖ Violent crime being directed against people

- Believed that there were certain physical characteristics that indicated a criminal nature
  - ❖ For instance, noted that criminals seemed to have a lower sensibility to pain evidenced by willingness of prisoners to submit to the pain of tattooing

- It is the criminal himself, and not his acts that threatens society, and thus the repression of crime actually means the repression of the criminal.

- The real problem is to determine how to sort the criminals based on the degree of danger that they represent.
  - ❖ Since criminals vary in their own adaptability to society, Garofalo felt that the means to repress them must also be adaptable.
  - ❖ Depending on the severity of the moral delinquency, Garofalo recommended punishments such as:
    - ◆ Deprivation of rights and liberties
    - ◆ Banishment
    - ◆ Marooning
    - ◆ Internment in overseas prison colonies
    - ◆ Death penalty

3.3.6   Enrico Ferri (1856–1929)

MAJOR IMPACT: Enrico Ferri added a social dimension to criminal behavior, contending that a number of biological, social, and organic factors caused deviant behavior, and that these causes were outside the criminal's control.

SELECTED PUBLICATION: *Criminal Sociology* (1881)

- Ferri argued against penal systems that stressed only punishment, and instead argued for crime prevention.

- The penal code of Argentina was based on Ferri's views, but the penal code that he drafted for his own country, Italy, was rejected by the then fascist government.

3.3.7   Charles Goring (1870–1919)

MAJOR IMPACT: Goring attempted to disprove the work of Lombroso by measuring the degree of correlation of criminal behavior within a family line.

SELECTED PUBLICATION: *The English Convict: A Statistical Study* (1913)

■ Compared brothers as well as fathers and sons, attempting to show that correlations for general criminality as measured by imprisonment were as high as for two other categories Goring measured:

❖ Ordinary physical traits and features

❖ Inherited defects, insanity, and mental disease

■ Attempted to show that correlations were the result of heredity, not environment, but was not able to conclude this was the case

3.4 Body type

CONSTITUTIONAL THEORY

A theory that looks at body type, or "constitution," to explain human behavior.

3.4.1 Considered a **constitutional theory**

3.4.2 Theories that explain criminality by reference to offender's:

■ Body types

■ Genetics

■ External observable physical characteristics

SOMATOTYPING

The classification of human beings into types according to body build and other physical characteristics.

3.4.3 **Somatotyping** is another name for body types.

3.4.4 Ernst Kretschmer (1888–1964)

MAJOR IMPACT: Kretschmer proposed a relationship between body build, personality type, and mental illness.

SELECTED PUBLICATION: *Physique and Character* (1921)

■ Kretschmer suggested three body types:

❖ Asthenic type

◆ Tall

◆ Thin

❖ Athletic type

◆ Muscular

❖ Pyknic type

◆ Rotund

■ Asthenics and athletic types were more prone to schizophrenia.

■ Pyknic cycloid types were more prone to manic depression.

■ Created a biopsychological constitutional typology

❖ Three basic mental categories

◆ **Cycloid personality**

❑ Individuals with heavyset, soft bodies

❑ Lacked sophistication and spontaneity

❑ Committed mostly nonviolent property types of offenses

CYCLOID PERSONALITY

Individuals with heavyset, soft bodies who commit mostly nonviolent property crimes.

♦ **Schizoid personality**

❏ Individuals with athletic, muscular bodies; could also be thin and lean

❏ More likely to be schizophrenic

❏ Likely to commit violent offenses

♦ **Displastic personality**

❏ Individuals who were highly emotional and unable to control themselves

❏ Thought to commit mostly sexual offenses and other crimes of passion

3.4.5 William Sheldon (1898–1977)

MAJOR IMPACT: Influenced by the work of Kretschmer, Sheldon, both a psychologist and medical doctor, identified four body types that could be related to specific behaviors

- Based his underlying concept on the fact that human beings begin life as an embryo, which has three different tissue layers

  ❖ Endoderm (inner layer)

  ❖ Mesoderm (middle layer)

  ❖ Ectoderm (outer layer)

- Studied 200 boys between the ages of 15 and 21 at Hayden Goodwill Institute in Boston.

- Identified four basic body types

  ❖ **Endomorph**

    ♦ Soft and round

    ♦ Overweight and a large stomach

    ♦ Low energy and moves slowly

  ❖ **Mesomorph**

    ♦ Athletic and muscular

    ♦ Larger bones and considerable muscle mass

  ❖ **Ectomorph**

    ♦ Thin and fragile

    ♦ Long, slender, poorly muscled extremities

    ♦ Delicate bones

  ❖ Balanced type

    ♦ Person of average build, without being overweight, thin, or exceedingly muscular

- Sheldon proposed that various temperaments and personalities were closely associated with each of these body types.
  - ❖ Ectomorphs were said to be "cerebrotonic"
    - ◆ Restrained
    - ◆ Shy
    - ◆ Inhibited
  - ❖ Endomorphs were said to be "viscerotonic"
    - ◆ Relaxed
    - ◆ social
  - ❖ Mesomorphs were said to be "somatotonic"
    - ◆ Bodily assertive
    - ◆ Most commonly associated with delinquency

For more on William Sheldon and the relationship of body types to behavior, visit Criminology Interactive online > Biological Theories > Theory Explained: William Sheldon.

3.4.6   Sheldon and Eleanor Glueck

- Conducted many studies on relationship of body type and criminal behavior, most of it focusing on juvenile delinquents

- In a 1950 study, compared 500 known delinquents with 500 nondelinquents from underprivileged neighborhoods.

- Concluded that mesomorphy was associated with delinquency

3.5   Genetics and crime

3.5.1   Genetics is the study of biological inheritance.

- Modern biological theorists look to genetics to find traits of criminality that may be passed down from parents.

3.5.2   Early biological theorists believed criminality was a trait that ran in families, suggesting the role of genetics and heredity in criminal behavior.

3.5.3   The premise is that if criminality is genetic, children of criminal parents are more likely to become criminals.

For more on studies of the relationship of genetics and crime, visit Criminology Interactive online > Biological Theories > Theory Explained: Genetics and Crime.

3.5.4   Richard Louis Dugdale (1841–1883)

MAJOR IMPACT: Dugdale, a social investigator, developed a detailed study of a family he called "the Jukes," tracing the prominence of criminal behavior through various generations in order to determine how deviant behavior may be passed down through families.

SELECTED PUBLICATION: *The Jukes: A Study in Crime, Pauperism, Disease, and Heredity* (1877)

- While working for the Prison Association of New York, discovered six members of the same family in a New York county jail in 1874

- Studied their family history, tracing lineage back to Max, a Dutch immigrant who arrived in New York in the early 1700s

- Two of Max's sons married into the Juke family, which consisted of six girls, all of whom were said to be illegitimate.

- Max's male descendants were described as violent and deviant. A female descendant, Ada, was particularly well known for tough behavior and became known as the "mother of criminals."

- By the time of the study, Dugdale was able to identify approximately 1,200 of Ada's descendants, which included:
  - ❖ 7 murderers
  - ❖ 60 habitual thieves
  - ❖ 90 or so other criminals
  - ❖ 50 prostitutes
  - ❖ 280 paupers

- Dugdale compared the Juke family to Jonathan Edwards's family, a pure-blooded Puritan preacher and one-time president of Princeton University.
  - ❖ Descendants of Edwards included:
    - ◆ American presidents and vice presidents
    - ◆ Many successful bankers and businesspeople
    - ◆ No one who was identified as having a run-in with the law

- Developed a theory derived from Darwin that suggested that the family's criminal history was based on a degenerative nature that was inherited and passed down

- Two flaws in the theory: The Jukes were not really one single family, but were in fact composed of several related families; almost of all the information about the Jukes came from anecdotes.

- Arthur H. Estabrook (1916) published a follow-up study and found:
  - ❖ 715 additional Juke descendents
    - ◆ 378 more prostitutes
    - ◆ 170 additional paupers
    - ◆ 118 other criminals

For more on Dugdale's research, visit Criminology Interactive online > Biological Theories > Theory Explained: Genetics and Crime.

3.5.5 Henry Herbert Goddard (1866–1957)

MAJOR IMPACT: Goddard conducted a study of several branches of the Kallikak family, who all descended from a Revolutionary War soldier. He found that family members who descended from a wayward girl and a Revolutionary war soldier were defective, while those descended from his union with a faithful Quaker girl were relatively untouched by deviance. Goddard also translated the Binet intelligence test into English, advocated wide intelligence testing and eugenics, promoting compulsory sterilization for those deemed defective in some way.

SELECTED PUBLICATION: *The Kallikak Family: A Study in the Heredity of Feeble-Mindedness* (1912)

- Studied two branches of the same family who lived in Pine Barrens, New Jersey, in 1912.
  - ❖ One branch began as a result of a sexual liaison between Martin Kallikak, a Revolutionary War soldier, and a barmaid.
    - ◆ As a result of this liaison, an illegitimate son (Martin Jr.) was born.
    - ◆ Four hundred eighty descendents of this union were identified.
    - ◆ Two hundred sixty-two "feebleminded" births and various other epileptic, alcoholic, and criminal descendants were produced.
  - ❖ Kallikak returned home after the Revolutionary War and married a righteous Quaker girl, creating a second branch of this family.
    - ◆ This branch produced only a few minor deviants.
- Goddard claimed that the feeblemindedness was a result of a regressive gene, and that selective breeding could eliminate this gene.
  - ❖ Goddard altered his views on such selective breeding techniques as his own theories developed.

3.5.6   **Eugenic criminology** (1920s and 1930s)

- Held that root causes of criminality were largely passed from generation to generation in the form of "bad genes"

- Replaced idea of "feebleminded criminal" with "defective delinquent"

- Movement called for sterilization of mentally handicapped women to prevent them from bearing additional offspring

  ❖ *Buck* v. *Bell* (1927)

    ◆ U.S. Supreme Court case that supported a Virginia statute permitting sterilization

3.5.7   Sir Francis Galton (1822–1911)

MAJOR IMPACT: Galton, variously described as a mathematician, meteorologist, naturalist, and a criminologist created the term eugenics, which called for the improvement of the human species through selective parenting and sterilization of those considered feebleminded.

- A cousin of Charles Darwin, he was heavily influenced by Darwin's work

- First Western scientist to systematically study heredity and its possible influence upon human behavior

- Became convinced that success in life was based on inherited abilities, which were passed down to offspring through a process of heredity

- Galton's work contributed to the development of the field of behavioral genetics.

- Credited with being one of the first researchers to look at the study of twins to explore the differences and similarities between monozygotic (identical) and dizygotic (fraternal) twins

- Credited with discovering that fingerprints were an index of a person's identity

3.5.8   Twin studies

- Provided a different mechanism for examining the role of genetics

- If inherited traits cause criminality, then it would be expected that twins would be similar in deviant behavior.

- Studies compared identical or monozygotic (MZ) twins with fraternal or dizygotic (DZ) twins.

  ❖ MZs are maternal twins and theoretically have 100% overlap in their genetic codes.

  ❖ DZs are fraternal twins and theoretically have no more genetic overlap than other siblings.

- If heredity determines criminality, then:
    - ❖ MZs should be more similar in their deviant behavior than DZs.
    - ❖ DZs should show no more similarity than other sibling pairs.
    - ❖ The similarity in behavior based on the level of genetic overlap is called concordance.
        - ◆ The studies done have generally found higher concordance rates for MZs than DZs.
- Karl O. Christiansen (1910)
    - ❖ Studied criminal behavior among 3,586 twins in one region of Denmark between 1881 and 1910
    - ❖ Reported that if one twin engaged in criminal behavior, the probability that the identical twin also would was 35%, compared with only 12% if the twins were not identical
- Sarnoff A. Mednick
    - ❖ Updated Christiansen's study
    - ❖ Concluded that genetic factors account for some of the variables associated with antisocial behavior
- Twin studies have been criticized on methodological grounds by many scholars.
    - ❖ The rates of difference vary and concordance levels are not perfect.
    - ❖ It is difficult to rule out environmental factors.

3.5.9 Adoption studies

- Cross-fostering analysis
    - ❖ Looks at rates of delinquency among adopted children based on the criminal status of both their biological and adoptive fathers
- Hutchings and Mednick (1977)
    - ❖ Used a sample of 72,000 individuals from Denmark's adoption register
    - ❖ Four categories are possible:
        - ◆ Adoptive and biological fathers are both criminals
        - ◆ Biological father is criminal, while adoptive father is not criminal
        - ◆ Biological father is not criminal, while adoptive father is criminal
        - ◆ Adoptive and biological fathers are both not criminals
    - ❖ If genetics play a dominant role, one would expect that the group with both the biological and adoptive fathers who are criminals would be the most criminal.

> ❖ The second most criminal group should be the group with the biological father who is a criminal, while the adoptive father is not a criminal.
>
> ❖ Hutchings and Mednick found support for these two groups as being the most criminal.
>
> ❖ Concluded that the genetic factor is important in explaining criminal behavior

3.5.10   General conclusions regarding twin/adoption studies

> ■ More recent studies into the genetics/heredity of criminality have shown less support than earlier, less scientifically sophisticated and methodologically sound studies.
>
> ■ Based on a review of the evidence, it is reasonable to conclude that it is likely that there are some genetic influences that may predispose individuals to criminality or that help promote that possibility.
>
> > ❖ These biological characteristics can take a variety of forms.
> >
> > ❖ It is unlikely that biology is destiny.
> >
> > > ◆ There is no "criminogenic gene."
> > >
> > > ◆ There is no gene or gene configuration that automatically creates criminality.
> >
> > ❖ The influence of various biological factors must be considered in the context of other kinds of internal and external factors.
> >
> > > ◆ Example of internal
> > >
> > > > ❑ Psychological/cognitive
> > >
> > > ◆ Example of external
> > >
> > > > ❑ Aspects of the social structure
>
> ■ One likely way that genetics may influence criminality is by impacting biological systems involved in early learning of law-abiding behavior.

3.5.11   Chromosome abnormalities, the XYY supermale, and Patricia Jacobs

MAJOR IMPACT: Patricia Jacobs, a British researcher, discovered that the prison population of 197 Scottish prisoners had chromosomes that were abnormal.

> ■ Jacobs research identified the XYY "supermale."
>
> > ❖ Examined 197 Scottish prisoners for chromosomal abnormalities through a relatively simple blood test know as karyotyping
> >
> > ❖ Twelve members of the group displayed chromosomes that were unusual:
> >
> > > ◆ Seven were found to have an XYY chromosome

- The incidence of XYY man in the prison population was placed at around 3.5% by Jacobs, quickly identified as potentially violent, and was termed a "supermale."
- To date, there have been nearly 200 studies of XYY males.
- Although not all researchers agree, taken as a group, these studies tend to show that supermales have these characteristics:
  - Height (often 6′1″ or taller)
  - Thinness
  - Suffer from acne or skin disorders
  - Tendency toward homosexuality
  - Have less than average intelligence
  - Are overrepresented in prisons and mental hospitals
  - Come from families with a lower than average history of crime or mental illness
- The media quickly created an image of the huge, dangerous hulk of a "supermale," perpetuating the most heinous of crimes spurred on by their extra Y chromosome.
- Little evidence suggests that XYY men actually commit crimes of greater violence than do other men, although they may commit somewhat more crimes overall.
- Studies done thus far are largely in agreement and demonstrate rather conclusively that males of the XYY type are not predictably aggressive.
- Mednick, et al. (1982) report that there is no evidence to support greater levels of violence among XYY males.
- XYY males constitute a very small percentage of the general population (about 3/1000) and the prison population (Ellison and Buckout, 1981).
- Even if XYY had been related to violence, it could only explain a very small fraction of cases and could not serve as a general explanation of criminality.

3.6 Neurological Factors

NEUROPHYSIOLOGY
The study of brain activity and the nervous system.

3.6.1 **Neurophysiology**

- The study of brain activity
- Neurophysiologists believe that neurological abnormalities can affect behavior.

3.6.2 Central nervous system

- Includes the nervous systems enclosed within the body portions of the skull and spine.

3.6.3   Central nervous system (CNS) testing

- Electroencephalogram (EEG)
  - ❖ Traditional method for monitoring brain activity
  - ❖ Creates graphic images of brain's activities by recording the electrical impulses in the brain (e.g., brain waves)
  - ❖ EEG is limited to surface activity.
  - ❖ Most common tool for research on relationship between CNS and criminal behavior
  - ❖ Some studies have found incarcerated individuals tend to have higher proportions of abnormal EEGs than do individuals in the general population.
  - ❖ A variety of differences have been reported.
    - ◆ The key is that such findings point to a role for an underlying organic dysfunction.
    - ◆ While such dysfunctions are not offered as a general explanation of criminality, they can be a factor in some cases.
  - ❖ These kinds of dysfunctions may affect the learning process, self-control mechanisms, decision making, etc.

- Neuropsychological tests
  - ❖ Examples:
    - ◆ X-rays
    - ◆ Computerized axial tomography (CAT)
      - ❑ Takes x-rays of the brain
    - ◆ Magnetic resonance imaging (MRI)
      - ❑ Permits viewing detailed images of the brain or other parts of the body
    - ◆ Spinal taps
      - ❑ Determines whether the brain has been damaged
  - ❖ Results of neurological tests
    - ◆ Suggest violent, impulsive individuals suffer from damage to specific brain areas that may occur before birth or at delivery
    - ◆ Criminals suffer injury with resulting unconsciousness earlier in life than noncriminals do.

- Positron emission tomography (PET)
  - ❖ Most sophisticated imaging tool to date
  - ❖ Monitors brain's radioactive substances showing which areas of the brain are working hardest when the individual is engaged in a particular thought process

❖ PET has been used to determine differences between the thought processes and emotions of men and women as well as differentiate between murderers and nonviolent criminals.

❖ More recently, PET has been used to reveal underlying causes of psychiatric illness and mental disease of aging.

3.6.4   Neuropsychological assessment data

■ The tests mentioned earlier allow for inferences about localization of brain dysfunction.

■ A variety of studies have demonstrated higher levels of localized dysfunction among delinquents and adult criminals.

■ Much of the evidence relates to cerebral cortex functioning.

❖ The cerebral cortex is the largest component of the human brain.

❖ The cerebral cortex is primarily associated with higher-order functioning.

◆ Decision making

◆ Identification of consequences

◆ Planning

■ One of the main areas of the cerebral cortex that has been identified is the frontal temporal lobe.

❖ Dysfunction in this area is associated with:

◆ Impaired self-control

◆ An inability to comprehend the consequences of one's behavior

■ There are still many unanswered questions about how the various types of dysfunctions impact behavior.

❖ Such physiological problems do not make criminal behavior inevitable.

❖ They interact with other factors to help increase the likelihood of behavioral problems.

■ These dysfunctions can result from a variety of causes.

❖ They are not necessarily genetic factors.

❖ They can result from injury, drug abuse, poor prenatal care, or illness.

NEUROENDOCRINOLGY

The study of the way the nervous system interacts with the endocrine system.

3.7   Neuroendocrinology

3.7.1   *The New Criminology* (1928)

■ Discussed the endocrine system and its relationship to crime

❖ The endocrine system is an integrated system of small organs that involve the release of extracellular signaling molecules known as hormones.

3.7.2 Research on animals and human beings demonstrates a relationship between hormones and behavior.

- Example: There are lower levels of certain hormones in men who are more dominant, aggressive, and hostile than in the average man.

- Research suggests that female hormones can reduce male sex drive and potency. This has led to chemical castration as a method of treating sex offenders.

- Premenstrual tension, which is common in about 25% of the female population, appears to be associated with the imbalance of two female hormones—estrogen and progesterone.

3.7.3 Hormones in the body have an effect on neurological activity.

3.7.4 Androgen (testosterone) and aggression

- Abnormally high levels of male sex hormones (androgens) have been found to produce aggressive behavior.

- High androgen levels in males also have been associated with:
  - ❖ Sensation seeking
  - ❖ Impulsivity
  - ❖ Reduced levels of verbal skills

- Hormones, like androgen, have been used by biocriminologists to help explain criminal behavior.

3.7.5 Research shows that hormonal changes are related to mood swings and behavior patterns.

- Hormones are believed to influence behavior because they can cause areas of the brain to become less sensitive to environmental stimuli.

- Androgens have been shown to influence parts of the brain that affect feelings and emotions.

3.7.6 Treating criminals with hormones has been successful.

- Mainly with sex offenders

- The long-term effects are still uncertain

- The evidence to date indicates that hormonal therapies alone are not terribly effective.

3.8 Sociobiology

3.8.1 Biological theories in the early twentieth century

- These theories fell out of favor. During this period, more stress was placed on sociological theories and influences.
  - ❖ Sociological theories and their developmental histories are chronicled in other chapters in the textbook.

SOCIOBIOLOGY

The belief that the biological characteristics of an individual are only one part in the equation of behavior. The other parts are the physical and social environments.

- ❖ Biological theories of criminality remained in disfavor will into the twentieth century.
- ❖ Today, biological theories generally receive, at best, lukewarm reviews and are still the targets of heavy criticism.

3.8.2   Edmund Wilson, in *Sociobiology: The New Synthesis* (1975), helped to revive some interest in biological theories of crime.

- ■ Sociobiology offers an interactive view while maintaining a strong biological core.
  - ❖ It still views human genes as the ultimate unit of life
  - ❖ Genes ultimately control destiny.
  - ❖ Sociobiology offers the deterministic view that most human actions are controlled by biological factors.
- ■ Emphasizes biological and genetic factors that affect how social behaviors are learned and filtered
- ■ Wilson's sociobiological view relies on fundamental aspects of some early biological approaches.
  - ❖ The preeminence of an innate survival drive
    - ◆ People are characterized as being controlled by the need to preserve their own genetics.
    - ◆ The dominant drive is to have one's gene pool survive.

3.8.3   Criticisms of sociobiology

- ■ Some have accused sociobiologists of dressing up old and dangerous ideas in new clothing.
- ■ Despite the interactionist trappings, at its core, it promotes biological determinism.
  - ❖ Determinism refers to the idea that people are not in control of their own actions.
  - ❖ Behavior is the result of biological circumstances beyond their control.
- ■ Such a view is seen by some as having destructive potential.
  - ❖ Deterministic models raise concerns about reducing individual/group responsibility for behavior.
  - ❖ Claiming that preservation of the gene pool (a survival instinct) is the dominant human motive also raises concerns.
    - ◆ Should we attribute human rights atrocities, such as the ethnic cleansing in Bosnia, to this innate drive?
    - ◆ Should we excuse such acts based on this explanation?
    - ◆ Should we expect that, as a species, we cannot move beyond this basic drive?

■ Sociobiology is considered by many criminologists to be methodologically unsound.

❖ Modern "trait" theories do not suggest that a single biological or psychological factor adequately explains all (criminal) behavior.

❖ Each individual is considered unique; therefore, explanations for each person's behavior will be, to some extent, different.

❖ There is considerable evolutionary evidence that variety, not uniformity, is central and key.

3.9   General critique of the biological perspective

3.9.1   Biological factors do not make behavior inevitable.

3.9.2   Humans are very learning dependent.

■ Behaviors are the result of complex interactions of internal and external factors.

■ Physiological, psychological, social, and physical environment factors all play a role.

3.9.3   Disregarding biology may be counterproductive.

■ All behaviors are, at some level, the result of biological activity.

■ The brain is the control center for behavior and is intertwined with other body functions.

■ There are some biological conditions that can differentially impact behavior in people.

■ This does not make the behaviors inevitable; the conditions become factors in the equation.

3.9.4   General concerns of criminologists

■ Biological explanations have been unpopular among criminologists for a variety of reasons.

❖ Most criminologists have roots in the social sciences.

❖ Many of the early attempts at biological explanations were seriously flawed.

❖ Their deterministic nature may be seen as inconsistent with the idea of free will, which is basis for law.

CHAPTER SUMMARY

➤ The biological perspective considers the mind to be the controlling factor in human behavior and the center of personality. In contrast to the classical perspective that focuses on free will and external forces, the biological perspective considers internal causes, especially genetic and physical make-up, as the sources of behavior. Human behavior, according to the biological perspective, is for the most part predetermined. Determinants of human behavior may be passed from generation to generation. Some human behavior, biological perspective theorists claim, has its roots in primitive developmental stages in the evolutionary process.

➤ The link between physical features and deviant behavior is one of the early concepts of the biological perspective. Franz Joseph Gall expanded that notion and founded the school of phrenology, which held that the physical features of the skull and brain caused specific behaviors. Gall's student, Johann Spurzheim, expanded Gall's notions and brought the idea of phrenology to the United States.

➤ The positivist school in the late nineteenth century represented the first use of the scientific method to quantify and study human behavior. Positivism rejected the notion of free will and focused on heredity and physical features as the determinants of human behavior. It also considered how evolutionary factors and instinct played a part in human development. Positivists also developed a medical model of criminal behavior. Because the cause of deviant behavior was physical, positivists claimed criminals could be medically treated.

➤ August Comte was the first figure to use the term positivism in relation to crime in 1851. The work of Charles Darwin, which suggested that human beings were the end product of a complex evolutionary process, was a strong influence during the positivist era. Other early figures in positivism included Ceasare Lombroso, who studied cadavers of executed criminals and examined prison inmates to identify bodily features that indicated criminal behavior. Theorists who followed include Raffaele Garofalo, who developed his own classification of criminals; Enrico Ferri, who claimed that criminals could not be responsible for their behavior since the causes of that behavior were outside their control; and Charles Goring, who unsuccessfully tried to disprove Lombroso's theories.

➤ Several theorist in the twentieth century linked body types to human behavior. Ernst Kretschmer established three body types that were directly related to human behavior. William Sheldon expanded Kretschmer's work to identify four different configurations of body types: endomorph, mesomorph, ectomorph, and balanced type. Sheldon went on to do studies that claimed that varying types of temperament and personalities were associated with each of the body types.

➤ Early biological theorists believed that criminal behavior ran in families and was, at least in part, genetically related. Richard Louis Dugdale studied the lineage of the Juke family in 1877. His study revealed that the descendants of Max, a Dutch immigrant who arrived in New York in the early 1700s, had an extreme pattern of criminal behavior. Dugdale was eventually able to prove that over 1,200 descendants of Ada, a female descendent of Max, had demonstrated criminal behavior. Herbert Goddard conducted a similar study of the Kallikak family. Goddard's study looked at two branches of the same family. The first branch was created when Martin Kallikak had an out-of-wedlock liaison with a barmaid. This produced descendents who were considered feebleminded and/or deviant. When Kallikak married a modest Quaker woman and produced heirs, only a few deviants could be found in the population of this second branch of the family.

➤ Twin studies and adoption studies are other ways that the biological theorists used to examine the role of genetics. Twin studies relied on the notion that if inherited traits caused criminal behavior, then it would be expected that twins would exhibit the same deviant behavior. Adoption studies considered the delinquency rates among adopted children based on the criminal behavior of their biological mothers and fathers. Biological researchers have also studied chromosome abnormalities as determinants of criminal behavior, although such research has not been conclusive.

➤ The study of brain activity, known as neurophysiology, has also been used in recent times to track the relationship of human behavior to physical reactions of the human brain. Neuroendocrinology, the relationship of hormones to human behavior, is a field that also considers the biological roots of human behavior. Sociobiology, which harkens back to earlier concepts of biological determinism, emphasizes genetic and biological factors as responsible for how social behaviors are learned and filtered.

STUDY QUESTIONS

1. What conclusions did phrenology make about the shape of the human head?
2. How did Darwin's theory affect the theories of the positivist school?
3. How did Lombroso apply atavism to criminality?
4. Which three body types did William Sheldon associate with which behavior?
5. What did family studies, such as the Juke and Kallikak families, have to say about the relationship between crime and genetics?
6. What do twin and adoption studies tell us about genetic connections to behavior?
7. What can PET and CAT tell us about the way the brain functions?

ONLINE@CRIMINOLOGY INTERACTIVE

Theory in Action

Case File #1: Crack Addict—Mark
Case File #2: Carrying Money at a Drug Deal—Hector

Review

Vocabulary Shootout
Essay Questions
Section Test

Readings and Research

Web Links

Chapter 4

The Psychological Perspective

CHAPTER OUTLINE

KEY IDEAS

➤ The psychological perspective contends that the individual's personality resides in the mind and is the key to understanding behavior, including deviant behavior.

➤ Psychiatric criminality considers the individual the essential point of analysis and identifies conditions such as psychopathy, which are disorders of the individual personality.

➤ Sigmund Freud, the founding father of the psychiatric tradition, did not devote study to criminology, but his theories have been applied to criminology in an approach called psychoanalytic criminology, which looks at the role of the personality in human behavior.

➤ Seymour Halleck developed the frustration-aggression theory, suggesting that criminal behavior occurs when individuals cannot adapt to the frustration that naturally occurs in the process of living.

➤ Modeling theory contends that human behavior stems from imitation of others and that deviant behavior is learned from individuals who exhibit that behavior.

➤ Behavior theory sees behavior as the result of the environment and its consequences, particularly the way that behavior is reinforced or discouraged through a series of rewards and punishment.

➤ Attachment theory looks at attachments between and among human beings, especially the relationship of a child to his parent, as the key to determining behavior.

➤ Self-control theory considers that the way an individual reacts and alters his behavior to outside influences is essential to his behavior.

➤ A general theory of crime, developed by Gottfredson and Hirschi, contends that a variation on self-control theory that encompasses a consideration of social bonds and relationships can explain all types of deviance.

KEY TERMS

attachment theory
behavior theory
disengagement
ego
Eros
frustration-aggression theory
id
modeling theory
neurosis
personality
psychiatric criminology
psychosis
psychoanalytical criminology
psychological perspective
psychopathy
psychotherapy
self-control theory
superego
Thanatos

**PSYCHOLOGICAL
PERSPECTIVE**

The individual's personality
resides in the mind and is the
key to understanding behavior,
including deviant behavior.

4.0   Psychological perspective

4.1   Major principles

4.1.1   Individual is the point of analysis.

4.1.2   The personality of the individual is the individual's motivating factor.

4.1 3   Crimes and other aberrant behavior are the result of the maladaptive or defective mind.

4.1.4   Psychological perspective seeks to understand and explain those defects, which are seen as having a variety of potential causes including mental disease, inappropriate or improper conditioning, imitation of inappropriate role models, and maladjustment to inner conflicts.

**For more on psychological theory, visit Criminology Interactive online >
Psychological Theories > Theory Explained: Basic Principles.**

4.2   Psychopath

4.2.1   "Psycho" comes from the Greek meaning "soul" or "mind." "Pathos" means suffering.

4.2.2   Definition: Psychopathology is a personality disorder that is distinguished by chronic antisocial or immoral behavior as well as the inability to empathize with others. It is often used interchangeably with sociopath.

4.2.3   Typical psychopathic behavior

- Psychopaths typically display a lack of conscience and poor impulse control.

- Psychopathy in and of itself does not necessarily lead to criminal or violent behavior.

- The degree to which the psychopath can hold his impulse controls in check helps to determine the ability to display no deviant behavior.

PSYCHIATRIC CRIMINOLOGY

The branch of psychiatry having
to do with the study of crime
and criminality.

4.3   Psychiatric criminology

4.3.1   Hervey M. Cleckley (1903–1984)

MAJOR IMPACT: Cleckley was a psychiatrist who was the first to describe psychopathy as a mental illness in which the victim is able to appear normal, but is suffering from a deep-seated mental disorder that is characterized by low level of guilt and conscience.

PUBLICATIONS: *The Mask of Sanity: An Attempt to Clarify Some Issues About the So-Called Psychopathic Personality* (1941), *The Three Faces of Eve* (1957), *The Caricature of Love* (1957)

- Described psychopath as a "moral idiot," or as one who does not feel empathy even though he is aware of what is happening around him

- One defining aspect of a psychopath is "poverty of affect."
  - ❖ Inability to imagine how others think and feel

- Some of the characteristics of a psychopath that Cleckley identified are:
  - ❖ Superficial charm and ability to project intelligence
  - ❖ Lacking signs of psychosis, such as delusions and hallucinations
  - ❖ Absence of nervousness
  - ❖ Inability to feel guilt or shame
  - ❖ Chronic lying
  - ❖ Pattern of antisocial behavior
  - ❖ Poor judgment and inability to learn from experience
  - ❖ Grandiose sense of self-worth
  - ❖ Unresponsiveness in general interpersonal relations

- **Psychopathy**
  - ❖ "A constellation of dysfunctional psychological processes as opposed to specific behavioral manifestations"
  - ❖ Indicators of psychopathy usually occur in early life, often in the teen years, and include lying, fighting, stealing, and vandalism.

- Even earlier indicators may include cruelty to animals, bedwetting, sleepwalking, and setting fires.

PSYCHOPATHY

A personality disorder, especially one manifested in aggressively antisocial behavior, which is often said to be the result of a poorly developed superego.

4.4 Psychoanalytic criminology

4.4.1 Sigmund Freud (1856–1939)

MAJOR IMPACT: Freud was almost single-handedly responsible for laying the groundwork for psychoanalytic criminology.

SELECTED PUBLICATIONS: *The Interpretation of Dreams* (1899), *Totem and Taboo* (1913), *On the Pleasure Principle* (1920), *The Ego and the Id* (1923)

- Freud was not a criminologist and did not devote a tremendous amount of attention to criminality.

- Freud was a determinist and a positivist. He placed some importance on biological factors, but felt the major source of behavior lies in the psychological make-up of the individual.

- Developed the term *psychoanalysis* in 1896.
  - ❖ Freud's entire theory of human behavior was based in psychoanalysis.

PSYCHOANALYTIC CRIMINOLOGY

A psychiatric approach developed by the Austrian psychiatrist Sigmund Freud that emphasizes the role of personality in human behavior, which sees deviant behavior as the result of dysfunctional personalities.

PERSONALITY

An individual's unique set of characteristics determines his temperament, motivation, and behavior.

NEUROSIS

Functional disorders of the mind or of the emotions involving anxiety, phobia, or other abnormal behavior.

PSYCHOSIS

A form of mental illness in which sufferers are said to be out of touch with reality.

PSYCHOTHERAPY

A form of psychiatric treatment based upon psychoanalytic principles and techniques.

ID

The aspect of the personality from which drives, wishes, urges, and desires emanate. More formally, the division of the psyche associated with instinctual impulses and demands for immediate satisfaction of primitive needs.

EGO

The reality-testing part of the personality; also referred to as the reality principle. More formally, the personality component that is conscious, most immediately controls behavior, and is most in touch with external reality.

SUPEREGO

The moral aspect of the personality; much like the conscience. More formally, the division of the psyche that develops by the incorporation of the perceived moral standards of the community, is mainly unconscious, and includes the conscience.

- ◆ Encompasses general notions of **personality**, **neurosis**, and **psychosis**
- ◆ Refers to specific concepts of transference, sublimation, and repression
- ❖ Considered criminal behavior as maladaptive or the product of inadequacies inherent in the offender's personality
  - ◆ Significant inadequacies may result in full-blown mental illness, which in itself can be a direct cause of crime.
- ■ Saw original human nature as assertive and aggressive
  - ❖ It is not learned but is rooted deeply in early childhood experiences.
  - ❖ Human beings all have deviant tendencies but most of us learn to control them during the socialization process by developing strong and effective inner controls.
- ■ **Psychotherapy**
  - ❖ Referred to in its early days as the "talking cure"
  - ❖ Focused on patient-therapist communication
  - ❖ Attempted to relieve patients of their mental disorders by using psychoanalytic principles and techniques

4.4.2   Components of personality

- ■ Made up of three components:
  - ❖ **Id**
    - ◆ Made up of primitive impulses and unconscious drives
    - ◆ Operates on the pleasure principle
      - ❑ Constantly seeks pleasure
    - ◆ Fundamental aspect of the personality from which drives, wishes, urges, and desires emanate
    - ◆ Fundamental drives include love, aggression, and sex.
  - ❖ **Ego**
    - ◆ The part of the personality that deals with everyday life
    - ◆ Operates on the reality principle
      - ❑ Conscious and rational
      - ❑ Subject to all of the rules of reality
    - ◆ Primarily concerned with how objectives might be best accomplished
    - ◆ Develops strategies for the individual that maximize pleasure and minimize pain
    - ◆ Recognizes that delaying gratification is necessary to achieve a more fulfilling long-term goal
  - ❖ **Superego**
    - ◆ The conscience, the moral guide to right and wrong
    - ◆ Based on the ethical principle

❖ Balances the ego's plan of action by dismissing some activities as ethically inappropriate while accepting others as morally viable

❖ "Ego-ideal"

❑ Part of superego

❑ Symbolic representation of what society values

❑ Less powerful in controlling behavior in the absence of the likelihood of discovery

4.4.3 Basic instincts

■ Freud talked about various basic instincts that are instrumental in creating behavior.

❖ Two dominant instincts are **Eros** and **Thanatos**.

❖ Eros

❑ The life instinct

• Often referred to as the survival instinct

• Very fundamental drive in humans

❖ Thanatos

❑ The death instinct

• The desire to return to an inanimate state

• The ultimate resolution to all conflict

• The desire to free oneself from the problems of the world

• The primary motive for suicide

• Freud subsequently characterized this as a major impetus for behavior and as an instinct for aggression.

■ Conflict between these opposing instincts has been offered as a source of criminal behavior.

EROS

Survival instinct.

THANATOS

A death wish.

For more on Sigmund Freud, visit Criminology Interactive online > Psychological Theories > Theory Explained: Sigmund Freud.

4.5 Frustration-aggression theory

4.5.1 Seymour Halleck

MAJOR IMPACT: Halleck theorized that deviant behavior sometimes represents an adaption to the stress of life and that, at times, criminal behavior can make those who are not empowered to feel powerful.

SELECTED PUBLICATION: *Psychiatry and the Dilemmas of Crime* (1971)

FRUSTRATION-AGGRESSION THEORY

A theory that holds that frustration, which is a natural consequence of living, is a root cause of crime. Criminal behavior can be a form of adaptation when it results in stress reduction.

- Halleck claimed that society cannot determine exactly what constitutes criminal behavior for which a person is liable and what can be excused for mental health reasons.

- All people will occasionally experience some form of mental illness, but the vast majority of people will not become criminals.

- Advocates psychological profiling for those deemed at risk of criminal behavior but finds fault with the current means of conducting psychological profiling.

- Served as the defense expert in the murder trial of Susan Smith, accused in 1994 of deliberately driving her car into a lake and watching as her two young sons drowned while still strapped in the car.

  - ❖ Halleck testified to Susan Smith's mental illness; however, she was found guilty of two counts of murder.

MODELING THEORY

This involves the process of learning by observing the behavior of others.

4.6 **Modeling theory** is a social learning theory that suggests that behavior is learned by observing others.

4.6.1 Laws of imitation

- Gabriel Tarde (1843–1904)

MAJOR IMPACT: Tarde was one of the first theorists to consider deviance as learned behavior, specifically developing three specific laws of imitation.

SELECTED PUBLICATIONS: *The Laws of Imitation* (1890), *Social Laws* (1908)

- ❖ Argued against biological theories of Lombroso
- ❖ Believed imitation was basis of any society
  - ◆ Imitation is the tendency of people to pattern their behavior after the behavior of others.
- ❖ Three laws of imitation
  - ◆ Law #1: Law of close contact
    - ❑ Individuals in close intimate contact with one another tend to imitate each other's behavior.
    - ❑ Could be something as trivial as clothing styles or something as serious as deviant behavior
  - ◆ Law #2: Law of imitation
    - ❑ Imitation moves from top down.
    - ❑ Inferiors tend to copy the way their perceived superiors act. Examples:
      - Poor people tend to imitate wealthy people.
      - Youngsters tend to emulate those older than themselves.

◆ Law #3: Law of insertion

❑ New acts and behaviors tend to replace or reinforce old ones.

❑ The criminal can learn how to be a better criminal or develop a better criminal technique by imitating those who are better at the crime.

❖ Epidemics of deviance

◆ Tarde believed that the media impacted crime.

◆ Because the media publicizes crime, copycat crimes often take place.

For more on imitation and Gabriel Tarde, visit Criminology Interactive online > Theory Explained: Gabriel Tarde.

4.6.2   Modeling theory of aggression

■ Albert Bandura (born 1925)

MAJOR IMPACT: Bandura specifically applied modeling theory to aggression and proposed that while all individuals are capable of aggression, those who become aggressively deviant do so by modeling specific patterns of behavior.

SELECTED PUBLICATIONS: *Social Learning and Personality Development* (1963), *Social Learning Theory* (1977), *Social Foundations of Thought and Action* (1986)

❖ Believed that people are not naturally born violent, but instead learn to be violent through their life experiences

❖ Reciprocal determinism

◆ The environment influences people and people influence the environment.

❖ The causes of any human behavior were a result of:

◆ That person's personality

◆ The effect of the environment on the person

◆ The effect of the person on the environment

❖ Aggressive behavior is learned, including the forms of that behavior, the frequency, and the targets selected for attack.

◆ Aggression can be provoked through:

❑ Physical assaults

❑ Verbal threats

❑ Thwarting a person's hopes

❑ Obstructing goal-seeking behavior

❑ Deprivation

◻ Reductions or negative changes in conditions

- A lowered standard of living
- Onset of disease
- A spouse leaving or caught cheating

◆ Individuals can see aggressive behavior as holding future benefits for them.

◻ Aggressive behavior is sometimes seen as a means to a desired end.

◆ Individuals may perceive that there are rewards for acting aggressively.

◆ Bandura also proposed that standing up for oneself can fuel aggression and improve the way one is treated by others.

◆ Everyone can regulate tendencies toward aggression.

◻ People use their own internal standards to reward or punish themselves for their behavior.

◻ Aggression may be inhibited in people who have religious, ethical, and/or moral standards.

◆ **Disengagement**

◻ People who are not inclined to aggression may still participate in it through disengagement, a process of constructing rationalizations that overcome internal inhibitions.

◆ BoBo the Clown studies

◻ BoBo was an inflatable, egg-shaped clown doll with a rounded weighted bottom, which constantly righted itself when struck.

◻ Bandura filmed a young woman hitting and kicking the clown and also striking the clown with a hammer.

◻ When the film was shown to a group of kindergarten children, they imitated the woman's behavior towards the same kind of inflatable clown.

◻ These children changed their behavior of non-action or nonviolence without being told to do so and without the promise of any rewards.

◻ Bandura described the children's behavior as modeling, behavior learned through observation.

◻ In later studies, a live clown was substituted for the inflatable BoBo and the results were the same.

◆ Bandura proposed that exposure to positive modeling examples could change the patterns of their behavior, including any deviant behavior.

DISENGAGEMENT
A process of constructing rationalizations that overcomes internal inhibitions.

❖ Criticisms of modeling theory

◆ Cannot comprehensively explain behavior

❑ There are differences in sibling behavior when early childhood experiences are likely similar.

❑ There are differences between genders in terms of the degree and type of deviant behavior, in spite of differences in social background and early learning experiences.

4.7 **Behavior theory** sometimes referred to as the stimulus-response approach to human behavior

4.7.1 Behavior is determined by the consequences it produces.

4.7.2 An individual's responses are called operant behavior; they operate on the environment to produce a consequence for the individual.

4.7.3 Environmental stimuli become cues that create conditioned responses from the individual.

4.7.4 Responses are conditioned according to the individual's past experiences.

4.7.5 Behavior theory is often used by parents seeking to control their children's behavior through reward and punishment.

4.7.6 Rewards and punishments

■ Rewards and punishments are divided into four categories.

❖ Positive rewards

◆ Increases the frequency of desired behavior by adding an item that is valued to the situation

◆ Example: When a child exhibits desired behavior and is rewarded with a toy

❖ Negative rewards

◆ Increases the frequency of desired behavior by removing something that is perceived as stressful from the situation

◆ Example: When a "good" child is permitted to skip certain activities

❖ Positive punishments

◆ Decreases the frequency of undesired behavior by adding something undesirable to the situation

◆ Example: When a child is spanked or put in time out

❖ Negative punishments

◆ Decreases the frequency of undesired behavior by removing something that is valued

◆ Example: When a toy is removed from a child who is not behaving

BEHAVIOR THEORY

An approach to understanding human activity that holds that behavior is determined by consequences it produces for the individual.

4.7.7 B. F. Skinner (1904–1990)

MAJOR IMPACT: Skinner, the major theorist of behavior theory, did extensive research, including animal studies that looked at behavior as a pattern of responses to rewards and stimuli. His studies eventually led to the basis for behavior modification.

SELECTED PUBLICATIONS: *Walden Two* (1948), *Science and Human Behavior* (1953)

- Focused on the characteristics of responses to external rewards and stimuli
    - ❖ Contended that all behavior is learned and can be unlearned
    - ❖ Concerned with observable behavior rather than psychological behavior that is not observable
    - ❖ Undesirable behavior can be eliminated, modified, or replaced by taking away the reward value or by rewarding a more appropriate behavior that is incompatible with the deviant one.

For more on behavior theory, visit Criminology Interactive online > Psychological Theories > Theory Explained: Behavior Theory.

4.8 Attachment theory

ATTACHMENT THEORY

The theory that a child's attachment to their parents is important for creating conformity even when those others are deviant themselves.

4.8.1 John Bowlby (1907–1990)

MAJOR IMPACT: A British child psychiatrist, Bowlby observed children in institutionalized situations in London and developed the attachment theory, which proposes that children, especially between 6 and about 30 months, are very likely to form emotional attachments to caregivers, and that strong attachment is essential to later emotional and personality development.

SELECTED PUBLICATIONS: *Attachment* (1969), *Separation* (1973), *Loss* (1980)

- Attachment theory contends:
    - ❖ There is a strong, natural, emotional bond between human beings.
    - ❖ Bonding involves the exchange of love, comfort, care, and pleasure between people.
    - ❖ Bonding begins at birth with the bonding of a child and its parents.
- Especially interested in maladjusted behavior of children who lacked a solid relationship with a mother figure
- Concluded that developing a healthy personality requires that an infant have a strong and continuous relationship with a mother figure.

- Identified three forms of attachment:
  - ❖ Secure attachment
    - ◆ The only healthy form of attachment
    - ◆ Occurs when a child feels confident that the mother figure is available and present in the infant's life
    - ◆ Secure attachments develop in early childhood when a developing infant is nurtured.
  - ❖ Anxious-avoidant attachment
    - ◆ Develops when a child feels rejected and fails to develop the confidence that the parent will care for him
  - ❖ Anxious-resistant attachment
    - ◆ Develops when the child feels uncertain regarding the parental bond causing the child (and later the adult) to be nervous, anxious, and fearful of his environment and to cling to partners or potential caregivers.

4.8.2 Nonsecure attachments lead to delinquenct behavior. Individuals who develop delinquent behavior will be those who:

- Were abandoned or institutionalized at an early age

- Experienced multiple placements in different homes

- Experienced the early absence of one or both parents

- Endured trauma in early childhood (physical, sexual, or other abuse)

4.9 **Self-control theory** considers the ways that an individual is able to change their responses, especially when faced with adversity.

SELF-CONTROL THEORY
Focused on the individual rather than on external sources of control.

  4.9.1 Four psychological types of self-control

- Impulse control, the ability to resist impulses that are socially unacceptable

- Self-control that suppresses unwanted thoughts, reasoning and analysis, and inference and guided intuition

- Self-control exercised over one's emotional and mood states

- Controlling performance, when an individual perseveres in the face of challenges

  4.9.2 High levels of self-control allow individuals to adjust to a wide variety of situations.

- Psychologists sometimes claim that today's personal and social problems stem from deficiencies or failures in self-control.
  - ❖ Some examples include drug and alcohol abuse, violence, unwanted pregnancy, and delinquency and criminality

4.9.3   General theory of crime

■ Michael R. Gottfredson (born 1951) and Travis Hirschi (born 1935)

MAJOR IMPACT: Gottfredson and Hirschi

PUBLICATION: *A General Theory of Crime* (1990)

❖ Gottfredson and Hirschi set forth this theory as a way to explain all types of delinquent and criminal acts, proposing that the ability to exhibit self-control depends on social bonds that are created in families and in society.

❖ Low self-control

◆ A person's impulsive personality gives in to the individual's low self-control.

◆ Low self-control occurs when social bonds such as attachment to family, involvement with friends and peers, are weak.

❖ Self-control

◆ Degree to which a person is likely to succumb to the temptations of the moment

◆ Acquired early in life as parents nurture children by keeping track of their behavior, using appropriate punishment, and taking action when any form of deviant behavior occurs

❖ The link between self-control and crime depends on opportunity presented when an individual encounters a situation.

■ Harold G. Grasmick

❖ Expanded on the work of Gottfredson and Hirschi

❖ Characterized individuals with low self-control as:

◆ Displaying impulsiveness

◆ Seeking immediate gratification

◆ Lacking tenacity

◆ Drawn to activities that are adventurous and exciting

◆ Preferring physical activity

◆ Indifferent or insensitive to the needs of others

◆ Predisposed to being self-centered

◆ Risk-taking

◆ Inclined to handling conflict through confrontation

❖ Those with higher levels of self-control are more inclined to delay gratification in order to achieve long-term gains.

CHAPTER SUMMARY

➤ The psychological perspective focuses on the individual in an attempt to understand how criminal behavior develops and how it is acted upon. Within the individual, the personality is seen as the major motivator. Crimes, then, result from abnormal, dysfunctional, or maladaptive mental processes of the personality. The psychological perspective seeks to understand and explain those defects, which are seen as having a variety of potential causes including mental disease, inappropriate learning, emulation of inappropriate role models, and poor adjustment to inner conflicts.

➤ Psychiatric criminology is a set of theories derived from medical science that focuses on the individual as a point of analysis. Key theorists of psychiatric criminology include Hervey M. Cleckley, one of the first theorists to use the term "psychopath" in association with mental illness. Psychopathy describes a personality disorder that is characterized by chronic antisocial or immoral behavior. Psychopaths demonstrate a lack of conscience or the ability to identify or imagine the feelings of others.

➤ Sigmund Freud was the founding father of psychiatric tradition and his theories have been applied to criminology in an approach known as psychoanalytic criminology. Freud saw deviant behavior as a dysfunction of personality and developed a theory of personality, which was made up of three components: the id (operates only on the pleasure principle); the ego (functions as the reality principle); and the superego (provides ethical guidance). Deviant behavior occurs when any of these three components are out of balance with each other. Though Freud did not touch on criminal behavior specifically, his principles have wide application to criminology, as well as to other fields of study.

➤ The frustration-aggression theory, developed by Seymour Halleck, contends that society cannot determine what criminal behavior is and what behavior should be excused for mental health reasons. According to Halleck, all people will occasionally experience some form of mental illness, but the vast number of people will not become criminals.

➤ The modeling theory asserts that people learn how to act by imitating others and therefore, that deviant behavior is learned or modeled behavior. Gabriel Tarde first suggested this theory in 1890 and developed three principles or laws that determined how imitation worked: the law of close contact, which suggests that individuals imitate those they are in close contact with; the law of imitation, which claims that imitation moves from top down; and the law of insertion, which states that new behaviors replace or reinforce old ones. A later theorist, Albert Bandura, specifically applied the modeling theory to aggression. His studies suggested the power of both negative and positive examples. Being exposed to positive examples, Bandura concluded, can change patterns of behavior, including deviant behavior.

➤ Behavior theory contends that behavior is determined by the environmental consequences that it produces. When behavior is rewarded with either positive or negative rewards, for example, that behavior increases. When it is punished with either positive or negative punishment, the behavior decreases. B. F. Skinner is the best-known proponent of behavior theory. Skinner focused on behavior that was unobservable rather than observed. Skinner's research suggested that undesirable or deviant behavior could be eliminated or modified by rewarding appropriate behavior.

➤ John Bowlby, an English child psychiatrist, first proposed the attachment theory. Attachment theory holds that there is a strong emotional attachment between and among human beings, especially between children and their parents. Delinquent behavior occurs when that attachment is insecure.

➤ Self-control theory contends that a person's ability to alter his responses to outside influences will determine their behavior. Some psychologists contend that such problems as drug abuse, alcoholism, and violence stem from lack of self-control.

➤ Related to self-control theory is the general theory of crime developed by Michael Gottfredson and Travis Hirschi. Their theory looks at the impulsive personality and its relationship to low self-control, as well as to the way low self-control weakens social bonds. This theory, they claim, can explain all kinds of delinquent and criminal acts.

STUDY QUESTIONS

1. According to the psychological perspective, what is considered the major motivator of human behavior?
2. What are the three major components of Freud's psychiatric theory?
3. What does modeling theory have to say about how deviant behavior is learned?
4. How does behavior theory mold behavior?
5. How does attachment theory evaluate family relationships?
6. How does self-control and the mechanisms associated with it impact deviant behavior?

ONLINE@CRIMINOLOGY INTERACTIVE

Theory in Action

Case File #1: Murder—Debra
Case File #2: Calling Friends for Party—Charlie

Review

Vocabulary Shootout
Essay Questions
Section Test

Readings and Research

Web Links

Additional Theorists

William Healy

Chapter 5

Sociological Theories I
Social Structure

MENU ▲   ▲ GLOSSARY

CHAPTER OUTLINE

KEY IDEAS

➤ Sociological theories focus on how an individual's position in society affects individual behavior. Specifically, this set of theories looks at social groups, institutions, and arrangements within groups to determine how and why criminal behavior takes place.

➤ The social structure approach, the subject of this chapter, investigates how the interactions of individuals and groups within and among economic and social conditions affects behavior.

➤ The social structure theory (known as social disorganization theory) considers how communities react to social change and uneven social and economic development of culture.

➤ The ecology theory grew out of studies conducted at the University of Chicago in the 1920s and 1930s. It looks at the organization of cities, particularly Chicago, and developed the notion of concentric zones, a series of zones organized like a target around a bull's-eye that were identified with particular social groups and activities.

➤ Another type of social structure theory, strain theory, considers deviance as adaptation in response to frustrating and undesirable social environments. Anomie specifically describes what happens when there is a breakdown between socially accepted goals and approved pathways to achieve those goals.

➤ Culture conflict theory considers that all conflict lies in the fact that individual groups have been socialized differently by different cultures.

➤ Related to culture conflict theory, subcultural theory looks at the smaller subcultures from within larger cultures of which they are a part, with a specific emphasis on how subcultures adopt and communicate their own set of values.

KEY TERMS

concentric zones
conduct norms
conformity
cultural transmission
culture conflict theory
distributive justice
drift
focal concerns
illegitimate opportunity
innovation
legitimate opportunity
primary conflict
reaction formation
rebellion
relative deprivation
retreatism
ritualism
secondary conflict
social disorganization theory
social ecology theory
social pathology
social structure approach
socialization
strain theory or anomie
subcultural theory
subcultures
symbolic interaction

5.0   Sociological theories I: Social structure

5.1   Major principles of sociological theories

    5.1.1   The study of social groups and the arrangement of society in general are pertinent to any study of criminology.

    5.1.2   The dynamics and organization of social groups can directly impact the occurrence of crime, and can offer insight into why and how that crime occurs.

    5.1.3   The level of organization or disorganization of a social group can contribute to the development of criminal behavior.

    5.1.4   An individual's location within society influences his behavior

SOCIAL STRUCTURE APPROACH

Theories that attempt to explain crime by reference to various aspects of the social fabric. Specifically, they look at the relationships among social institutions and describe the types of behavior that tend to characterize groups of people as opposed to individuals.

5.2   Major principles of **social structure approach**

    5.2.1   A person's location or position within society has a direct impact on criminal behavior.

    5.2.2   Approach focuses on social and economic conditions of life, including:

- Poverty
- Alienation
- Social disorganization
- Weak social control
- Personal frustration
- **Relative deprivation**
- Differential opportunity
- Alternative means to success
- Deviant **subcultures** and subcultural values that conflict with conventional values

RELATIVE DEPRIVATION

The feeling that because of social inequality, they are not offered equal opportunities to achieve legitimate success.

SUBCULTURES

Collections of values and preferences that are communicated to subcultural participants through the process of socialization.

5.3   Social structure theories

    5.3.1   Attempts to understand crime by considering the economic and social structures of society

    5.3.2   Focuses particularly on low socioeconomic status as a cause of crime

    5.3.3   Crime is seen primarily a lower-class occurrence.

5.3.4   Types of social structure theories:

- **Social disorganization theory**

- **Strain theory**

- **Culture conflict theory**

For more on the social structure approach, visit Criminology Interactive online > Social Structure Theories > Theory Explained: Introduction to Social Structure Theories.

5.4   Social disorganization theory

5.4.1   Initially developed from the ideas of the ecological school of criminology, which focused on urban communities, especially those in Chicago in the early twentieth century

5.4.2   The ecological school looked at the natural environment of the community as a major determinant of human behavior. Major theorists include:

- Emile Durkheim (1858–1917) (Discussed in more detail under Anomie section, 5.5.2)

  - Believed that crime is both a normal and functional characteristic of society

    - Crime is a basic part of human social nature.

      - For crime not to exist, virtually all members of society would have to be alike in action and thought.

      - As long as human differences exist, so will crime.

        - Based on a basic Darwinian principle— variety is the evolutionary norm and necessity

  - Durkheim also proposed that crime can be, and often is, useful and healthy for a society.

    - Based on the principle of evolution that variety creates change/progress

    - Crime opens the door for social change.

  - Crime can call attention to social problems.

SOCIAL DISORGANIZATION THEORY

A condition said to exist when a group is faced with social change, uneven development of culture, maladaptiveness, disharmony, conflict, and lack of consensus.

STRAIN THEORY OR ANOMIE THEORY

A sociological approach that posits a disjuncture between socially and subculturally sanctioned means and goals as the cause of criminal behavior.

CULTURE CONFLICT THEORY

A theory that sees conflict as major social processes, set in motion by the differences in values and cultures among groups of people.

- Ferdinand Toennies (1855–1936)

MAJOR IMPACT: Toennies developed the theory that the earliest forms of society developed as families and small communities, based in togetherness and mutually helpful relationships. As these communities developed into towns and then cities, the emphasis on social ties has been lost.

SELECTED PUBLICATION: *Community and Society* (1912), *Marx* (1921)

❖ Toennies' theory of society was based on evolutionary principles that showed how communities had changed since ancient times.

- Georg Simmel (1858–1918)
  ❖ Pioneered concept of social structure
  ❖ Attempted to explain the recurring forms of normal human behavior in everyday life in terms of economics, politics, and aesthetics

- W. I. Thomas (1863–1947) and Florian Znaniecki (1882–1958)

MAJOR IMPACT: Thomas and Znaniecki studied Polish immigrants in America, especially as it related to crime, and developed the term social disorganization to describe the way immigrants reacted to their new environment. Thomas went on to develop the symbolic interaction perspective, which proposed that individuals impart their own meaning to words and acts.

SELECTED PUBLICATION: *The Polish Peasant in Europe and America* (1920)

❖ Noted the increase in crime in immigrant populations that had been displaced, and created the idea of social disorganization to explain the immigrants' inability to integrate norms and cultures from their original culture to their new one

❖ Thomas's work later shifted to the field of social psychology and more particularly, the **symbolic interaction** perspective.

◆ Proposed the idea that individuals bring their own particular meaning to words and acts

◆ In symbolic interaction theory, a person's response to something (the symbol) was based both on the objective setting of the act, word, or situation, and on the subjective responses of individuals.

◆ Thomas believed that people responded to both the objective characteristics of a symbol and to what that symbol meant to them personally.

SYMBOLIC INTERACTION

Developed from a belief that human behavior is the product of purely social symbols communicated between individuals.

For more on the ecological approach, visit Criminology Interactive online > Social Structure Theories > Theory Explained: The Chicago School and Social Process Theories > Theory Explained: Introduction to the Chicago School.

5.4.3   **Social ecology theory** (ecological school of criminology)

- Developed at the University of Chicago in the 1920s and 1930s as a study of urban environments, using Chicago and the surrounding area as a laboratory of research.

- Social ecology grew out of the work of biologists who studied the way organisms interacted with their environment.

- Focuses on how the structure of society changes based on its natural resources and its reaction to other human groups

- Social ecologists developed a disease model built around the concept of **social pathology**.

  ❖ The concept of social pathology was the idea that aspects of society may be somehow pathological or "sick," and may produce deviant behavior among those who live in these conditions.

- Examined the role that social institutions play in the development of criminal lifestyles, with a particular emphasis on how breakdowns in social institutions lead to deviant behavior

- The ecological study of crime

  ❖ Explored the interaction between the environment and deviant behavior

  ❖ Identified how neighborhood conditions (like poverty) affected the distribution of crime

- Ernest W. Burgess (1886–1966) and Robert E. Park (1864–1944)

  MAJOR IMPACT: Using Chicago as a model, researched the relationship between ecology and crime, and founded the ecological school of criminology, a perspective that became known as social ecology.

  ❖ According to Burgess and Park, the city was a living, growing thing much like a human body, and the various parts of the city were seen as organs that served different functions.

- Studies of Chicago's high-crime areas suggested that a criminal's world has its own set of order and rules.

  ❖ **Concentric zones**

    ◆ Developed to study Chicago, but thought to be applicable to other cities

    ◆ Can be visualized as a target, similar to one used in archery. This theory divides the city into five zones:

      ❑ Zone 1: central business district (center of target)

        • City's business zone, and includes light manufacturing, retail trade, and commercialization

SOCIAL ECOLOGY THEORY

Also commonly called the "Chicago School" of criminology, is a type of sociological approach, which emphasizes demographics (the characteristics of population groups) and geographics (the mapped location of such groups relative to one another) and sees the social disorganization, which characterizes delinquency areas as a major cause of criminality and victimization.

SOCIAL PATHOLOGY

A concept that compares society to a physical organism and sees criminality as an illness.

CONCENTRIC ZONES

A conception of the city (Chicago) as a series of distinctive circles radiating from the central business district used to describe differences in crime rates.

- Zone 2: zone of transition
  - Surrounds the central business district; zone offers a transition from residential to business use
  - Occupied primarily by those of low income
  - Home to immigrant groups who have recently relocated
  - General features include deteriorated housing, factories, and abandoned buildings
  - May also include some high-cost luxury housing
- Zone 3: zone of working-class homes
  - Less deteriorated than Zone 2
    - Occupied primarily by those with an income that allows them to have typical comforts of a city, and even some luxuries
- Zone 4: area of middle-class dwellers
  - Populated largely by professionals, small business owners, and those of management status
  - Single-family homes, typically with their own yard and garage
- Zone 5: commuters' zone
  - Many of the occupants commute to city for employment.
  - Consists of suburbs and satellite towns
- ◆ As a general rule, residents of inner-city zones tended to migrate to outer zones as their economic positions improved.

For more on concentric zones, visit Criminology Interactive online > Social Structure Theory > Theory Explained: Concentric Zones Theory and Social Process Theories > Theory Explained: Concentric Zone Theory.

- Clifford Shaw (1896–1957) and Henry McKay (1899–1980)

MAJOR IMPACT: Shaw and McKay applied the concentric zone model to their study of juvenile delinquency, concluding that as groups moved outward into different zones, the areas they left behind stayed relatively the same. This led to their theory of cultural transition, the idea that **socialization** transmitted delinquency through successive generations of individuals who lived in the same area.

SELECTED PUBLICATION: *Juvenile Delinquency and Urban Areas* (1969)

SOCIALIZATION

The lifelong process of social experience, whereby individuals acquire cultural patterns of their society.

- ❖ Conducted studies of arrest rates for juveniles in Chicago during the years 1900 to 1906, 1917 to 1923, and 1927 to 1933
  - ◆ These years represented high rates of neighborhood transitions when immigrant groups moved most rapidly from the inner city outward.
- ❖ This pattern was repeated as new immigrant groups settled into the zone of transition.
- ❖ Shaw and McKay found that delinquency remained relatively constant over time within the zone of transition (Zone 2).
- ❖ This led them to conclude that delinquency was caused by characteristics of the environment in which the immigrants lived rather than by some trait of the groups themselves.
- ❖ Some disorganization developed when local communities could not solve common problems.
  - ◆ The amount of disorganization depended upon the degree of mobility and racial diversity in the community.

- ■ **Cultural transmission**
  - ❖ The theory that delinquency is passed down through successive generations of the same zone

CULTURAL TRANSMISSION

The theory that delinquency is passed down through successive generations of the same zone.

5.5   Strain theory

5.5.1   Sees delinquency as an attempt to solve problems, usually in response to undesirable or unsatisfying social conditions or environments

5.5.2   Anomie

- ■ Emile Durkheim (1858–1917)

MAJOR IMPACT: A noted French sociologist, Durkheim developed the idea that crime was necessary, normal, and functional, and developed the concept of anomie, which describes the loss of belonging that an individual feels when he is not personally integrated in society.

SELECTED PUBLICATION: *Suicide* (1897)

- ❖ A noted French sociologist, Durkheim saw crime as:
  - ◆ Necessary
    - ❑ The concept of wrong is necessary to give meaning to right.
    - ❑ Inevitable; even a community of saints will create sinners
    - ❑ If society is to permit positive deviation, it must expect negative deviation as well.
  - ◆ Functional
    - ❑ If deviation is not permitted, societies become stagnant.
    - ❑ Crime helps prepare society for such changes; it is one of the prices we pay for freedom.

- ◆ Normal
  - ❑ No society is exempt from crime.
- ❖ Durkheim was responsible for making the concept of anomie an integral part of sociology and criminology.
- ❖ Durkheim described two types of societies (somewhat similar to those described by Toennies, section 5.4.2).
  - ◆ Mechanical society
    - ❑ People are homogeneous.
    - ❑ Similar to primitive societies
    - ❑ Dominated by the collective conscience
    - ❑ Reason for law is to discourage individuals from acting in a way that threatens the collective conscience.
  - ◆ Organic solidarity
    - ❑ People are more heterogeneous
    - ❑ Representative of more modern societies
    - ❑ Characterized by an increased need for a division of labor
    - ❑ Traditional forms of social control of behavior are not effective.
    - ❑ Social isolation and loss of identity often occurs.
    - ❑ A state of anomie, or a lack of norms, replaces the former state of solidarity, providing an atmosphere in which crimes and other antisocial acts develop.

- ■ Robert K. Merton (1910–2003)

MAJOR IMPACT: A sociologist who spent most of his career at Columbia University, Merton expanded the concept of anomie to include the disconnect between socially accepted goals and an individual's ability to achieve those goals. Merton's work identified the strain felt by the individual as a result of the disconnection, an approach that has been called strain theory.

SELECTED PUBLICATION: "Social Structure and Anomie" published in *American Sociological Review*, Vol. 3

- ❖ Durkheim's theory of anomie and the notion that crime is normal led to Merton's contributions toward understanding criminal behavior.
  - ◆ To achieve goals such as wealth, status, and personal happiness, most individuals rely on socially approved methods: education, hard work, and saving financially.

♦ Strain results when individuals do not have access to the tools or the socially approved ways to meet these goals, and they resort to crime and deviance as a way to achieve them.

♦ This led Merton to develop the theory known as strain theory.

♦ The fact that not everyone accepts the legitimacy of socially approved goals offers a further complication.

♦ Merton identified five adaptations, which represent different combinations of goals and means:

❏ **Conformity**

- Individuals strive for goals that society holds as legitimate and uses normal ways to achieve these goals.

- Most common form of adaptation; is used by most middle- and upper-class individuals

❏ **Innovation**

- Individuals accept that the goals of society are legitimate but replace legitimate means to achieve these goals and uses non-approved means.

- Characteristic of many lower-class individuals who have been socialized to desire socially approved goals but do not have ready access to the approved tools to acquire them

- These individuals turn to crime when they are deprived of socially approved tools for success.

- Poverty does not cause crime; rather, the pressure an individual feels to achieve material success leads to crime.

❏ **Ritualism**

- Individuals accept the goals that society holds as legitimate, but show little interest in achieving them.

- Ritualists may get an education, be employed in an acceptable occupation, and appear to lead a typical middle-class lifestyle, yet may not strive for the traditional symbols of success, choosing to live an otherwise independent lifestyle.

CONFORMITY

Striving for socially approved goals and following normal means of achieving them. Most people adapt this way; if not, according to Merton, the very existence of society would be threatened.

INNOVATION

A case of adaptation in which the emphasis on the approved goals of society is maintained while legitimate means are replaced by other, nonapproved means.

RITUALISM

A mode of adaptation where the goals themselves are not rejected, but there is very little interest in attaining traditional symbols of success.

RETREATISM

Individuals reject both the socially legitimate goals and the approved means for achieving them.

REBELLION

This mode of adaptation focuses on the substitution of society's goals and means for other ones.

❐ **Retreatism**

- Individuals reject both the socially legitimate goals and the approved means for achieving them.

- Retreatists may become:
  - Dropouts
  - Drug abusers
  - Gang members
  - Homeless persons
  - Participants in an alternative lifestyle like communal living

- Individuals who rely on retreatism are often isolated from the larger society around them.

- Least common form of adaptation

❐ **Rebellion**

- Individuals reject society's goals and the socially approved means to achieve them, replacing them with new goals.

- Examples of individuals who may fit this category:
  - Political radicals
  - Revolutionaries
  - Antiestablishment agitators

- This adaptation is an attempt to alter social structure rather than to adapt to it.

For more on the Robert Merton and his theories, visit Criminology Interactive online > Social Structure Theories > Theory Explained: Robert Merton.

5.5.3 Relative deprivation

■ Steven F. Messner and Richard Rosenfeld

MAJOR IMPACT: Messner and Rosenfeld expanded Merton's anomie theory to include relative deprivation, a theory proposing that there is an economic and social divide between the rich and poor who live close to one another.

SELECTED PUBLICATION: *Crime and the American Dream* (2006)

❖ Messner and Rosenfeld focus on the notion of the American Dream and claim that inconsistencies within the American Dream are the cause of most criminal activities.

❖ The American Dream induces pressure on the social environment and suggests that any behavior is appropriate when pursuing this dream.

❖ The American Dream is both a goal and a process.

 ◆ The existence of the American Dream implies that there will always be losers and winners.

 ◆ When the losers face the fact that they have lost, they feel justified in pursuing the American Dream through illegal means.

 ◆ This rationalization leads to criminal behavior.

■ Judith and Peter Blau

MAJOR IMPACT: Judith and Peter Blau contended that people judge their own position in life by comparing themselves to things and other individuals they know.

SELECTED PUBLICATIONS: *Exchange and Power in Social Life* (1964), *A Formal Theory of Differentiation in Organizations* (1970)

❖ Individuals who grow up impoverished in the inner city develop an increasing sense of relative deprivation as they witness well-to-do lifestyles in nearby neighborhoods.

❖ Relative deprivation creates feelings of:

 ◆ Anger

 ◆ Frustration

 ◆ Hostility

 ◆ Social injustice

❖ Two types of relative deprivation:

 ◆ Personal

  ❏ Individuals feel deprived when comparing themselves to other people.

  ❏ This results in feelings of social isolation and personal stress.

 ◆ Group

  ❏ Social groups feel a communal sense of injustice.

  ❏ Individuals in this social group may participate in social movements and actively attempt to change the social system.

  ❏ Relative deprivation as a group activity can be a powerful force for social change.

5.5.4 Distributive justice

■ Related to relative deprivation

■ John Rawls (1921–2002), best known proponent of distributive justice

■ In a *Theory of Justice* (1971, revised 1999), argued for the notion of justice and fairness and, contended that an individual's perception of his rightful place in the reward structure of society impacts behavior.

DISTRIBUTIVE JUSTICE

The notion that rightful rewards for those in society are based on cultural expectations.

- Socially privileged individuals, as well as those who are less privileged, feel slighted if they feel they have not been rewarded for their behavior or their accomplishments.

- Cultural expectations determine the rightful distribution of rewards.

5.5.5   General strain theory

- Robert Agnew (b. 1953)

MAJOR IMPACT: Agnew reformulated the strain theory into a comprehensive theory called general strain theory, which described strain as a kind of coping strategy to deal with the social and emotional repercussions of negative social relations.

SELECTED PUBLICATION: *Juvenile Delinquency: Causes and Control* (2004)

- ❖ General strain theory expands on traditional strain theory in several ways:
  - ◆ Includes all types of negative reaction between an individual and others
  - ◆ Claims that strain has a cumulative effect on delinquency
  - ◆ Offers a more comprehensive explanation of cognitive, behavioral, and emotional adaptations
  - ◆ Describes a wider variety of factors that cause strain and delinquent adaptations to that strain
- ❖ Strain occurs when others do the following:
  - ◆ Deny or attempt to deny an individual the means to achieve socially approved goals
  - ◆ Remove or threaten to remove something an individual values, such as a loved one
  - ◆ Demonstrate or threaten to demonstrate negative behavior to a individual, such as insults or physical abuse
- ❖ Strain creates a predisposition for delinquency when it is chronic or repetitive.
- ❖ Several factors determine whether strain will result in criminal behavior, including personality, intelligence, social support, and bonds with criminal peers.
- ❖ Negative affect states, which refer to anger and related emotions, can cause strain and lead to delinquency, particularly in adolescents.

For more on general strain theory, visit Criminology Interactive online > Social Structure Theories: Theory Explained: Introduction to Strain Theory.

5.6 Culture conflict theory

5.6.1 Proposes that criminality is caused by a conflict of values between differently socialized groups over what is acceptable

5.6.2 Thorsten Sellin (1896–1994)

MAJOR IMPACT: Sellin developed the culture conflict theory in which he maintained that conflict is a result of the major the differences in values and cultures among groups of people.

SELECTED PUBLICATIONS: *Culture Conflict and Crime* (1938)

- **Conduct norms**

- Forms the fundamental basis for human behavior in regard to values acquired through childhood socialization

- The conflict in norms between groups that have been socialized differently results in crime.

- Crime, then, is really a disagreement over what is acceptable.

  ❖ What has been called a crime in some social groups is a natural part of life for others, and criminal events occur when one does not take measures to protect oneself.

  ❖ Victims of crime are not so much victims as they are unprepared.

- Sellin identified two types of culture conflict:

  ❖ **Primary conflict**

    ◆ A fundamental cultural conflict

    ◆ Example: an immigrant father who kills his daughter's lover following an old-world tradition that demands that a family's honor be kept intact

    ◆ When primary conflict occurs, norms move from one culture to another. This conflict continues until the acculturation process has been completed.

  ❖ **Secondary conflict**

    ◆ Arises when smaller cultures clash with the larger culture

    ◆ Criminal laws are based on middle-class values and these values may conflict with other norms, such as those of the inner city or lower class, to create crime.

    ◆ Example: Many lower-income groups consider gambling and prostitution, both illegal activities, a way of life.

5.6.3 Subcultural theory

- Subculture is a group that possesses a collection of values and preferences that is communicated to participants of a smaller group through the process of socialization.

CONDUCT NORMS

The shared expectations of a social group relative to personal conduct.

PRIMARY CONFLICT

Occurs when an individual is caught between two different cultures governing behavior.

SECONDARY CONFLICT

Over a period of time, smaller cultures existing within a larger culture begin , to create their own set of values where there are enough differences to cause conflict.

- Subcultures differ from the larger culture because they are made up of smaller groups of people and do not conform to the rules of the traditional culture.

- **Subcultural theory** considers the way that various subcultures contribute to crime.

- Frederic M. Thrasher (1892–1970)

  ❖ A sociologist and a member of the Chicago School of sociology in the 1920s, Thrasher believed gangs were a part of the psychological and group processes of adolescents in poor communities.

  ❖ Believed gangs were formed spontaneously in a particular area through normal associations with individuals and were then integrated and structured through conflict

  ❖ Over a period of time, gangs developed loyalties, solidarity, morale, and attachments to the area.

- William F. Whyte (1914–2000)

  ❖ From 1937 to 1940, Whyte studied members of an Italian slum and published a study called "Cornerville."

  ❖ Developed a subcultural theory, which found that members of a typical slum could achieve success through the activities of the slum culture, including gambling.

- Walter B. Miller (1920–2004)

  ❖ Miller created the concept of **focal concerns**.

    ◆ A lower-class culture is characterized by:

      ❑ System values that establish and maintain the way of life

      ❑ Attitudes that go against norms of the middle class and may be considered as purposely nonconforming

  ❖ Miller's specific focal concerns:

    ◆ Trouble is a fundamental feature of lower-class culture

      ❑ Examples of trouble include men fighting or having sexual adventures while drinking, or women involved in sexual encounters with negative consequences.

    ◆ Lower-class men need to develop the characteristic of toughness, either spiritually or physically, or they risk being seen as weak.

      ❑ The need to be tough in lower-class male culture may be related to the fact that many of these men were raised in female-headed families.

    ◆ The ability to outsmart others, which Miller called "smartness," is another essential trait of lower-class individuals.

- ◆ Excitement, or the search for thrills, characterizes lower-class lifestyles.
  - ❐ The pursuit of excitement is often an attempt to overcome boredom.
  - ❐ Examples of behaviors that produce excitement include drinking, fighting, gambling, or sexual adventuring.
- ◆ The notion of fate influences the lower-class lifestyle.
  - ❐ The concept of luck forms behavior.
  - ❐ This may stem from the fact that many lower-class individuals feel their lives are influenced by factors over which they have little control.
- ◆ Autonomy is a primary characteristic of lower-class lifestyles.
  - ❐ Manifests itself in statements like "I can take care of myself" and "No one's going to push me around"
  - ❐ Problems develop when norms of autonomy, especially in environments like schools or other institutions, interfere with the lower-class concept of autonomy.

For more on Walter B. Miller, visit Criminology Interactive online > Social Structure Theories > Theory Explained: Walter B. Miller.

- ■ Gresham Sykes (b. 1922) and David Matza (b. 1930)
  - ❖ Criminal behavior in a subcultural environment is not caused by poverty, but is the result of the values system of the subculture
  - ❖ Sykes and Matza suggested that offenders can overcome feelings of responsibility when involved in crime by employing types of justifications:
    - ◆ Denying responsibility, or justifying the injury by saying it was not caused by the offender, but rather by his background of poverty
    - ◆ Denying injury, or claiming that the injury is not serious because the victim can afford it
    - ◆ Denying the victim, or contending that the victim deserved the injury
    - ◆ Condemning the condemners, or claiming society is worse than the offenders; therefore, the offender cannot be responsible
    - ◆ Appealing to higher loyalties, contending the injury was caused because the offender had to defend his honor, his family's honor, or his gang's honor

DRIFT

A state of limbo that makes deviant acts possible.

❖ **Drift**

♦ David Matza introduced the concept of drift, which claims that delinquents tend to participate in crime when weak or ineffective values are present.

♦ A criminal moves between criminal and legal behaviors, choosing the behavior that serves him best at the time.

For more on Gresham Sykes and David Matza, visit Criminology Interactive online > Social Structure Theories > Theory Explained: Sykes and Matza.

■ Franco Ferracuti and Marvin Wolfgang

MAJOR IMPACT: Ferracuti and Wolfgang developed the theory that violence is a learned behavior in response to problematic life circumstances and that learning to be violent occurs in a subculture that demonstrates the advantages of violence over other behaviors.

SELECTED PUBLICATION: *The Subculture of Violence: Toward an Integrated Theory of Criminology* (1967)

❖ Subcultures are characterized by rituals that glorify violence, including songs and stories, macho models, and status as demonstrated by gun ownership.

❖ The violent see violence as a legitimate behavior.

❖ Ferracuti and Wolfgang studied data rates of homicide between racial groups in the Philadelphia area and determined that the rate of homicide for nonwhite men and women was approximately 9 to 10 times the rate as for white men and women.

❖ Ferracuti and Wolfgang offer explanations:

♦ Subcultures do not conflict with the larger society of which they are a part.

♦ The subculture of violence does not require that all individuals share the basic value of violence or that they express violence in all situations.

♦ Violence and deviance in a subculture generally falls within a limited age group, ranging from late adolescence to middle age.

♦ A propensity for violence in a subculture depends on learned behavior.

♦ Subcultures generally don't see violence as criminal or immoral, so deviant individuals do not have to struggle with feelings of guilt about their crimes.

■ Richard A. Cloward (1926–2001) and Lloyd E. Ohlin (1918–2009)

MAJOR IMPACT: Cloward and Ohlin developed the differential opportunity theory, derived from strain theory, which focused on the notion of **illegitimate opportunity** structure, a structure not approved by wider society, and **legitimate opportunity structure**, an opportunity structure available to middle-class culture.

SELECTED PUBLICATION: *Delinquency and Opportunity* (1960)

ILLEGITIMATE OPPORTUNITY
Standard illegitimate avenues used to reach cultural goals.

LEGITIMATE OPPORTUNITY
Standard legitimate avenues used to reach cultural goals.

❖ Identified four types of lower-class youths:

◆ Type I seek to become middle class by improving their economic position.

◆ Type II do not want to improve their economic position in order to enter middle class.

◆ Type III seek higher economic rewards without entry to middle class.

◆ Type IV retreat from society through drug and alcohol.

For more on Richard A. Cloward and Lloyd E. Ohlin, visit Criminology Interactive online > Social Structure Theories > Theory Explained: Cloward and Ohlin.

■ Albert K. Cohen (b. 1918)

MAJOR IMPACT: Cohen proposed the notion of **reaction formation**, claiming that nonmainstream children who can never achieve middle-class values reject them entirely.

REACTION FORMATION
The process by which a person openly rejects that which he or she wants or aspires to but cannot obtain or achieve.

SELECTED PUBLICATION: *Delinquent Boys: The Culture of the Gang* (1955)

❖ Suggested that a measuring rod exists that holds young people accountable to middle-class ideals such as school performance, neatness, nonviolent behavior, and language proficiency

❖ Nonutilitarian delinquency

◆ Youths who choose delinquent behavior are alienated from middle-class lifestyles and achieve status identity from subcultural peers through destructive behavior.

❖ Status frustration

◆ Children, especially those from deprived backgrounds, experience status frustration because they are aware they can't achieve middle-class goals.

❖ Collective behavior of youth

◆ When youths experience alienation from middle-class ideals, they create a delinquent subculture in order to deal with problems of adjustment.

For more on Albert K. Cohen, visit Criminology Interactive online > Social Structure Theories > Theory Explained: Albert Cohen.

CHAPTER SUMMARY

➤ Sociological theories differ from psychological theories discussed previously in that they focus on how an individual's location or position in society, rather than the individual himself, affects behavior. All sociological theories are based on the same principles. First, sociological theorists study social groups, institutions, arrangements, and groups to explain and interpret behavior. Second, the dynamics and organization of social groups directly affect the occurrence of crime and can offer insight into why and how that crime occurs. Third, the level of organization or disorganization can determine the nature and frequency of criminal behavior. Last, an individual's location or position in society influences his behavior.

➤ The social structure approach specifically looks at crime based on the interaction of individuals and groups with social and economic conditions, including poverty, alienation, and personal frustration.

➤ Social disorganization theory, closely aligned with the ecological school of criminology and the human ecology movement of the early twentieth century, looked at communities in order to explain how a community directly determines the quality of life for its members. Emile Durkheim, an early theorist in the field, believed that crime was a natural part of all societies and that law was a symbol of social solidarity. Ferdinand Toennies argued that the earliest forms of communities were based on family relationships that then expanded into larger units of villages, towns, and communities. Georg Simmel, who pioneered the concept of social structure, contended that the recurring forms of normal behavior in everyday life were based on types of human activity, specifically economic, political, and aesthetic. W. I. Thomas specifically studied recent immigrants and their response to community, positing that those who were new to the United States responded in one of three ways: conforming, developing innovations, or rebelling.

➤ The ecology theory, also known as the ecological school of criminology, emerged out of the University of Chicago in the 1920s and 1930s. Social ecology considered the community a living, growing organism and activities that threatened its stability were considered a pathology or disease. Ernest Burgess and Robert E. Park, who developed the social ecology model, studied Chicago specifically and created the notion of concentric zones. The center of the five zones is the central business zone. Zone 2 surrounds the business district and is a zone of transition, populated primarily by those of low income. Zone 3 is characterized by working-class homes, Zone 4 by middle-class dwellers, and Zone 5 by suburban dwellers who commute back and forth for work to Zone 1. According to Burgess and Park, residents of inner-city zones move outward as their economic positions improve. Clifford Shaw and Henry McKay applied the concentric zone theory to a study of juvenile delinquency and immigrants, finding that the amount of crime in Zone 2 did not decrease as its inhabitants moved outward, which led to the conclusion that the delinquency was caused by the nature of the environment, rather than the immigrants themselves.

➤ Strain theory, the second major type of social structure theory, considers delinquency as an adaptive, problem-solving behavior usually in response to frustrating and undesirable social environments. The classic statement of strain theory is anomie, a term originally coined by Emile Durkheim to explain how the breakdown of social norms leads to alienation, isolation, and personal loss. The theory of anomie was expanded upon in 1938 by Robert K. Merton. Merton used anomie to describe what happens when there is a disconnect between socially accepted goals and the socially approved way to attain those goals. Individuals who feel the strain to succeed but are deprived of socially approved means to achieve them resort to crime and deviance as alternatives. The situation is complicated further, Merton argues, because not everyone agrees on which socially approved goals are legitimate.

➤ Steven F. Messner and Richard Rosenfeld offered a contemporary view of anomie called relative deprivation. Relative deprivation claims that our society coerces individuals to achieve the American Dream by any means possible, including resorting to criminal activity. Judith and Peter Blau suggest that people experience relative deprivation when they compare their own situations unfavorably to those in higher economic class. Related to relative deprivation is the notion of distributive justice, which suggests that the rewards that individuals expect to receive for achieving their goals depends on cultural expectations.

➤ General strain theory, developed by Robert Agnew, expands on traditional strain theory. According to Agnew, strain occurs when an individual is prevented from achieving a valued goal such as financial success or autonomy, loses something of value such as a loved one, or is the victim of negatively valued stimuli, such as verbal insults or physical abuse. The effects of strain are cumulative and create a predisposition for delinquency in the form of negative affective states or emotions such as anger, fear, depression, and disappointment.

➤ A third type of social structure theory—culture conflict theory—suggests that the root of conflict is caused by differences in culture and socialization. This conflict is the cause of criminality. Thorsten Sellin, a major theorist in culture conflict theory, suggested that individuals develop conduct norms through socialization. The clash of norms between groups that have been socialized differently causes crime.

➤ Related to culture conflict theory is subcultural theory. Subcultures are smaller groups within a larger subculture whose values are communicated to each other through socialization. Several leading theorists contributed to the understanding of subcultural theory. Frederic M. Thrasher, a sociologist who was a member of the Chicago School, looked at gangs as a subculture in the 1920s. William F. Whyte, another important subcultural theorist, studied an Italian community in Boston and developed the theory that residents of this slum could achieve success only through illegal activities including racketeering and bookmaking.

➤ Walter Miller took the study of subcultures further by identifying a series of concerns of lower-class culture. These included a system of interrelated attitudes, practices, behaviors, and values that characterized the lower-class way of life.

➤ Gresham Sykes and David Matza were concerned with explaining how members of subcultures could oppose the larger culture of which they are a part. They proposed several ways that offenders could escape responsibility when involved in committing a crime.

➤ Franco Ferracuti and Marvin Wolfgang looked at violent subcultures and claimed that violence was a learned behavior that was inherent in a subculture through both ritual and habit. Richard A. Cloward and Lloyd E. Ohlin proposed the differential opportunity theory, identifying two types of socially structured opportunities for success: illegitimate opportunity structure (opportunities for success not approved by the larger culture) and legitimate opportunity structure (opportunities available to all individuals). Delinquent behavior, then, may result from the availability of illegitimate opportunities that are made legitimate because the subculture makes that opportunity legitimate.

➤ Albert K. Cohen focused on gang behavior and developed the notion of reaction formation. Young people in society from all backgrounds are subject to a middle-class measuring rod, according to Cohen. This measuring rod is a set of expectations related to everything from school performance to neatness to nonviolent behavior. When youths are not equipped to measure up to these standards, they often exhibit reaction formation, which sometimes takes the form of hostility toward middle-class values. The collective solution to this problem of alienation occurs when youths band together to create a delinquent subculture.

STUDY QUESTIONS

1. What is the concentric zone theory? What attributes does each zone exhibit?
2. How does social disorganization theory interpret social change and economic development?
3. How does anomie describe the isolation that occurs as a result of the breakdown of social norms?
4. How does relative distribution relate to the concept of the American Dream?
5. What is the definition of a subculture? What is the relationship of a subculture to the larger culture of which it is apart?

ONLINE@CRIMINOLOGY INTERACTIVE

Theory in Action

Case File #1: Murderer for Hire—Marcello
Case File #2: Cooking Crack—Lucas

Review

Vocabulary Shootout
Essay Questions
Section Test

Readings and Research

Web Links

Chapter 6

Sociological Theories II
Social Process and Social Development

CHAPTER OUTLINE

KEY IDEAS

➤ Social process and social development theories are two sociological theories that consider crime to be the end product of various processes, including inappropriate socialization and inadequate social learning.

➤ Social process theories explain behavior by looking at the way that individuals and society interact.

➤ Learning theory is a social process theory that suggests that everyone learns behavior in the same way. Edwin H. Sutherland developed differential association, which looked at the way that individuals learn criminal behavior in differential association with others.

➤ The way that self-control affects delinquent behavior is the foundation for social control theory, which suggests that social learning and socialization increases self-control and reduces the need for individuals to act in delinquent ways. Important to social control theory is containment theory, which demonstrates that there are pushes toward and pulls away from crime. These pushes and pulls are mediated by containment.

➤ Labeling theory is a social process theory that contends that once a person is "tagged" or identified as a criminal, their choices for legitimate activities are limited.

➤ John Braithwaite developed the process of reintegrative shaming, which suggests that condemning the crime instead of the criminal allows the criminal a chance for redemption and the possibility of reintegrating into society.

➤ Dramaturgy, which states that individuals play a variety of roles at the same time, can be used to describe how society treats individuals who have been labeled as deviants differently than those who are in the mainstream.

➤ The life course perspective is a social development theory that looks at the patterns that criminal behavior follows over the life cycle.

➤ A related theory, age-graded theory, considers the way that an individual's connection to society at various points in his life can help account for when deviance occurs. Marriage and job stability, this theory claims, are strong deterrents to deviance in later life.

KEY TERMS

attachment
belief
commitment
containment theory
control-balance theory
differential association
differential reinforcement
disintegrative shaming
dramaturgy
imitation
involvement
labeling theory
learning theory
life course theory
moral enterprise
reintegrative shaming
social bond theory
social capital
social control theory
social development perspective
tagging
total institutions

6.0   Social process and social development

6.1 Major principles of social process and **social development perspectives**

    6.1.1   Crime is the end product of various social processes, especially inappropriate socialization and social learning.

    6.1.2   Various factors have a role in the social process:

- Interpersonal relationships

- Social bonds

- Self-control

- The consequences of societal reactions to behavior, especially deviance

6.2   Social process theories

    6.2.1   Assumes that everyone has the potential to violate the law

    6.2.2   Contends that criminality is learned by interacting with others through socialization and is not an innate human characteristic

    6.2.3   Reference groups with which one identifies, including family, peers, and work groups, contribute to the process of socialization.

    6.2.4   Individuals who are not well-disposed to conformity are more likely to be influenced by the social situations and experiences that lead to crime.

    6.2.5   Once individuals make a choice to commit a crime, they continue to commit crimes because their social group reinforces this behavior.

    6.2.6   Types of social process theories:

- **Learning theory**
    - ❖ Emphasizes the role of communication and socialization as the way that individuals learn patterns of criminal behavior and the values that support that behavior

- **Labeling theory**
    - ❖ Emphasizes the significance of society's response to the criminal

- **Social control theory**
    - ❖ Focuses on the bonds that people share with institutions and individuals around them

- **Reintegrative shaming**
    - ❖ Emphasizes the outcomes of the labeling process

■ **Dramaturgy**

❖ Demonstrates how people can effectively manage the impressions they make on others

6.2.7 Learning theory

■ Basic principles of learning theory

❖ All behavior is learned in much the same way.

❖ Individuals learn criminal behavior from others by adopting the norms, values, and behaviors that are conducive to crime.

❖ Criminal behavior is learned through social interaction and is not an inherent characteristic of individuals.

DRAMATURGY

A theoretical point of view, which depicts human behavior as centered around the purposeful management of interpersonal impressions.

For more on major principles of social process theories, visit Criminology Interactive online > Social Process Theories > Theory Explained: Major Principles.

For more on learning theory, visit Criminology Interactive online > Social Process Theories > Theory Explained: Emergence of Learning Theory.

■ Edwin H. Sutherland (1883–1950)

MAJOR IMPACT: Sutherland developed the theory of **differential association**, one of the earliest and most influential forms of learning theory, which claimed that criminal behavior is learned through interactions with others who display criminal values and engage in criminal behavior.

SELECTED PUBLICATIONS: *Principles of Criminology* (3rd ed., 1939), *Principles of Criminology* (1924), *White Collar Crime* (1949)

DIFFERENTIAL ASSOCIATION

The sociological thesis that criminality, like any other form of behavior, is learned through a process of association with others who communicate criminal values.

❖ Nine propositions of differential association theory:

◆ Criminal behavior is learned.

◆ Criminal behavior is learned in interaction with others through communication.

◆ The primary learning of criminal behavior occurs within intimate personal groups.

◆ Learned criminal behavior includes the techniques of committing crime as well as the adoption of the attitudes and rationalizations that motivate criminal behavior.

◆ The meaning of these drives and motives is learned from an understanding of legal definitions as favorable or unfavorable.

- When definitions that favor violating the law are stronger than definitions that are unfavorable, an individual will choose crime.

- Differential associations vary in frequency, duration, priority, and intensity.

- The process of learning criminal behavior involves the same processes that are involved in any other learning.

- Criminal behavior and noncriminal behavior are an expression of the same needs and values; therefore, crime cannot be fully explained by examining general needs and values.

For more on Edwin Sutherland and Differential Association Theory, visit Criminology Interactive online > Social Process and Development Theories > Theory Explained: Edwin Sutherland > Differential Association Theory.

- Ronald L. Akers (b. 1939) and Robert Burgess

MAJOR IMPACT: Akers, with Burgess, developed the differential association-reinforcement theory, integrating the principles of operant conditioning with differential association.

SELECTED PUBLICATIONS: "A Differential Association-Reinforcement Theory of Criminal Behavior," *Social Problems*, Vol. 14 (1966); *Deviant Behavior: A Social Learning Approach* (1973)

- Organized Sutherland's nine principles into seven:
  - Criminal behavior is learned according to the principles of operant conditioning.

  - Criminal behavior is learned in nonsocial situations that are reinforcing or discriminative and through social interaction in which the behavior of other persons is reinforcing or discriminative for criminal behavior.

  - The principal part of the learning of criminal behavior occurs in those groups that compromise the individual's major source of reinforcements.

  - The learning of criminal behavior, including specific techniques, attitudes, and avoidance procedures, is a function of the effective and available reinforcers, and the existing reinforcement contingencies.

  - The specific class of behaviors that are learned and their frequency of occurrence are functions of the reinforcers, which are effective and available, and the rules or norms by which these reinforcers are applied.

  - Criminal behavior is a function of norms that are discriminative for criminal behavior, the learning of which takes place when such behavior is more highly reinforced than non-criminal behavior.

- ◆ The strength of criminal behavior is a direct function of the amount, frequency, and probability of its reinforcement.
- ❖ Akers later proposed that the same learning process creates both deviant and conforming behaviors.
  - ◆ Two primary learning mechanisms:
    - ❑ **Differential reinforcement**, also called instrumental conditioning
      - • Behavior is determined by the frequency, amount, and probability of rewards and punishments.
    - ❑ **Imitation**
      - • Individuals observe and model the behavior of others.
  - ◆ These two learning behaviors occur in a process of differential association involving communication and identification with others.
  - ◆ The frequency, intensity, and length of associations determine whether or not behavior becomes deviant.

DIFFERENTIAL REINFORCEMENT

A learning theory that asserts that people have different conditioning histories and therefore, learn differently.

IMITATION

The theory that those who are socially inferior copy the behaviors of those who are superior.

For more on Burgess and Akers and Punishment vs. Rewards, visit the Criminology Interactive online > Social Process Theories > Theory Explained: Burgess and Akers.

■ Daniel Glaser

MAJOR IMPACT: Glaser developed differential identification theory, a theory that purports that an individual turns to criminal behavior when he intimately identifies himself with real or imaginary individuals who consider criminal behavior acceptable.

SELECTED PUBLICATION: "Differential Association and Criminological Prediction," *Social Problems*, Vol. 8 (1960)

- ❖ All individuals identify with others and these identifications vary from being weak to being strong.
  - ◆ The process, not the magnitude, of identification determines behavior.
  - ◆ Identifying with a person or with an idea of what a person represents can be more important than the actual association.
- ❖ Role models can be ideas rather than actual individuals.
- ❖ Economic conditions, frustrations with social position, morals, and participation in group activity all play important roles in differential identification.
- ❖ Just as identification with criminal individuals can result in criminal behavior, identification with noncriminals offers the possibility of rehabilitation.

6.2.8   Social control theory

- These theories focus on how social and psychological integration with others constrains or regulates criminal impulses.

- Social control theorists look to identify the features of the personality and the environment that prevent individuals from committing crimes.

- Social control theorists focus on how social integration develops as a process.

- An individual's involvement with positive social institutions and with others determines his ability to resist criminality.

- Social control theories try to determine why people obey rules instead of breaking them.

CONTAINMENT THEORY

The aspects of the social bond that act to prevent individuals from committing crimes and keep them from engaging in deviance.

- Walter C. Reckless (1898–1988)

MAJOR IMPACT: Reckless proposed **containment theory**, which looks at the processes that allow individuals to resist or fail to resist social pressures to violate the law. Reckless characterized the resistance as similar to a biological immune response—just as some people resist diseases they are exposed to, some people are able to resist criminal behavior.

SELECTED PUBLICATION: *The Crime Problem* (4th ed., 1967)

❖ External containment refers to the ability of a social group to hold an individual's behavior in check by providing meaningful roles for that individual.

❖ Inner containment refers to the ability of the individual to compel himself to follow acceptable norms and is far more effective in preventing criminal behavior than external containment.

◆ Inner containment is enhanced when individuals have positive self-image, socially appropriate and realistic goals, a high degree of tolerance for frustration, and behavior that adheres to the norms and values of society.

❖ Pushes toward crime

◆ Describes the factors in an individual's background that might cause them to engage in criminal behavior, including a delinquent subculture, deprivation, biological tendency toward deviance, and maladjustment.

❖ Pulls toward crime

◆ Defined as all the perceived rewards crime may offer, such as financial gain, sexual satisfaction, and higher social status

❖ Containment, if effective, prevents such pushes and pulls from leading the individual toward crime.

For more on social control, visit Criminology Interactive online > Social Process Theories > Theory Explained: Social Control Theory.

■ Travis Hirschi (b. 1935)

MAJOR IMPACT: Hirschi proposed social bond theory, which suggested that the connections between individuals and social groups are responsible for controlling human behavior and that deviance and crime may result if this bond is weak or nonexistent.

SELECTED PUBLICATION: *Causes of Delinquency* (1969)

❖ Four elements of the social bond:

◆ **Attachment**, or an individual's shared interest with others

❑ Interpersonal conflicts or alienation can negatively impact attachment.

◆ **Commitment**, especially the amount of energy a person invests in conforming

❑ Examples: getting an education, building a business, having a reputation for being virtuous

◆ **Involvement**, the amount of energy an individual expends on legitimate pursuits

❑ An individual who is busy with legitimate pursuits will have little opportunity for deviance.

◆ **Belief**, or a shared set of values by individuals within a society or group

❑ Acknowledges that the criminal believes in the rules, but violates them because he has little respect for them

ATTACHMENT

Important for creating conformity even when those others are deviant themselves.

COMMITMENT

Hirschi's idea that the emotional investment one builds up in conventional activities and pursuits of achievement will bond them to nondelinquent behavior.

INVOLVEMENT

Hirschi's bond of social control that measures the degree of activity available for conventional or unconventional behavior.

BELIEF

Constitutes the acknowledgment of society's rules as being fair.

For more on Travis Hirschi, visit the Criminology Interactive online > Social Process Theories > Theory Explained: Travis Hirschi.

■ Travis Hirschi and Michael Gottfredson

MAJOR IMPACT: Hirschi and Gottfredson collaborated to create a general theory of crime built on a classical model: Crime is a natural consequence of individuals seeking pleasure and avoiding pain.

SELECTED PUBLICATION: *A General Theory of Crime* (1990)

❖ Hirschi and Gottfredson claimed that most crimes have the goal of satisfying the desires of the moment.

❖ Criminal offenders have little control over their own desires.

❖ Those who lack self-control impulsively choose the desires of the moment, which often includes crime with a disregard for the legal consequences.

❖ Social bonds are effective in helping individuals maintain of self-control.

❖ Self-control, or lack of self-control, can explain all kinds of behavior, including criminal behavior.

For more on self-control, visit Criminology Interactive online > Social Process Theories > Theory Explained: Self-Control Theory.

CONTROL-BALANCE THEORY
The theory that combines ideas from control and deterrence theories, some propensity theories, and subject theories.

■ Charles R. Tittle

MAJOR IMPACT: Tittle proposed an innovation to traditional control theories called **control-balance theory**, which claimed that too much control was as harmful as too little.

SELECTED PUBLICATION: *Control Balance Theory: Toward a General Theory of Deviance* (1999)

❖ Control ratio

◆ An individual is subject to a certain amount of control that is balanced by the amount of control that person exerts over others.

◆ The control ratio suggests how likely it is that the individual will turn to deviance, as well as the form that deviance will take.

❖ Control surplus (high levels of control or overcontrol)

◆ Individuals with a control surplus develop behavior that exercises control over others.

◆ This control can lead to such deviant behaviors as exploitation and decadence typical of those seen in white-collar crime and political corruption.

◆ Control surpluses create the need for autonomy.

❑ Autonomous deviance develops when the need to extend control over others results in deviance.

❖ Control deficit (low levels of control)

◆ Creates a deviant situation as an attempt to avoid control

◆ Deviance caused by control deficit can take the form of predation (physical violence, theft, sexual assault), defiance (vandalism, curfew violations, general challenges to society), and submission (passive obedience to others).

❖ Control imbalance creates deviance when individuals realize that criminal acts can push the control ratio in their favor.

❖ Opportunity plays an important role.

◆ The criminal must also have the opportunity to act deviantly; control surplus or deficit alone do not increase the likelihood of deviance.

6.2.9   Labeling Theory

■ Frank Tannenbaum (1893–1969)

MAJOR IMPACT: Tannenbaum developed labeling theory to describe the way that labeling individuals as criminals negatively impacts their behavior.

SELECTED PUBLICATION: *Crime and the Community* (1938)

❖ **Tagging**
  ◆ Term used to explain how offenders are labeled as a result of arrest, conviction, and sentencing
  ◆ Tagging creates further delinquency as the community reacts to the tag instead of the individual.

❖ Tannenbaum proposed that crime had two opposing definitions:
  ◆ The definition of the delinquent
  ◆ The definition of the community at large

❖ Conflict occurs when these values clash.
  ◆ The community demands suppression.
  ◆ The community defines the offender as evil, rather than the criminal act.

❖ Dramatization of evil
  ◆ Term used by Tannenbaum to explain how an offender comes to be seen as bad by the community
  ◆ Dramatization of evil led Tannenbaum to develop the theory of symbolic interactionism.
  ◆ Once a person has been defined as bad, there are few legitimate opportunities for the offender and soon he finds that other individuals who have been categorized as bad are the only ones he can associate with. This, in turns, leads to continued crime.

For more on labeling theory, visit Criminology Interactive online > Social Process Theories > Theory Explained: Introduction to Labeling Theory.

For more on symbolic interactionism, visit Criminology Interactive online > Social Process Theories > Symbolic Interactionism.

■ Edwin Lemert (b. 1912)

MAJOR IMPACT: Lemert developed two concepts that form the core of labeling theory: primary deviance, which refers to acts that occur before the individual defines himself as a criminal, and second deviance, acts that occur after the individual has identified himself as a criminal.

SELECTED PUBLICATION: *Social Pathology: A Systematic Approach to the Theory of Sociopathic Behavior* (1951)

❖ Primary deviance
  ◆ Deviance is caused by a variety of factors that occur before the individual identifies himself as a criminal,

TAGGING
Like labeling, the process whereby an individual is negatively defined by agencies of justice.

including the need to solve an immediate problem or in reaction to the expectations of his subculture.

◆ Community reaction to these acts determines whether secondary deviance occurs.

❖ Secondary deviance

◆ Deviance that occurs after an individual is officially labeled by the community that causes him to continue the criminal behavior as a method of defense, attack, or adjustment.

◆ Causes tagged individuals to internalize the negative labels that the community has placed on them

◆ Society, then, causes deviance through the same mechanisms it has developed to stop it.

For more on Edwin Lemert, visit Criminology Interactive online > Social Process Theories > Theory Explained: Edwin Lemert.

■ Howard Becker (b. 1928)

MAJOR IMPACT: Becker studied marijuana use in a deviant subculture of jazz musicians to determine the processes by which an individual becomes labeled as an outsider, or one who does not live by the rules of the group.

SELECTED PUBLICATION: *Outsiders: Studies in the Sociology of Deviance* (1963)

❖ Becker found that deviance is created by society, rather than by the individual who commits the deviant acts.

❖ The path to deviance follows a pattern that leads to a commitment to a criminal identity and participation in a career of deviance.

❖ **Moral enterprise**

◆ Describes the efforts of an interest group to impose its moral values as law

◆ The group that imposes its moral agenda successfully does not necessarily represent a consensus point of view.

❑ The group is simply more effective than others at using the system to impose legislation.

❖ Transitory deviance

◆ After the first deviant event, deviance is unlikely to occur again, but if the individual is labeled deviant, deviance will likely become a pattern.

❖ The successful deviant needs to acquire the techniques and resources necessary to commit deviant acts.

MORAL ENTERPRISE

A term that encompasses all the efforts a particular interest group makes to have its sense of propriety enacted into law.

- ❖ As the deviant career progresses, the individual who has been labeled deviant takes on society's negative label and is likely to become a deviant.
- ❖ Becker's typology of delinquents:
  - ◆ The pure deviant: an individual whose deviant behavior is accurately assessed as deviant by society
  - ◆ The falsely accused deviant: an individual who is innocent of deviance but somehow is labeled as deviant
    - ❏ Innocent individuals who are accused or incarcerated develop a negative self-concept and subsequently develop relationships and behaviors that are the same as those of the true deviant.
    - ❏ Labeling alters the life of the falsely accused as much it does the pure deviant.
  - ◆ The secret deviant: an individual who violates social norms, but does so in secret so that society does not impose consequences
    - ❏ Due to the lack of consequences, the secret deviant does not experience negative reaction from the community.
- ❖ According to Becker, those who label others are moral entrepreneurs.
  - ◆ There are two related types of moral entrepreneurs: creators who create rules and enforcers who enforce them (criminal justice system).
  - ◆ Becker suggests that society needs a checks and balances system to help inform those who create and enforce the rules,

- ■ Critique of Becker's theory
  - ❖ The impact of labeling has been questioned.
    - ◆ Some research has shown that labeling does not have a negative impact on self-image. Some criminals even seek out labels.
    - ◆ Studies show that individuals can shed their labels.
    - ◆ Research shows that contact with the criminal justice system does not always have negative consequences.

For more on Howard Becker, visit Criminology Interactive online > Social Process Theories > Theory Explained: Howard Becker.

6.2.10   John Braithwaite

MAJOR IMPACT: Braithwaite and colleagues extended labeling theory to include the process reintegrative shaming, whereby an individual who is labeled deviant can be brought back to conformity.

SELECTED PUBLICATION: *Crime, Shame and Reintegration* (1989)

- Reintegrative shaming is built on the premise that deviance can have a stigmatizing effect, but that effect occurs in interaction with others.

- Two kinds of shame exist:

  ❖ **Disintegrative (stigmatizing) shaming**, which destroys the bond between the offender and the community and offers no opportunity to integrate the shamed offender back into that community

    ◆ The technique American judges use when they compel an offender to post a sign saying "a violent felon lives here" or a bumper sticker on his car saying "I am a drunk driver"

    ◆ Sets offender apart as an outcast—often for the rest of the offender's life

    ◆ This form of shaming strongly suggests that the offender will commit more crimes because the offender has been labeled as someone who cannot be trusted to obey the law.

    ◆ Disintegrative shaming creates the situation that traditional labeling theory describes as secondary deviance.

      ❐ Individuals who have been so shamed and humiliated reject the society that has rejected them.

      ❐ This creates subcultures of individuals in similar situations, all of who feel as if they are outsiders.

  ❖ Reintegrative shaming is an attempt to strengthen the moral connection between the offender and the community to bring the offender back into that community.

    ◆ The goal is to condemn the crime, not the criminal.

    ◆ Identifies the harmfulness the individual has caused, but offers a new start

    ◆ Gives offenders an opportunity to become law-abiding citizens by offering diversionary programs that allow offenders to express remorse, experience forgiveness, and avoid incarceration.

DISINTEGRATIVE SHAMING
The process of destroying the moral connection between the offender and the community without the intention of reconnecting the two.

For a summary of the impact of labeling theory, visit Criminology Interactive online > Social Process Theories > Theory Explained: Labeling Closing Statement.

6.2.11   Erving Goffman (1922–1982)

MAJOR IMPACT: Erving Goffman developed the concept of dramaturgy, which states that individuals play a variety of roles as they interact with others.

SELECTED PUBLICATIONS: *The Presentation of Self in Everyday Life* (1959), *Stigma: Notes on the Management of Spoiled Identity* (1963), *Asylums: Essays on the Social Situations of Mental Patients and Other Inmates* (1961)

■ Individuals present themselves more or less effectively when performing a specific role.

■ Through communications, both verbal and nonverbal, individuals control the situations in which they are involved.

■ Some individuals may find themselves discredited when information is introduced about them, especially information they have tried to hide.

■ Interaction and performance may change substantially when discrediting information is revealed.

   ❖ Goffman suggests that society responds significantly differently to discredited or stigmatized individuals.

   ❖ Society believes that those with a stigma are not quite human.

      ◆ Society tends to generalize a wide range of imperfections called stigmata on the basis of a single imperfection. These may be physical, such as birthmarks; behavioral, such as theft; or ideational, such as low rank in a pecking order.

   ❖ Goffman focused on how mainstream and stigmatized individuals interact.

      ◆ Discredited individuals are known to others before they come into contact with them.

      ◆ When this happens, normal people expect to encounter further stigmatized behavior.

      ◆ If discrediting information is not communicated to those the stigmatized individual encounters, he may attempt to pass as normal by misrepresenting himself.

   ❖ Societal reactions are instrumental in the formation of group identities.

      ◆ When discredited individuals join like-minded groups, they may form alliance against the larger society and justify their deviant behavior.

■ Goffman describes the phenomenon of **total institutions**, facilities from which individuals can rarely come and go and in which intense communal life is required. Individuals in total institutions eat, sleep, play, learn, and worship together.

TOTAL INSTITUTIONS

Facilities from which individuals can rarely come and go and in which communal life is intense and circumscribed.

❖ Examples of total institutions include seminaries and convents, military camps, prisons, and mental hospitals.

❖ Goffman believed that residents of total institutions bring "presenting cultures" with them to their respective facilities.

◆ In the case of prisons, some inmates carry street culture into correctional facilities.

❖ Disculturation

◆ A period during which residents of total institutions give up their parts of their presenting cultures that are not consistent with existing institutional culture.

For more on societal reactions, visit Criminology Interactive online > Social Process Theories > Theory Explained: Societal Reactions.

6.3   Social development perspective

6.3.1   Considers that development begins at birth and occurs primarily within a social context

6.3.2   Socialization is only one feature of the social context.

6.3.3   Human development occurs on many levels simultaneously including psychological, biological, cultural, interpersonal, and familial.

6.3.4   Social development theories are integrated.

6.3.5   Concepts in social development theories:

■ Focus is on individual rates of offending; seeks to understand increases and decreases in rates of offending over an individual's lifetime.

■ Use longitudinal measurements of delinquency and offending

■ Focus special attention on the transitions that people face as they move through the life cycle.

■ **Life course theorists** have identified at least seven developmental tasks that American adolescents must confront:

❖ Establishing identity

❖ Cultivating symbolic relationships

❖ Defining physical attractiveness

❖ Investing in a value system

❖ Obtaining an education

❖ Separating from family and achieving independence

❖ Obtaining and maintaining meaningful employment

LIFE COURSE THEORY

Developmental theory that states individuals and their influencing factors change over time, usually in patterned ways.

6.3.6   The life course perspective

- Has its roots in a 1986 National Academy of Sciences (NAS) panel report
    - ❖ The panel report emphasized the importance of the study of criminal careers and of crime over the life course.
    - ❖ Defined criminal career as "the longitudinal sequence of crimes committed by an individual offender"
    - ❖ Described criminal careers in terms of four dimensions:
        - ◆ Participation
            - ❑ The percentage of the population that is criminally active
            - ❑ Depends on the scope of criminal acts and the length of the observation period
        - ◆ Frequency
            - ❑ Refers to the number of crimes committed by an individual offender during specific time periods
            - ❑ Frequency generally varies over the life course, even for habitual offenders.
        - ◆ Duration
            - ❑ Refers to the length of the criminal career
        - ◆ Seriousness
            - ❑ Refers to the severity of the crime. Some offenders with long criminal careers commit only petty crimes while others are serious habitual offenders, and still others commit offenses with a mixed degree of seriousness.

For more on life course theory, visit Criminology Interactive online > Social Process Theories > Theory Explained: Life Histories.

- Robert J. Sampson and John H. Laub

MAJOR IMPACT: Sampson and Laub were the first to identify life course criminology, a form of criminology built on social learning principles that considers criminal behavior as a result of many different influences that are present through a lifetime.

SELECTED PUBLICATION: *Crime in the Making: Pathways and Turning Points through the Life Course* (1993) (Sampson and Laub first identified life course criminology.)

- ❖ Life course researchers examine trajectories and transitions through the life span.
    - ◆ A trajectory is a path of development that is marked by a sequence of transitions such as changes in career, marriage, parenthood, and criminal behavior.

- ◆ Transitions are marked by specific life events such as a first job or the onset of crime.
- ◆ Age differentiation (or age grading) recognizes that some forms of behavior have more impactful consequences than others.
- ◆ Three sets of dynamic concepts are important to the life course perspective:
  - ❐ Activation: the ways that delinquent behavior continues, accelerates, and diversifies after initiation
  - ❐ Aggravation: a sequence of activities that increase in seriousness over time
  - ❐ Desistance: a slowdown in the frequency of offending (deceleration), a reduction in its variety (specialization), or a reduction in seriousness (de-escalation)
- ❖ Linked lives describe the ways in which human lives are involved in relationships with family and friends across the life span.
  - ◆ Family, friends, and coworkers influence the life course of most people.

For more on Robert J. Sampson and John H. Laub, visit the Criminology Interactive online > Social Process Theories > Theory Explained: Robert J. Sampson and John H. Laub.

- ■ Glen H. Elder, Jr. (b. 1934)

MAJOR IMPACT: Elder identified four important life course principles that have come to make up life course theory.

SELECTED PUBLICATIONS: "The Life Course as Developmental Theory," *Child Development*, Vol. 69, No. 1 (1998); "Urban Poverty and the Family Context of Delinquency: A New Look at Structure and Process in a Classic Study," *Child Development*, Vol. 65 (1994)

- ❖ Elder's principles included:
  - ◆ The principle of historical time and place
    - ❐ The life course of individuals is shaped by the historical times and places they experience over their lifetime.
  - ◆ The principle of timing in lives
    - ❐ The developmental impact of a succession of life transitions or events is contingent on when they occur in a person's life.

- ◆ The principle of linked lives
  - ❏ Lives are interdependent and social, and historical influences are expressed through a network of shared relationships.
- ◆ The principle of human agency
- ❖ Individuals create their own life course by the choices they make and the actions they take.

6.3.7   Age-graded theory

- ■ Sheldon (1896–1980) and Eleanor (1898–1972) Glueck

MAJOR IMPACT: The Gluecks conducted early research of delinquent boys and determined that family dynamics play an important role in the development of delinquency, and that delinquency tends to persist through adulthood. This research laid the foundation for the development of life course theory and especially for age-graded theory.

SELECTED PUBLICATION: *Unraveling Juvenile Delinquency* (1950)

- ❖ The Gluecks studied the cause of crime on four levels: sociocultural, physical, intellectual, and emotional/temperamental. They found that family dynamics played an important role in the development of criminality.

For more on Sheldon and Eleanor Glueck, visit the Criminology Interactive online > Social Process Theories > Theory Explained: Sheldon and Eleanor Glueck.

- ■ John Laub and Robert Sampson discovered 60 cartons of data that had been done by the Gluecks at Harvard Law School and reanalyzed their data, concluding that children in the study who turned to delinquency had had trouble at school and at home and had friends who were involved in delinquency.
  - ❖ Laub and Sampson found that marriage and job stability were particularly important in reducing the frequency of offending in later life.
  - ❖ Laub and Sampson developed an age-graded theory of informal social control that suggested that delinquency was more likely to occur when an individual's connection to society is weak or broken and that adult transitions like marriage explain variations in criminal behavior unaccounted for by childhood deviance.
  - ❖ Although it incorporates elements of **social bond theory**, age-graded theory also emphasizes the significance of continuity and change over the life course.

SOCIAL BOND THEORY

A theory that looks at the rather intangible link between individuals and the society of which they are a part and the role socialization plays in that link.

SOCIAL CAPITAL

The degree of positive relationships with other persons and with social institutions that individuals build up over the course of their lives.

❖ **Social capital**

- ◆ Refers to positive relationships individuals build up over the course of their lives with other people and with social institutions

- ◆ Social capital can be enhanced by such experiences as education, consistent employment, and strong personal connections, including a strong marriage and family.

- ◆ Social capital impacts directly on life course trajectories.

  - ❏ The greater a person's social capital, the less the chance of criminal activity.

CHAPTER SUMMARY

➤ Social process and social development theories, founded on the same principles as other sociological theories (see Chapter 5, 5.1), see crime as the end product of various social processes, especially inappropriate socialization and social learning. In particular, these two approaches stress the role of the following in affecting behavior: interpersonal relationships, social bonds, self-control, and the consequences of society's reactions to deviance.

➤ Social process theories explain behavior by considering the interaction between individuals and society. Although these theories assume that every individual has the potential to break the law, they also suggest that criminality is not an innate human characteristic. Rather, social process theories see criminal behavior—in fact, all behavior—as learned as a result of the socialization process. Groups that are essential to socialization include family, peers, work groups, and the overall social group with which an individual identifies. According to social process theories, individuals who are not predisposed to conformity are more likely to be influenced by social forces and, potentially, criminality. Once an individual chooses criminal behavior, this behavior is likely to continue because it is reinforced by a society that has established deviant behavior as accepted behavior.

➤ There are several types of social process theories: learning theory, labeling theory, social control theory, reintegrative shaming, and dramaturgy.

➤ Learning theory in its broadest sense contends that all behavior is learned in much the same way.

➤ Differential association, developed by Edwin H. Sutherland, was one of the first and most influential forms of learning theory. Sutherland proposed that criminal behavior developed as a result of an individual's differential association with others who communicate criminal values and promote criminal behavior. Sutherland's contention that criminal behavior is learned as opposed to being driven by biology became the prevailing theory of the latter part of the twentieth century.

➤ Ronald Akers and Robert Burgess added the idea of reinforcement to Sutherland's differential association theory to create differential association-reinforcement theory. This theory focused on the notion that criminal behavior is learned through operant conditioning. Akers went on to develop the social structure-social learning theory, which integrates social structure and learning and argues that an individual's location in the social structure determines the learning style of that individual.

➤ Daniel Glaser also built upon Sutherland's theory to create a theory he called differential identification. Glaser's argument relies on the premise that individuals pursue criminal behavior when they identify themselves with real or imaginary persons that see criminal behavior as acceptable.

➤ Social control theory contends that socialization and social learning create self-control and reduces the need for individuals to behave in antisocial or delinquent ways. The opposite is also true: When adequate social constraints on antisocial behavior are not in place, delinquent behavior results. Social control theorists attempt to identify the factors that inhibit people from committing crimes rather than seek the cause of criminal action. Ultimately, social theorists conclude that when individuals are involved with positive social institutions, they are more likely to avoid criminal behavior.

➤ An important theory in social control theory is containment theory, which was proposed by Walter C. Reckless. Reckless claimed that crime occurred when an individual failed to resist the social pressure to violate the law. Reckless theorized that there are "pushes" toward crime and "pulls" away from crime. Pushes would include an upbringing that involves criminal behavior, deprivation, biological propensities toward deviant behavior, and maladjustment. The process of containment blocks such pushes and pulls and prevents the individual from committing a crime.

➤ Travis Hirschi proposed the social bond theory, claiming that when socialization is successful, a bond forms between individuals, which has four elements: attachment to parents, peers, or school; commitment to activities that are conventional and accepted; involvement in activities that are accepted; and belief in a common value.

➤ Charles Tittle proposed the control-balance theory, arguing that too much control can be as harmful as too little. The control ratio, or the amount of control an individual feels versus the amount of time the individual controls others, predicts the likelihood of that individual displaying criminal behavior as well as the form that behavior will take.

➤ Labeling theory, first proposed by Frank Tannenbaum, suggests that once a person is tagged or identified as a criminal, his legitimate choices are limited. Edwin Lemert developed two core concepts of labeling theory: primary and secondary deviance. Primary deviance is the initial deviant act that occurs before the individual decides to identify himself as a criminal. Secondary deviance is subsequent criminal activity that results in the individual identifying himself as a criminal. It was Howard Becker who brought labeling to the forefront of criminology; specifically, exploring ways that individuals identified themselves as outsiders and how that definition contributed to their deviant behavior.

➤ Reintegrative shaming is a concept developed by John Braithwaite that suggests that labels can be stigmatizing, but only in interactions with others in society. Two kinds of shame exist, according to Braithwaite: disintegrative shaming, which destroys the moral connection between the offender and the community and does not seek to reconnect the two, and reintegrative shaming, which condemns crime rather than the individual, to bring the individual back into the community.

➤ Dramaturgy, developed by Erving Goffman, suggests that individuals play a variety of social roles at the same time, and that interaction with others helps to support these roles. Later, Goffman described how labeled individuals differ from those who are considered normal by the way society treats them.

➤ The social development perspective focuses on how an individual's rate of crime increases or decreases over a lifetime. In particular, social development theories consider how lifetime transitions impact behavior.

➤ Life course perspective contends that criminal behavior tends to follow a pattern throughout a life cycle. This perspective describes four dimensions of deviances: participation, frequency, duration, and seriousness.

➤ Robert J. Sampson and John H. Laub examined what they called "trajectories and transitions" through the life span. Trajectories are paths of development characterized by a sequence of transitions. A transition is a specific life event, like a first job or the first onset of crime.

➤ Life course researcher Glen H. Elder, Jr., introduced four important principles that summarize life course theory: historical time and place (person's life course is determined by the times in which he is living), timing (the significance of life events is determined by when they occur in an individual's life), the linked lives (shared relationships affect behavior), and human agency (individuals determine their own life course by the choices they make).

➤ Research on the impact of life course was begun as early as the 1930s by Sheldon and Eleanor Glueck who studied the careers of delinquent boys. Their conclusion was that family dynamics played a significant role in criminality.

➤ Based on the research of the Glueck, Laub and Sampson proposed age-graded theory in 1994, which indicated that two events in the life course—marriage and job stability—were essential to reducing the frequency of criminal behavior later in life.

STUDY QUESTIONS

1. What are the social process and development theories discussed here? Describe each one.

2. What are the basic principles of learning theory?

3. How does self-control impact deviant behavior?

4. What is likely to happen to an individual who has committed a crime and is labeled or tagged as a result?

5. What two processes involve shaming as a way of dealing with criminal behavior?

6. When considering the life course perspective, what are the distinguishing characteristics of trajectories and transitions?

ONLINE@CRIMINOLOGY INTERACTIVE

Theory in Action

Case File #1: Juvenile Drug Runner—Javier
Case File #2: Looking in Window—Michael

Review

Vocabulary Shootout
Essay Questions
Section Test

Readings and Research

Web Links

Additional Theorists

Terrie E. Moffit
Terence P. Thornberry

Chapter 7

Sociological Theories III
Social Conflict

CHAPTER OUTLINE

KEY IDEAS

➤ Social conflict theories consider crime to be the result of class struggle and focus on the power relationship in the economic, political, and social structure as the primary source.

➤ The consensus model of social conflict holds that society is made up of a shared value set and that the members of society work toward the greater good.

➤ The pluralist perspective proposes that society is made up of individuals with diverse values and beliefs and that law maintains and mediates peace among these groups.

➤ The conflict perspective also contends that society is made up of individuals with diverse values, but that conflict can never be resolved and that law is a tool of the powerful used against the powerless.

➤ Karl Marx, though not a criminologist, was one of the best-known writers on social conflict and claimed that society was made up of two classes, the proletariat (workers) and the bourgeoisie (the powerful who control the workers). Conflict occurs in a capitalist society when these two forces oppose each other and the outcome of this conflict is the overthrow of capitalism and the creation of a communist society.

➤ Radical criminology purports that crime is caused primarily because those in power take power away from those who are not. Law is used by the state to maintain this social order.

➤ Critical criminology focuses on economic and political factors to critique the social relationships that lead to crime.

➤ Feminist criminology, based on feminism, contends that society's inequalities are primarily based on gender and that crime is a male act of aggression. Radical feminism takes that theory one step further to suggest that if male dominance were eliminated, crimes against women would increase.

➤ Deconstructionist theories, including two important subtheories—anarchist criminology and constitutive criminology—consider innovative alternatives to social and criminal problems.

➤ Peacemaking criminology asserts that the solution to crime can be achieved through compassion and by offering services to the criminal and the victim. Victims, offenders, and their communities should all come together to heal the harm caused by crime.

KEY TERMS

anarchist criminology
androcentricity
bourgeoisie
constitutive criminology
feminist criminology
participatory justice
peace model
peacemaking criminology
pluralist perspective
power-control theory
proletariat
radical criminology
radical feminism

7.0 Sociological theories III: Social conflict theories

7.1 Major principles

    7.1.1 Crime is the product of class struggle.

    7.1.2 Focus of social conflict perspective:

- The nature of power relationships between and among social groups

- The uneven distribution of wealth within society

- The economic and social structure of society as it relates to social class and social control

 For more on social conflict theory, visit Criminology Interactive online > Social Conflict Theories> Theory Explained: Introduction.

7.2 The consensus perspective

    7.2.1 Consensus model

- Based on the belief that most members of society basically agree on what is right and wrong and members of society work for greater good

    7.2.2 Principles of consensus perspective

- Belief in a system of core values, including what is right and wrong

- Belief that laws reflect the consensus of the people

- Assumption that the law serves all people equally

- Idea that those who violate the law are somehow improperly socialized or defective

    7.2.3 Roscoe Pound (1880–1964)

MAJOR IMPACT: Pound was a legal scholar who championed the consensus perspective and developed the belief that law is a tool for developing society.

SELECTED PUBLICATIONS: *The Spirit of the Common Law* (1921), *Law and Morals* (1924), *Criminal Justice in America* (1930)

- Pound claims that in civilized society men and women must be able to be assured that:
    - ❖ Others will not be intentionally aggressive against them
    - ❖ They control what they have created for their own use.
    - ❖ Those with whom they deal in society will act in good faith
    - ❖ Others in society will not cause unreasonable risk of injury upon others.
    - ❖ Those in charge of maintaining society will restrain those who are out of bounds.

7.3   The **pluralist perspective**

7.3.1   This perspective claims that any complex society is made up of a variety of values and beliefs and that not everyone agrees on what the law should say.

7.3.2   Law, then, is a peacekeeping tool that allows officials and agencies within the government to settle disputes effectively between individuals and among groups.

7.3.3   Basic principles of pluralist perspective include:

- Society is made up of many and diverse social groups.

- Each group has its own characteristic set of values, beliefs, and interests.

- Society agrees that laws are useful as mechanisms for dispute resolution.

- The legal system is value-neutral and free of petty disputes that characterize relationships among groups.

- The legal system and those who run it are concerned with the best interests of society.

7.3.4   The best way to resolve conflict is through the peacekeeping activities of an unbiased government exercising objective legal authority.

PLURALIST PERSPECTIVE
An analytical approach to social organization, which holds that a multiplicity of values and beliefs exist in any complex society, but that most social actors agree on the usefulness of law as a formal means of dispute resolution.

7.4   The conflict perspective

7.4.1   Claims that conflict is a natural aspect of social life that can never be fully resolved

7.4.2   The criminal justice system coerces those who are powerless to comply with the rules established by those in power.

7.4.3   Law is a tool of the powerful and is used to prevent others from taking control of essential social institutions.

7.4.4   Those in power constantly work to stay in power.

7.4.5   Key elements of the conflict perspective:

- Society is made up of diverse social groups.

- Each group has different notions of what is right and wrong.

- Conflict between groups is unavoidable.

- Law is the tool of power.

- Those in power work to maintain their power against those who would take power from them.

**For a definition of social conflict, visit Criminology Interactive online >
Social Conflict Theories> Theory Explained: Definition.**

7.4.6 Social class

- Maintains that there are distinctions between individuals on the basis of such characteristics as race, religion, education, speech, accent, child-rearing habits, housing, tastes, and so on
    - ❖ Individuals are ascribed to a class by others and by themselves because of certain characteristics.
        - ◆ Ascribed characteristics are those with which a person is born, such as race or gender.
        - ◆ Achieved characteristics are those that are acquired, such as education, income, or profession.
- Most social scientists identify at least three social classes: upper, middle, and lower.

7.4.7 Karl Marx (1818–1883)

MAJOR IMPACT: Marx's writings about capitalism and its inherent conflicts led to the communist movement and the rise of communist societies in the twentieth century.

SELECTED PUBLICATIONS: *The Communist Manifesto* (1848), *Das Kapital* (1867)

PROLETARIAT

The working class.

BOURGEOISIE

The class of people that owns the means of production.

- Marx identified two fundamental classes in capitalist society:
    - ❖ **Proletariat**
        - ◆ The working class who are uneducated and without power
    - ❖ **Bourgeoisie**
        - ◆ The upper class, who are wealthy and control the means of productions
- The struggle between these two classes is inevitable and the outcome, according to Marxists, is the replacement of capitalist society with a classless or communist society.

For more on Karl Marx, visit Criminology Interactive online > Social Conflict Theories > Theory Explained: Karl Marx.

7.4.8 Willem Bonger (1886–1940)

MAJOR IMPACT: Bonger expanded Marxist principles by describing the natural condition of capitalism as a constant struggle between the haves and have-nots.

SELECTED PUBLICATION: *Criminality and Economic Conditions* (1905)

- Believed that only those who lack power are subject to the law
- Contended crime is caused by economic, cultural, and social conditions

7.4.9   George Bryan Vold (1896–1968)

MAJOR IMPACT: Vold contributed the Marxist ideology by claiming that conflict is a universal reaction and that as conflict intensifies, the loyalty of the members of the groups in conflict become stronger.

SELECTED PUBLICATION: *Theoretical Criminology* (1958)

7.4.10   Ralf Dahrendorf (b. 1929)

MAJOR IMPACT: Dahrendorf claimed that the root of conflict is power and authority, and that change can destroy or construct the social order by increasing cohesiveness in society.

SELECTED PUBLICATION: *Class and Class Conflict in Industrial Society* (1959)

7.4.11   Austin T. Turk

MAJOR IMPACT: Turk claimed that social order represents a pattern of conflict and that law is simply no more than a powerful tool for social groups to control others.

SELECTED PUBLICATION: *Criminality and the Legal Order* (1969) (Austin Turk claims that social order is primarily a pattern of conflict.)

For more on the basic principles of social conflict, visit **Criminology Interactive online > Social Conflict Theories > Theory Explained: Basic Principles.**

7.5   Radical criminology

7.5.1   An intellectual development based on three important concepts:

- The ideas of nineteenth century utopian and political theorists, including: Marx, Engels, Hegel, Simmel, Bonger, and Weber

- The rise of conflict theory in the social sciences

- The radicalization of American intellectual thought in the 1960s and 1980s

7.5.2   Contemporary radical criminology claims that crime is caused by social conditions that make the wealthy more politically powerful, but render powerless those who are less fortunate.

7.5.3   William J. Chambliss and Robert Seidman

MAJOR IMPACT: Chambliss and Seidman proposed a concept that integrated early conflict theorists with the Marxist radical approach.

SELECTED PUBLICATIONS: *Law, Order, and Power* (1981) (Chambliss and Seidman proposed a concept that bridged earlier conflict theorists and the more radical approach of the Marxists.)

RADICAL CRIMINOLOGY

A perspective that holds that the causes of crime are rooted in social conditions that empower the wealthy and the politically well organized, but disenfranchise those less fortunate. Also called Marxist or critical criminology.

- Emphasized social class, class interests, and class conflict
- Presented a Marxist perspective without references to capitalism as the cause of crime
- Chambliss and Seidman presented four propositions:
  - ❖ The conditions of one's life create one's values and norms.
  - ❖ Society, then, is made up of disparate and conflicting sets of norms.
  - ❖ The set of norms of a specific group are not necessarily part of the law but are related to the political and economic status of that group.
  - ❖ The higher a group's political or economic status, the more likely it will be that its views will be reflected in laws.
- Crime is defined by the ruling class as any activity that goes against their interests.

7.5.4 Richard Quinney (b. 1934)

MAJOR IMPACT: Richard Quinney developed a methodology that used Marxist propositions to explain crime.

SELECTED PUBLICATIONS: *Critique of the Legal Order: Crime Control in Capitalist Society* (1984); *Class, State, and Crime: On the Theory and Practice of Criminal Justice* (1988)

- Marxist propositions that explain crime:
  - ❖ American society is an advanced capitalist system.
  - ❖ The state serves the interests of the capitalist ruling class.
  - ❖ Criminal law is created by the ruling class and maintains the existing social and economic order.
  - ❖ The governmental elite creates agencies to control crime to support their efforts to establish and maintain for the purpose of establishing domestic order.
  - ❖ The features of advanced capitalism demand that the subordinate classes remain oppressed by whatever means necessary.
  - ❖ The only way to eradicate crime is to eradicate the capitalist society and create a new society based on socialist principles.
- Quinney argued that almost all crimes committed by members of the lower classes are necessary for their survival.
  - ❖ Crime is a natural part of a capitalist society because it is a response to materialism.
  - ❖ This further underscores the need for a socialist society

For more on Richard Quinney, visit Criminology Interactive online > Social Conflict Theories > Theory Explained: Richard Quinney.

7.5.5   Two schools of today's radical criminology:

- Structural Marxism
    - ❖ Considers capitalism as an ongoing process in which the law and justice system work to maintain power relationships
    - ❖ Maintains that even the rich are subject to laws that prevent them from engaging in forms of behavior that might undermine the system
- Instrumental Marxism
    - ❖ Considers criminal law and the justice system as ways that the powerful control the poor and keep them powerless
    - ❖ Claims that the legal system maintains power relationships and ensures that those in power will continue to be in control
    - ❖ Jeffrey H. Reiman
        - ◆ In *The Rich Get Richer and the Poor Get Prison* (6th ed., 2002), Reiman contends that the criminal justice system is biased against the poor and that well-to-do members of society control the criminal justice system.

For more on Jeffrey H. Reiman, visit Criminology Interactive online > Conflict Theories > Theory Explained: Jeffrey Reiman.

7.6   Critical criminology

- Critical criminology offers a critique of the relationships that cause crime.

7.6.1   Gresham M. Sykes (b. 1922)

- In "Critical Criminology," *Journal of Criminal Law and Criminology*, Vol. 65 (1984), Sykes defines critical criminology as an inquiry into how criminal law is based on norms and how various norms are related to behavior.

7.6.2   Elliott Currie

MAJOR IMPACT: Currie developed the premise that market societies—those societies that stress individual gain—are especially prone to crime.

SELECTED PUBLICATION: "Market, Crime, and Community," *Theoretical Criminology*, Vol. 1, No. 2 (1958)

- Currie identifies eight mechanisms that produce crime in a market society:
    - ❖ Livelihood is destroyed: There is a long-term absence of opportunities for stable and rewarding work.
    - ❖ Growing extremes in economic inequality and material deprivation

❖ The lack of public services and support systems, especially for families and children

❖ The lack of networks of mutual support, supervision, and care

❖ The growth of a materialistic and neglectful culture

❖ The marketing of the technology of violence, including the availability of guns, an emphasis on technologies of destruction (such as the military), and violence on television and in other media

❖ The lack of social or political alternatives

7.7   Emerging conflict theory

7.7.1   Left-realist criminology developed as a response to concerns with street crime, the fear of crime, and victimization.

■ Claims that radical and critical criminologists romanticize street crime and street criminals as political resisters in an oppressive capitalist society

■ Left-realists focus on a practical assessment of crime and the needs of crime victims, and emphasize social justice.

■ Takes the perspective that those most often affected by crime are victims and their families, offenders, and criminal justice personnel

■ Left-realism is a natural consequence of increasingly conservative attitudes toward crime and criminals.

■ Walter DeKeseredy
   ❖ Popularized left-realist notions in North America

■ Jock Young
   ❖ Perpetuated left-realist views in England through the publication of *The New Criminology: For a Social Theory of Deviance*

■ Left-realists view victims of crime as the poor and powerless who fall prey to criminals with similar backgrounds.

■ The criminal justice system should be modified to reduce use of force.

FEMINIST CRIMINOLOGY

A developing intellectual approach that emphasizes gender issues in criminology.

RADICAL FEMINISM

A theory whose primary focus is on the way in which power is constructed and dominated by males in society.

7.7.2   Feminist criminology

■ Beginning in the 1980s, feminist theory was applied to criminology.

   ❖ Strands of feminist thought informing feminist criminology include liberal feminism, **radical feminism**, socialist feminism, and Marxist feminism.

■ Claims that conflict in society occurs because of inequalities based in gender, although they vary on how much inequality exists

- Intends to redirect the thinking of mainstream criminologists to include gender awareness

- Feminist criminology claims that there are inequalities because of patriarchal forms of thought.

  ❖ Patriarchy is a set of social relations in which the male gender appropriates the labor power of women and controls their sexuality.

  ❖ Crime is often seen as an act of aggression in which men are biologically characterized as having an aggressive nature that needs to be channeled and controlled.

    ◆ Women, then, are passive actors and excluded from criminological study, which makes them more susceptible to continued victimization by men.

    ◆ Early works in the field of feminist criminology include *Women and Crime* (1985) by Rita J. Simon and *Sisters in Crime* by Freda Adler.

      ❏ In their works, Simon and Adler:

        • Explained the difference in crime rates between men and women as being caused by socialization rather than biology

        • Claimed women were taught to believe in personal limitations and this resulted in lower aspirations

        • Said that as gender equality increased, male and female criminality would take on similar characteristics

- Kathleen Daly and Meda Chesney-Lind

MAJOR IMPACT: Daly and Chesney-Lind developed the notion of **androcentricity**, which offers a single-sex perspective of criminality.

SELECTED PUBLICATION: "Feminism and Criminology," *Justice Quarterly*, Vol. 5, No. 4 (1988)

ANDROCENTRICITY
The belief that society is male-centered.

  ❖ Five elements of feminist thought that distinguish it from other types of social and political thought:

    ◆ Gender is a complex, social, historical, and cultural phenomenon, rather than simply a biological one.

    ◆ Gender and gender relations create fundamental social order.

    ◆ Gender relations are based on the notion that men are superior and have social, political, and economic dominance over women.

    ◆ Knowledge and the ability to attain knowledge are reflected in men's views of the natural and social worlds.

    ◆ Women need to be at the center of intellectual inquiry.

- Susan Caulfied and Nancy Wonders

MAJOR IMPACT: Caulfield and Wonders categorized the five major contributions that have been made by feminist criminology.

SELECTED PUBLICATION: "Gender and Justice: Feminist Contributions to Criminology," in Gregg Barak, ed., *Varieties of Criminology: Readings from a Dynamic Discipline* (1994)

- ❖ Contributions made by feminist criminology:
  - ◆ Gender is the organizing principle of contemporary life.
  - ◆ Power is important in shaping social relationships.
  - ◆ Social context helps shape human relationships.
  - ◆ Social reality is a process and a development of research methods that take this into account
  - ◆ A commitment to social change is a crucial part of feminist scholarship.

- Schools of feminist thought:
  - ❖ Radical feminism
    - ◆ Views men as aggressive
    - ◆ Sees men as controlling women by taking advantage of women's biological dependence and their comparative lack of physical strength
    - ◆ Believes that men control the law and women are defined as subjects
    - ◆ The elimination of male domination will decrease male violence against women.
  - ❖ Liberal feminism
    - ◆ Blames present inequalities on the development of separate traditional attitudes about the roles of men and women
    - ◆ Demands an end to the unequal division of power and labor between genders to eliminate inequality and promote social harmony
  - ❖ Socialist feminism
    - ◆ Views gender oppression as a result of, and a natural outgrowth of. capitalism
  - ❖ Alternative framework developed by women of color
    - ◆ Feminism should have a heightened sensitivity to the complex interplay of gender, class, and race oppression.

- John Hagan (b. 1946)

MAJOR IMPACT: Hagan developed the **power-control** theory that holds that the distribution of crime and delinquency has its roots in the power relationships of domestic settings and family life.

SELECTED PUBLICATION: *Structural Criminology* (1989)

POWER-CONTROL THEORY

A perspective that holds that the distribution of crime and delinquency within society is to some degree founded upon the consequences that power relationships within the wider society hold for domestic settings and for the everyday relationships between men, women, and children within the context of family life.

❖ Power-control theory finds that crime reflects the structure of the family.

❖ Most middle- and upper-middle-class families follow a paternalistic model in which the father works and the mother supervises the children.

◆ The behavior of girls is affected by the father and mother through male domination and female role modeling.

◆ Boys have more of an ability to deviate from social norms, thereby resulting in higher levels of delinquency.

❖ The paternalistic model is often absent in lower- and lower-middle-class families.

7.7.3 Postmodern criminology

■ Developed primarily in Europe after World War II, postmodern criminology applies notions of social change to criminal theory.

■ Proposes that sexism, racism, capitalism, and professional interests compromise scientific research.

■ Theories that fall under the umbrella of postmodernism:
❖ Chaos theory
❖ Discourse analysis
❖ Typology theory
❖ Catastrophe theory
❖ Laconian thought
❖ Gödel's theorem
❖ Constitutive theory
❖ Anarchic criminology

■ Deconstructionist theories
❖ Deconstructionist theories challenge existing criminological perspectives and suggest that they be replaced with approaches more relevant to the postmodern era.
❖ **Anarchist criminology**
◆ Embraces alternative methods to social and criminal problems and seeks to demythologize the concepts behind criminal justice
❖ **Constitutive criminology**
◆ Claims that crime is created through a social process in which offender, victim, and society are all involved

7.7.4 Peacemaking criminology

■ Has its roots in Christian and Eastern philosophies

■ Suggests that crime can be reduced if social control agencies and the citizens create solutions to social problems and alleviate human suffering

ANARCHIST CRIMINOLOGY
Seeks to demythologize the concepts behind the criminal justice system and the legal order on which it is based.

CONSTITUTIVE CRIMINOLOGY
The study of the process by which human beings create an ideology of crime that sustains it (the notion of crime) as a concrete reality.

PEACEMAKING CRIMINOLOGY
A perspective that holds that crime control agencies and the citizens they serve should work together to alleviate social problems and human suffering, thus reducing crime.

- Peacemaking criminology focuses on:
  - ❖ How violence is perpetuated through social policies based on traditional criminological theory
  - ❖ The role of education in peacemaking
  - ❖ Conflict resolution within community settings
- Richard Quinney and John Wilderman summarize peacemaking criminology this way:
  - ❖ The Western rational mode is conditional, limiting knowledge primarily to what is already known.
  - ❖ Each life is a spiritual journey and extends beyond the self.
  - ❖ By moving beyond the self and developing love and compassion, we can end suffering.
  - ❖ Crime can be eliminated by ending suffering through peace and social justice.
- Quinney and Wilderman suggest that crime can be controlled by adopting a **peace model** based on cooperation.
- Restorative justice is a modern social movement that attempts to reform the criminal justice system.
  - ❖ A modern social movement meant to reform the criminal justice system
  - ❖ Stresses healing rather than retribution
  - ❖ Restoration, or repairing the harm done by crime and rebuilding relationships in the community, is the primary goal of restorative justice.
  - ❖ Peace model
    - ◆ Focuses on developing a consensus on quality-of-life issues including major crimes, property rights, the rights to use of new technologies, and the ownership of information
  - ❖ **Participatory justice**
    - ◆ All parties to a dispute accept a kind of binding arbitration by neutral parties.
    - ◆ Alternative dispute resolutions are important in the application of the peacemaking perspective.
    - ◆ Examples of alternative participatory justice programs include dispute resolution centers and neighborhood justice centers.

PEACE MODEL

An approach to crime control that focuses on effective ways for developing a shared consensus on critical issues that have the potential to seriously affect the quality of life.

PARTICIPATORY JUSTICE

A relatively informal type of criminal justice case processing that makes use of local community resources rather than requiring traditional forms of official intervention.

♦ Relies on cooperative efforts to resolve disputes rather than by the adversarial-like proceedings that are seen as characteristic in most American courts.

For more on Richard Quinney, visit Criminology Interactive online > Conflict Theories > Theory Explained: Richard Quinney.

For more additional theorists Stephen Spitzer, Jeff Farrel, and Herbert Blalock, visit Criminology Interactive online > Conflict Theories > Theory Explained: Stephen Spitzer, Jeff Farrel, and Herbert Blalock.

CHAPTER SUMMARY

➤ Social conflict theories see crime as a result of a class struggle. These theories emphasize the power relationships between social groups, the distribution of wealth, ownership as a means of production, and economic and social structure in terms of social class and control.

➤ There are three perspectives in social conflict theory that are discussed in this chapter: the consensus perspective, the pluralist perspective, and the conflict perspective.

➤ As was discussed in Chapter 1, the consensus model is based on the idea that there is agreement among most people about what is right and wrong, and those members of society work toward the greater good. Roscoe Pound, the dean of Harvard Law School in 1916, was one of the first and strongest proponents of the consensus model. According to Pound, individuals do not expect people to act aggressively toward each other in a civilized society. Pound also proposed that citizens are in control of what they have acquired or created for their own use, that they act in good faith, that they do not participate in acts that will hurt others, and that any behavior that is harmful to society will be restrained by those who maintain the society.

➤ The pluralist perspective suggests that society is made up of a diverse set of values and beliefs. Theorists of pluralism claim that the law exists to maintain the peace between individuals and among groups. In addition, pluralism contends that society generally agrees about the role of laws and the legal system, and that the legal system functions objectively.

➤ The conflict perspective asserts that conflict in society can never fully be resolved. Like the pluralistic perspective, the conflict perspective contends that society is made up of diverse social groups that have different ideas about what is right and wrong. Conflict between groups, then, cannot be avoided. Ultimately, law is the tool of the powerful and furthers the interests of those who make the law.

➤ Karl Marx is one of the best-known writers on social conflict. According to Marx, a capitalist society is composed of two classes: the proletariat (the working class that has no power) and the bourgeoisie (the class that is in power because they control the means of production). The struggle between classes, then, occurs in any capitalist society. The natural outcome is the overthrow of capitalism and the creation of a classless or communist society.

➤ Several theorists used Marx's works as a springboard to develop deeper theories of crime and social conflict. In 1905, Willem Bonger expanded Marx's basic ideas by proposing that there was a link between crime and economic and social conditions, and that crime was a normal response to cultural conditions. George Bryan Vold created the notion of theoretical criminology along Marxist lines, claiming that crime is a political definition thrust upon those who are not powerful by the powerful, who create the law. Ralf Dahrendorf's work considers conflict inevitable and claims that it is out of conflict that change—either destructive or constructive—occurs. Austin Turk developed theories that positioned crime as the natural consequence of intergroup struggle and as the result of laws of those in power forcing their form of justice on those without power.

➤ Radical criminology is derived from such nineteenth century theorists as Marx and Engels. Radical criminology rose to special prominence in the 1960s and

1970s. The contemporary version of radical criminology contends that crime is caused by social conditions that give power to the wealthy and take power away from those who are less fortunate. In 1971, William J. Chambliss summarized radical criminology by stating that behavior is considered criminal because the state uses coercive power over the middle class. In 1974, Richard Quinney used six Marxist propositions to explain crime. He also claimed that American society is an advanced capitalist economy whose sole purpose is to serve the dominant economic class. Criminal law, then, is used by the state to perpetuate the existing social order.

➤ While radical criminology calls for social change in the conditions that lead to crime, critical criminology critiques the social relationships that lead to crime. In 1974, critical criminologist Gresham Sykes explained critical criminology as an inquiry into the way criminal law is internalized by different segments of society. Earlier, Elliot Curries identified seven mechanisms that create crime, focusing on economic and political reasons.

➤ Emerging conflict theory includes left-realist criminology. A natural outgrowth of concern with street crime and everyday victimization, left-realist criminology finds fault with radical-critical criminologist theory for romanticizing street crime and street criminals. This approach focuses on those most affected by crime: the victims and their families, offenders, and criminal justice personnel. Walter DeKeseredy popularized the notion of emerging conflict theory in the United States, while Jock Young was the major source of left-realist notions in England.

➤ Beginning in the 1970s, feminist criminology, based on several theories of feminism, emerged. These theories contend that the inequalities in society are based on gender. Crime is considered an act of aggression that characterizes men as aggressive by nature. The works of Rita Simon and Freda Adler in 1975 asserted that the difference in criminal activity between women and men had to do with socialization. Kathleen Daly and Meda Chesney-Lind suggested that gender differences in crime have developed because criminologists have traditionally studied only males.

➤ Radical feminism takes feminist criminology one step further by suggesting that men are fundamentally aggressive and violent. If male dominance is eliminated, the theory contends, crimes against women would decrease. In 1989, John Hagan built on notions of radical feminism by claiming that power relationships are part of everyday domestic settings and relationships.

➤ Postmodern criminology is a collection of criminological perspectives that focus on social change that is part of the postmodern philosophy developed after World War II. At its core, postmodernism questions whether anything can be known.

➤ Deconstructionist theories are postmodern theories that have two threads: anarchist criminology (looks at alternatives to social and criminal problems) and constitutive criminology (considers how individuals shape their world and, in turn, are shaped by it).

➤ Peacemaking criminology has its roots in Christian and Eastern philosophies and asserts that social control agencies and citizens should work together to alleviate social problems and human suffering. Richard Quinney and John Wilderman, the leading advocates of peacemaking criminology, contend that a solution to crime can be achieved through nonviolent criminology of compassion and service. Their system of restorative justice is based on a view of crime as not simply lawbreaking, but an offense against governmental authority. According to peacemaking criminologists, victims, offenders, and their communities should be engaged to heal the harm caused by crime.

STUDY QUESTIONS

1. What are the distinctions between the consensus, pluralist, and conflict perspectives?
2. What was Karl Marx's contribution to criminological theory?
3. How did Willem Bonger, George Vold, and Austin Turk apply Marx's theories?
4. Identify and describe the two schools of radical criminology.
5. What was the left-realist view of radical and critical criminologies?
6. How does feminist criminology use the term *androcentricity* to describe society?
7. What are some of the fundamental ways that peacemaking criminology seeks to deal with violent and criminal behaviors?

ONLINE@CRIMINOLOGY INTERACTIVE

Theory in Action

Case File #1: Shipyard Worker—Gus
Case File #2: Drug Dealer at Car—Mario

Review

Vocabulary Shootout
Essay Questions
Section Test

Readings and Research

Web Links

Additional Theorists

Friedrich Engels
Georg Simmel
Max Weber
Wilhelm Friedrich Hegel
Stephen Spitzer
Jeff Farrel
Herbert Blalock

Chapter 8

Measuring Crime

CHAPTER OUTLINE

KEY IDEAS

➤ Measuring crime is central to criminology. It impacts decision making, theory validation, and resource allocation.

➤ Crime measurement data is gathered in two ways. Primary data are gathered directly by the researcher. Secondary data are collected by an entity for a variety of different research purposes, which is then used in different ways for various research.

➤ Gathering crime statistics is a new phenomenon, but censuses, which measure population, have been taken for thousands of years.

➤ Thomas Malthus was an economist in modern times who looked at statistics and made predictions about the way demographics would impact the world. As a result of Malthus's work, a movement called Malthusian thought developed, and investigators in the early 1800s began studying crime rates throughout Europe, defining a form that has been called the statistical school of criminology.

➤ In 1929, the Uniform Crime Reporting program began to provide crime statistics for use by agencies throughout the United States.

➤ Because of the limitations of the Uniform Crime Reporting program, the National Crime Victimization Survey now provides yearly data. The FBI's National Incident-Based Reporting System also reports every year.

➤ The *Sourcebook of Criminal Statistics* offers yearly data as well, organized in tables that cover all aspects of criminal justice.

➤ Crime statistics are frequently supplemented by self-report surveys in which individuals report their own criminal behavior.

➤ Crime statistics from both surveys and reported statistics can tell us important things about crime, including the environmental distribution, the relationship between age and crime, the correlation between social class and crime, and the relationship between race and criminal behavior.

KEY TERMS

chivalry hypothesis
National Incident-Based Reporting System (NIBRS)
primary data
secondary data
self-report surveys
Sourcebook of Criminal Statistics
Uniform Crime Reporting (UCR)

8.0 Measuring crime

8.1 Measuring crime is a complex process.

    8.1.1 Crime can be measured in many ways, for various purposes.

       ■ No individual approach provides a complete picture of crime.

       ■ Different approaches have strengths and limitations.

    8.1.2 The way crime is measured is important.

       ■ Decisions are made based on data from measurements, such as:
          ❖ The validity of theories
          ❖ The effectiveness of programs/policies
          ❖ The allocation of resources

    8.1.3 Three major reasons for measuring crime (Adler, et al., 1998)

       ■ To test theories

       ■ To gain knowledge about various types of offenses

       ■ To provide data to criminal justice system agencies to aid in decision making

    8.1.4 All of these data influence how the public perceives crime and crime control.

For more on measuring crime, visit Criminology Interactive online > Introduction to Crime > Defining and Measuring Crime: Introduction to Measuring Crime.

8.2 Sources of data

    8.2.1 Data can be gathered using a variety of methods.

       ■ Data take two basic forms:
          ❖ **Primary data** is gathered directly by a researcher specifically for the purpose of a particular study.
          ❖ **Secondary data** has been collected previously for a different research purpose and can take the form of statistics from government agencies and private foundations or businesses.

8.3 History of crime statistics

    8.3.1 Gathering statistics specifically about crime is a relatively new phenomenon, but population statistics have been collected since pre-Roman times.

PRIMARY DATA

Data gathered for a distinct purpose.

SECONDARY DATA

Data collected for reasons other than a specific research project, usually by government agencies, private foundations, or private businesses.

8.3.2 Thomas Robert Malthus (1766–1834)

MAJOR IMPACT: Malthus, an English political economist and demographer, predicted that human population would grow exponentially, creating a future of warfare, crime, and starvation.

SELECTED PUBLICATION: *Essay on the Principle of Population as It Affects the Future Improvement of Society* (1798)

8.3.3 André Michel Guerry (1802–1866)

MAJOR IMPACT: Guerry, a French lawyer and statistician, published a work that considered the relationship between social and moral variables, which included graphic examples such as tables and maps to chronicle rates of suicide and crime in France by gender, age, and region of France, as well as seasons of the year.

SELECTED PUBLICATION: *Essai sur la statistique morale de la France* (1833)

- Guerry found that rates for suicide and crime remained relatively stable over time, but they varied according to different geographic areas of France.

8.3.4 Adolphe Quételet (1796–1864)

MAJOR IMPACT: Quételet was a Belgian astronomer and mathematician who applied probability and statistics to the social sciences and developed a statistical analysis to crime in several European countries.

SELECTED PUBLICATION: *Of the Development of the Propensity to Crime* (1831)

- Assessed the degree to which crime rates vary with climate, gender, and age

- Quételet's studies indicated that:
  - ❖ Violent crimes increase in hot weather.
  - ❖ Property crimes increase in frequency during the colder months.

- Developed the concept of thermic law, which claimed that morality undergoes seasonal variation

- *Compte generale*
  - ❖ First officially published crime statistics in London in 1828
  - ❖ Influenced Quételet's ideas about crime and social variables

- Comparisons or correlations were calculated to make connections between economic conditions and rates of various types of crime

❖ Joseph Fletcher

  ◆ Completed study of English statistical data covering the years 1810 to 1847

  ◆ Concluded that prison commitments increased as price of wheat increased

❖ Gerog von Mayr (1841–1925)

  ◆ German writer, whose data covered the years 1836 to 1861

  ◆ Discovered that rate of theft increased with the price of rye in Bavaria

■ Statistical school

  ❖ Works of statisticians like Guerry and Quételet formed the historical basis for what has been called the statistical school of criminology.

    ◆ The statistical school foreshadowed development of both sociological criminology and the ecological school.

8.4 Crime statistics today

  8.4.1 U.S. crime statistics: Uniform Crime Report, National Incident-Based Reporting System, Bureau of Justice crime statistics

UNIFORM CRIME REPORTS (UCR)

A summation of crime statistics tallied annually by the Federal Bureau of Investigation (FBI), consisting primarily of data on crimes and arrests reported to the police.

■ **Uniform Crime Reports (UCR)**

  ❖ An annual summation of crime statistics

  ❖ Relies on data collected from local police department on reported crimes and arrests

  ❖ History of the UCR

    ◆ Conceived of in 1929 by the International Association of Chiefs of Police to meet the need for reliable crime statistics

    ◆ Part I offenses

      ❑ Initial UCR data were structured in terms of seven major offense categories:

        • Murder

        • Rape

        • Robbery

        • Aggravated assault

        • Burglary

        • Larceny

        • Motor vehicle theft

      ❑ An eighth offense, arson, was added in 1979.

- ◆ Crime index
  - ❑ Provides a rate that can be compared over time, and from one geographic area to another for comparisons between/among groups
  - ❑ Rates are reported per 100,000 people.
- ❖ Present status of the UCR
  - ◆ Approximately 17,000 city, county, and state law enforcement agencies report data.
  - ◆ Agencies voluntarily provide information on crimes that have been reported to police and cleared by arrest.
  - ◆ All data are verified.
  - ◆ Each month, the participating law enforcement agencies report on 29 offense categories.
- ❖ Part I and Part II offenses
  - ◆ Part I offenses
    - ❑ Also called index crimes or major offenses
    - ❑ Eight offenses are divided into two categories that are collectively considered the most serious:
      - • Crimes against the person
        - • Criminal homicide
        - • Forcible rape
        - • Robbery
        - • Aggravated assault
      - • Crimes against property
        - • Burglary
        - • Larceny-theft
        - • Arson
        - • Motor vehicle theft
    - ❑ The reporting of these crimes to police tends to be more reliable than less serious crimes.
    - ❑ Data on these crimes are used as an indicator of changes in crime over time.
  - ◆ Part II offenses
    - ❑ Includes all other offenses except traffic violations, and are generally less serious
    - ❑ Offenses in this category include:
      - • Embezzlement
      - • Vandalism
      - • Fraud
      - • Simple assault

- Forgery and counterfeiting
- Stolen property (receiving, etc.)
- Vagrancy
- Weapons (carrying, etc.)
- Prostitution and related offenses
- Sex offenses (statutory rape, etc.)
- Drug law violations
- Gambling
- Offenses against the family (nonsupport, etc.)
- Driving under the influence
- Liquor law violations
- Public drunkenness
- Disorderly conduct
- Curfew violations
- Loitering
- Runaway
  - ❐ Part II offenses are less likely to be reported to police.
- ❖ Limitations of the UCR
  - ◆ Methodological problems
    - ❐ The UCR focuses only on crimes reported to the police, hence it may underestimate the true incidence of criminal activity.
      - Reasons for failure to report:
        - Fear of perpetrator
        - Shame, especially when women have been victimized in a sexual encounter
        - Fear that the victim may have of not being believed
        - Fear of participation in the justice system, such as going to court to testify against the offender
    - ❐ Hierarchical rule
      - For some crimes, only the most serious offense is reported when multiple offenses are committed.
      - For some crimes, each act is counted as a separate offense.
      - Legal definitions of crimes differ across states and between states and the FBI.

- ◆ Reporting practice problems
    - ❏ Police reports are voluntary.
    - ❏ The reports vary in accuracy and completeness.
    - ❏ Reporting is affected by political agendas.
    - ❏ White-collar crimes are not counted.
- ❖ Strengths of the UCR
    - ◆ The report provides comprehensive coverage of a range of crimes.
- ❖ Conducts incident-driven **National Incident-Based Reporting System (NIBRS)**
    - ◆ Designed to provide more in-depth data
    - ◆ Each offense and arrest is counted as an incident.
    - ◆ A wider range of information is recorded (52 items).
        - ❏ Information about the offense:
            - • Location where it happened
            - • Whether a weapon was involved or used
            - • Whether the offender was under the influence of drugs or alcohol
            - • Whether there was a racial, religious, or gender-based motivation behind the offense
        - ❏ Information about the parties includes:
            - • Demographics such as:
                - • Gender of victim/offender
                - • Age of victim/offender
                - • Race of victim/offender
                - • Any known relationship between the victim and offender
                - • Circumstances that might have motivated the crime
        - ❏ Information about the property (if any) involved:
            - • Value of property damaged
    - ◆ It reports on 22 crime categories representing 46 specific offenses
        - ❏ Group A offenses (extensive crime data are collected on the offenses in this category)
            - • Arson
            - • Assault offenses
                - • Aggravated assault
                - • Simple assault
                - • Intimidation

NATIONAL INCIDENT-BASED REPORTING SYSTEM (NIBRS)
A new form of the UCR that will collect data on each single incident and arrest within 22 crime categories.

- Bribery
- Burglary/breaking and entering
- Counterfeiting/forgery
- Destruction/damage/vandalism of property
- Drug/narcotic offenses
  - Drug/narcotic violations
  - Drug equipment violations
- Embezzlement
- Extortion/blackmail
- Fraud offenses
  - False pretenses/swindling/confidence games
  - Credit card/automatic teller machine fraud
  - Impersonation
  - Welfare fraud
  - Wire fraud
- Gambling offenses
  - Betting/wagering
  - Operating/promoting/assisting gambling
  - Gambling equipment violations
  - Sports tampering
- Homicide offenses
  - Murder and non-negligent manslaughter
  - Negligent manslaughter
  - Justifiable homicide
- Kidnapping/abduction
- Larceny-theft offenses
  - Pocket picking
  - Purse snatching
  - Shoplifting
  - Theft from a building
  - Theft from coin-operated machine or device
  - Theft from a motor vehicle
  - Theft of motor vehicle parts or accessories
  - All other forms of larceny
- Motor vehicle theft
- Pornography/obscene material

- Prostitution offenses
  - Prostitution
  - Assisting or promoting prostitution
- Robbery
- Sex offenses, forcible
  - Forcible rape
  - Forcible sodomy
  - Sexual assault with an object
  - Forcible fondling
- Sex offenses, nonforcible
  - Incest
  - Statutory rape
- Receiving stolen property
- Weapon law violations

❑ Group B offenses (those for which only arrest data are reported)
  - Bad checks
  - Curfew/loitering/vagrancy violations
  - Disorderly conduct
  - Driving under the influence
  - Drunkenness
  - Nonviolent family offenses
  - Liquor law violations
  - Peeping Tom
  - Runaway
  - Trespass of real property
  - All other offenses

◆ Advantages of NIBRS over UCR
  ❑ NIBRS is totally computerized; the UCR is not.
    - Data collection is not restricted to a limited number of offense categories.
    - Definitions meet local, state, and national reporting needs.
    - Details on individual crime incidents are recorded and analyzed.
    - Arrests and clearances can be matched with specific incidents or offenses.
    - All offenses in an incident are recorded and counted.

- Distinctions can be made between attempted and completed crimes.
- Detailed crime analyses can be made within and across law enforcement jurisdictions, and regional law enforcement agencies can share information easily.

For more on the Uniform Crime Reports, visit Criminology Interactive online > Introduction to Crime > Identifying and Measuring Crime: Uniform Crime Reports.

- Bureau of Justice Statistics (BJS)
  - ❖ Conducts the National Crime Victimization Survey (NCVS)
    - ◆ Data is officially reported in *Criminal Victimization in the United States*, the nation's primary source of information on criminal victimization.
    - ◆ Data is based on a significant number of households, representing over 130,000 individuals age 12 or older each year.
    - ◆ The survey is conducted by the U.S. Census Bureau, with the Bureau of Justice Statistics.
    - ◆ Reports data on the extent of victimization for the following crimes:
      - ❒ Rape
      - ❒ Sexual assault
      - ❒ Robbery
      - ❒ Assault
      - ❒ Theft
      - ❒ Household burglary
      - ❒ Motor vehicle theft
    - ◆ Provides the largest forum for victims to describe the impact of crime and characteristics of violent offenders
    - ◆ The NCVS measures:
      - ❒ Characteristics of crimes
        - Time and place of occurrence
        - Number of offenders
        - Use of weapons
        - Economic loss
        - Nature of injury
      - ❒ Characteristics of victims
        - Gender
        - Race

- Ethnicity
- Marital status
- Household composition
- Income
- Education level

❏ Perceived characteristics of offenders

- Age
- Race
- Gender
- Relationship to victim

❏ Circumstances surrounding the offense

- Type of interaction

❏ Police reporting factors

- Why reported/not reported

◆ NCVS findings:

❏ An estimated 720 million victimizations reported to the NCVS for individuals 12 or older

❏ Between 1993 and 2005, the violent crime rate decreased 58%, from 50 to 21 victimizations per 1,000 persons age 12 or older.

❏ Property crime declined 52% from 319 to 154 per 1,000 households

❏ In 2005, according to victims, 47% of violent crimes were reported to the police, up from 43% in 1993.

❏ The proportion of property crimes reported to the police also increased to 40% in 2005, from 33% in 1993.

❏ The rate of firearm violence increased between 2004 and 2005, from 1.4 to 2.0 victimizations per 1,000 individuals age 12 or older.

❏ Males were most vulnerable to violence by strangers (54% of the violence against males), while females were most often victimized by nonstrangers (64%).

❏ In 2005, males, blacks, and persons age 24 or younger continued to be victimized at higher rates than females, whites, and persons age 25 or older.

◆ Redesigned and tested in 1989, with first redesign results reported in 1993

❏ New questions were added to accommodate heightened interest in certain types of victimizations.

❑ Improvements in technology and survey methods were incorporated in the redesign.

❑ Survey now includes improved questions and cues that aid victims in recalling victimizations.

❑ Survey interviewers now ask more explicit questions about sexual victimizations.

❑ Advocates have also encouraged victims to talk more openly about their experiences.

◆ Critique of the NCVS

❑ It provides narrower coverage than the UCR

❑ Overreporting occurs

• Respondents may embellish crime reports and may even concoct criminal incidents for purposes of self-aggrandizement.

❑ Underreporting occurs

• Several factors may affect underreporting, including embarrassment, fear of self-incrimination, and faulty memory.

❑ Inconsistent interviewing/recording also threatens the validity.

• Different interviewers are used, which may result in reporting accurately.

❑ Potential sampling error is another threat to validity

❑ Definitions of crimes measured by the NCVS do not necessarily correspond to any federal or state statutes making comparisons difficult.

❑ Changes in NCVS categories have resulted in an inability to easily compare NCVS findings of even a decade ago with current NCVS data.

◆ Strengths of the NCVS

❑ It addresses the serious issue of unreported crime.

❑ It provides in-depth information on victimizations.

❑ The data are considered "a relatively unbiased, valid estimate of all victimizations for target crimes." (Siegel, 2000, p. 58)

❑ It is a tremendous aid in gathering data on domestic violence.

For more on the National Crime Victimization Survey, visit Criminology Interactive online > Introduction to Crime > Identifying and Measuring Crime: National Crime Victimization Survey.

❖ Publishes the *Sourcebook of Criminal Justice Statistics* each year

  ◆ Consists of approximately 1,000 tables covering all aspects of criminal justice in the UnitedStates

  ◆ Data is collected from over 100 different sources.

  ◆ Data is organized into six sections of tables:

    ❐ Characteristics of the criminal justice systems
      • Corrections
      • Courts
      • Finance
      • Judges
      • Law enforcement

    ❐ Public attitudes toward crime and criminal justice-related topics
      • Capital punishment
      • Crime
      • Courts
      • Drugs
      • Guns
      • Police
      • Public confidence
      • Students
      • Schools
      • Social and other issues
      • Terrorism

    ❐ Nature and distribution of known offenses
      • Alcohol and drugs
      • Crime, law enforcement officers
      • Students
      • Victimization

    ❐ Characteristics and distribution of persons arrested
      • Arrests
      • Clearances
      • Seizures

    ❐ Judicial processing of defendants
      • Juvenile courts
      • Large county courts
      • State courts
      • U.S. Court of Appeals

SOURCEBOOK OF CRIMINAL STATISTICS

An annual report on crime statistics organized in tables that provides characteristics of the criminal justice system, attitudes toward crime, and the distribution of offenses.

- U.S. district courts
- U.S. Sentence Commission Guidelines
- U.S. Supreme Court
- ❏ Person under correctional supervision
  - Adults under correctional supervision
  - Community supervision
  - Death row
  - Federal prisoners
  - Jail inmates
  - Juveniles
  - State prisoners

8.4.2 Crime surveys

■ Are generally **self-report surveys**
  ❖ Confidential interview
  ❖ Anonymous questionnaire

■ Self-report format
  ❖ These surveys were created in response to problems with official statistics

■ The major concern is with the validity of responses.
  ❖ Concerns about the validity of self-report data are especially acute when asking about involvement in criminal activity.

■ Target populations
  ❖ Self-report surveys can be done with any group.
  ❖ This format is particularly well suited for use with juveniles.

■ Limitations of crime surveys
  ❖ Underreporting
    ◆ People are unwilling to report illegal acts.
    ◆ Those engaging in the most crime are also at greatest risk by responding and this creates a bias.
    ◆ People forget some acts that they committed.
    ◆ Confusion may exist about what is being asked.
  ❖ Overreporting
    ◆ There may be some exaggeration of criminal acts because of faulty memory, status issues, and for shock value.
    ◆ Responses that do occur often represent an excess of trivial offenses.

■ Strengths of crime surveys
  ❖ They allow researchers to address perceived biases in race, gender, and class biases in official statistics

SELF-REPORT SURVEYS

Surveys in which individuals report on their own criminal activity.

❖ They provide a validity check for official statistics

❖ They are useful for assessing undetected crime, especially with regard to drug use

❖ They allow for the simultaneous measurement of other factors, such as attitudes and values, personal characteristics, and family and educational factors

■ Trends in criminal activity

   ❖ Monitoring trends serves several important functions:

      ◆ It aids in monitoring overall crime

      ◆ It helps assess influences of various factors on crime

      ◆ It helps in the evaluation of effectiveness of policies/programs

   ❖ The crime rate exhibited a slow increase between 1930 and 1960.

      ◆ In the early 1940s crime decreased sharply, probably due to large numbers of young men who entered military service.

   ❖ More rapid rise from 1960 until 1990s

      ◆ This may be linked to World War II

         ❏ End of war and the return of millions of young men to civilian life, birth rates skyrocketed between 1945 and 1955 creating a postwar baby boom

         ❏ By 1960, baby boomers were entering their teenage years.

         ❏ A disproportionate number of young people in the U.S. population produced a dramatic increase in most major crimes.

      ◆ Other factors contributing to the increase in this time period:

         ❏ Modified reporting requirements

         ❏ Growing professionalization of some police departments

         ❏ The 1960s were tumultuous years due to the Vietnam War, the civil rights struggle, growth of secularism, dramatic increases in the divorce rate, diverse forms of liberation, and the influx of psychedelic and other drugs.

      ◆ From 1960 to 1980, crime rates rose from 1,887 to 5,950 per 100,000 members of the U.S. population.

   ❖ Since the 1990s, there has been a gradual decline

      ◆ This is possibly due to:

         ❏ An aging out of the post-World War II baby-boomer generation

         ❏ Stricter laws

          ❑ Expanded justice system and police funding

          ❑ Changes in crime-fighting technologies

          ❑ Economic and demographic factors

          ❑ Family planning practices, which kept birth rates relatively low among members of the baby-boomer generation

        ◆ Between 1993 and 2003, the crime index decreased from 5,897 to 4,063 offenses per 100,000 people in the U.S. population.

      ❖ The key issue is what the source(s) of this decline is/are.

        ◆ Age distribution and crime

          ❑ Strong associations have been found between age and criminal activity; the young exhibit the highest crime rate.

          ❑ The higher the percentage of young people in the population, the higher the crime rate.

        ◆ Baby boomers and the crime rate

          ❑ This group reached the peak of their crime-prone years in the 1960s and this is reflected in the crime rate for that time period.

          ❑ As boomers aged, there was a corresponding decline in the crime rate.

        ◆ Other factors

          ❑ At the same time, there were other social changes that have been characterized by stricter, more harsh approaches to crime control.

    ■ Researchers/consumers of all such data must:

      ❖ Be cognizant of potential differences

      ❖ Be careful when interpreting the data

For more on crime surveys and their limitations, visit Criminology Interactive online > Introduction to Crime > Identifying and Measuring Crime: Underreporting of Crime.

8.5   Measuring crime characteristics

    8.5.1   The frequency with which a given crime is committed is essential to any analysis.

    ■ Information about crime statistics allows officials to determine criminal trends.

    ■ Trends in criminal activity

      ❖ The crime rate exhibited a slow increase between 1930 and 1960 and a more rapid rise from 1960 until 1980.

      ❖ Since 1980, there has been a gradual (overall) decline.

- Future trends
  - ❖ Some predict there will be a rise in the early twenty-first century when the children of boomers reach their crime-prone years.
  - ❖ It is hard to predict why the crime rate dropped, and it is equally hard to predict what might happen.

8.5.2 Environmental and temporal factors

- Patterns in the crime rate and distribution can be linked to environmental and temporal factors.
  - ❖ Information on where and when crimes are committed is useful.
  - ❖ It informs prevention (policy/practice)
- When do crimes occur?
  - ❖ Most reported crimes occur during summer months.
    - ◆ Homes are vacant because of vacations.
    - ◆ Doors and windows are left open.
    - ◆ Temperatures are higher, day and night.
      - ❏ Crime increases with higher temperatures up to a certain point; then crime may decline.
      - ❏ This relationship is still being debated; it may not apply to all crimes.
  - ❖ More reported crimes occur at night.
    - ◆ Mostly between 6:00 P.M. and 6:00 A.M.
  - ❖ More crimes occur on the first day of the month than on any other day.
    - ◆ The arrival of government issued checks
- Where do crimes occur?
  - ❖ The highest rates are in large urban areas
    - ◆ Most crimes occur in cities.
  - ❖ There are a variety of factors associated with these higher crime rates:
    - ◆ Population density
    - ◆ Economic conditions
    - ◆ Age distributions
    - ◆ Quality/prevalence of law enforcement

8.6 Measuring characteristics of criminals

8.6.1 Characteristics of criminals

- Research focuses on the characteristics of crimes, but also on those who commit them.

- This allows researchers to categorize offenders in a variety of ways that are useful.
  - ❖ They help address why some people are more likely to engage in criminal behavior.

8.6.2   Age and crime (adapted from Adler, et al., 1998; Siegel, 2000)

- Age and crime are inversely associated.
  - ❖ Crime is fundamentally committed by young people.
  - ❖ Thirteen to seventeen-year-olds represent 6% of the population.
    - ◆ They commit 30% of the index crimes.
    - ◆ They represent 18% of all arrests.
    - ◆ Those under 25 represent over 50% of all arrests.
- Arrest rates decline after age 30.
  - ❖ Those over 45 represent 32% of population; however, they are arrested for only 8% of the index crimes.
  - ❖ Those over 50 represent 2% of the arrests.
  - ❖ The aging-out phenomenon
    - ◆ Refers to a decline in criminal activities with age
      - ❑ This implies that offending patterns are influenced by a variety of factors besides age alone.
        - • The relationship between age and offending varies for different people.
        - • Other factors can include:
          - · Economic status
          - · Interpersonal relationships
          - · Lifestyle
          - · Substance abuse

8.6.3   Gender and crime

- Historically, males commit more crimes.
- Two early explanations for gender differences:
  - ❖ The first focuses on the differences between males and females
  - ❖ The second focuses on the notion of the **chivalry hypothesis**
    - ◆ The low crime rate for females is attributable to lenient treatment by the criminal justice system.
    - ◆ The crime rate for females is more a result of the reaction of the male-dominated justice system than the actual crimes committed by females.
- In the mid-twentieth century, the focus shifted to socialization.
  - ❖ Gender differences in crime rates were attributed to differential socialization practices.

CHIVALRY HYPOTHESIS

Old conceptions of men doing things for women and perhaps showing leniency toward female offenders, which some argue, may explain the differences in arrest and incarceration rates for women.

- ◆ Females are socialized to be less aggressive.
- ◆ Young girls are more closely supervised.

- ■ The gap between male and female crime rates has been narrowing since the 1960s.

- ■ Alternate/competing explanations
  - ❖ Chivalry in the criminal justice system is dead.
  - ❖ Female crime has increased, but mostly for nonviolent, petty property, and drug-related crimes.

- ■ There is still disagreement about the form and extent of female crime.
  - ❖ Female crime tends to be linked to socioeconomic position.

8.6.4   Socioeconomic status and crime

- ■ Researchers disagree about this relationship.
  - ❖ Part of the disagreement relates to how class is determined.
  - ❖ There are also issues over sources of data
    - ◆ Official statistics show a strong relationship, but the data are potentially biased.
    - ◆ Self-report data shows fewer class differences.
      - ❑ Concern remains over differences in types of crimes.
        - • The overall amounts are similar, but the nature of the crimes is different.
        - • Lower-class youths are more involved in serious crimes.

- ■ Though the relationship between social class and criminal behavior is unclear, there is a clear relationship between social class and incarceration.
  - ❖ The poor and uneducated are the most likely to be in prison.
  - ❖ Education level and incarceration
    - ◆ In 2003, only 32% of prison inmates had completed high school. (Bureau of Justice Statistics, 2003)
    - ◆ In 2007, approximately 86% of the general population, age 25 to 29, had finished high school. (U.S. Census Bureau, 2007)
    - ◆ Income level and incarceration (general income figures are from the U.S. Census Bureau, 2007)
      - ❑ In 2007, 31% of prison inmates had an income of $15,000 or more prior to their incarceration.
      - ❑ In 2007, the median household income in the United States was $50,233.
      - ❑ In 2007, the poverty level for a family of four was $20,650.

8.6.5   Race and crime

- Blacks and crime
  - ❖ In 2006, blacks exhibited the highest arrest rate, representing 28% of arrests for all crimes, while they made up only approximately 13% of the U.S. population.
  - ❖ In 2006, blacks were arrested in 30.3% of the delinquency cases, more than twice the percent they represent in the total population.
  - ❖ From 1976 to 2004, blacks were the offenders in 52.2% of the homicides, while whites were offenders in 45.8% of the homicides.
  - ❖ From 1976 to 2004, blacks were homicide victims in 46.9% of the cases, while whites were homicide victims in 50.9% of the cases.

- American Indians and crime
  - ❖ American Indians are also disproportionately represented in crime statistics.
    - ◆ Rates for violent victimization for both males and females were higher for American Indians than for all races.
    - ◆ American Indians experienced violence at a rate of 10,100 per 100,000 American Indians, more than twice the rate for the nation (41,100 per 100,000) for the years 1992 to 2001.
  - ❖ American Indians and the crime of murder
    - ◆ From 1976 to 2001, an estimated 3,738 American Indians were murdered.
      - ❏ After 1995, the annual American Indian murder rate decreased about 45%, from 6.6 to 3.6 murders per 100,000 residents in 2001.
      - ❏ From 1976 to 1999, 7 in 10 American Indian juvenile murder victims were killed by another American Indian.
  - ❖ Violent crime and age
    - ◆ The violent crime rate in every age group below age 35 was significantly higher for American Indians than for all persons.
    - ◆ Among American Indians ages 25 to 34, the rate of violent crime victimizations was more than two-and-a-half times the rate for all persons the same age.
  - ❖ Violent crime and gender
    - ◆ Rates of violent victimization for both males and females were higher for American Indians than for all races.

◆ American Indian females were less likely to be victims compared to American Indian males.

◆ The rate of violent victimization among American Indian women was more than double that among all women.

❖ Violent crime and victim-offender relationship

◆ Offenders who were strangers of the victims committed most of the robberies (71%) against American Indians.

◆ American Indians were more likely to be victims of assault and rape/sexual assault committed by a stranger or acquaintance rather than an intimate partner or family member.

❖ Alcohol use by offender

◆ American Indian victims of violence were more likely than all victims to report an offender who was under the influence of alcohol at the time of the crime.

◆ Overall, about 62% of American Indian victims experienced violence by an offender using alcohol, compared to 42% for the national average.

❖ American Indian incarceration rates

◆ They are 38% higher than the national rate.

◆ Less than 33% of the nation's correctional population is confined in prisons/jails, but almost 50% of American Indians under correctional supervision are in prison or jail.

CHAPTER SUMMARY

➤ Measuring crime is a complex process that can be carried out in different ways for different purposes. How crime is measured is central to decision making in criminology and affects how theories are validated, how programs are judged, and how resources are allocated. There are three basic reasons for measuring crime: to test theories, to gain information about offenses, and to provide data to the criminal justice system for effective decision making. Data can be gathered two ways. Primary data is gathered directly by the researcher involved. Secondary data is data that has been previously collected, usually for a different research purpose, and often collected by government agencies, private foundations, or private businesses.

➤ Although collecting crime statistics is relatively new, population statistics in the form of censuses have been taken for thousands of years. Thomas Robert Malthus, an economist in the late 1700s, was the first to look at statistical data and make predictions regarding demographics and its impact. As a result of the development of Malthusian thought, researchers throughout Europe began to collect and scrutinize what were called "moral" statistics as a way to evaluate crime and conflict. André Michele Guerry was one of the first investigators in this movement, calculating the per capita crime rates in provinces in France in the early 1800s. Guerry's work was followed by Adolphe Quételet, who published a statistical analysis of crime in European countries that showed how crime was affected by climate, gender, and age of offender. The works of Guerry and Quételet form what is called the statistical school of criminology.

➤ In 1929, the Uniform Crime Reporting (UCR) program was created to provide crime statistics that could be used by agencies throughout the United States. UCR data is organized by Part I offenses, which are categorized as crimes against the person and crimes against property, and Part II offenses, which include all other offenses except traffic violations. While the UCR provides a comprehensive coverage of a range of crimes, it has certain limitations, including methodological problems and reporting practices problems.

➤ In part because of these limitations of the UCR, the Bureau of Justice Statistics developed the National Crime Victimization Survey (NCVS) and summarizes its data annually. The FBI collects data for both the UCR and the more detailed National Incident-based Reporting System (NIBRS), which also reports yearly. Offenses in the NIBRS are categorized as Group A (detailed data is reported and include homicide, gambling, fraud, and sex offenses) and Group B (more minor offenses for which only arrest data is reported).

➤ The Bureau of Justice Statistics conducts the NCVS in an attempt to address the issue of unreported crime. The NCVS measures the characteristics of crimes, victims, and offenders, as well as circumstances surrounding the offense and police reporting factors.

➤ The Bureau of Justice publishes the *Sourcebook of Criminal Statistics* each year, which offers 1,000 tables covering all aspects of criminal justice. Data are organized by characteristics of the criminal justice systems, public attitudes toward crime, nature and distribution of offenses, characteristics and distribution of persons arrested, judicial processing of defendants, and persons under correctional supervision.

➤ Crime surveys are generally self-report surveys where individuals report on their own criminal activity. They can take place in a confidential interview or through an anonymous questionnaire. While crime surveys are particularly useful for documenting trends in criminal activity, they are limited because they may be influenced by under- and overreporting.

➤ The frequency with which a given crime is committed has important implications. Crime trends follow increases and decreases in crime rates over time and determine the source of the increase and decline. For instance, while crime experienced a rapid rise between 1960 and 1980, there has been a gradual decline since 1980. Some reasons for this decline may include age distribution (the young tend to exhibit the highest crime rate) and the "get tough on crime" approach.

➤ There are a number of environmental conditions that affect crime rate and distribution. Statistics indicate that most crimes occur during the summer months and at night. More crimes occur on the first day of the month than on any other day.

➤ Statistics can help determine why certain people are more likely to engage in criminal behavior. Statistics on age and crime, for instance, indicate that while individuals between the ages of 13 and 17 represent 6% of the population, they commit 30% of crime and represent 18% of all arrests. Those over 25 represent 50% of all arrests. Arrests decline after the age of 30, and those over 50 represent only 2% of all arrests.

➤ The relationship between gender and crime is also of interest to researchers. Historically, males are roughly three-and-a-half to five times as likely as females to commit crime. There are two possible explanations for this gender difference. The first is that there are key differences between males and females, including the fact that females are physically weaker, more passive, and are less equipped to commit crimes. The second explanation is the chivalry hypothesis—the justice system is simply more lenient toward females. The gap between male and female crimes has been narrowing since the 1960s, which has been explained by the feminist theory as being the result of an equalization of economic and social roles.

➤ Social class or socioeconomic status have also been closely correlated with crime, although there is disagreement about the relationship between the two. This disagreement in part has to do with how class is determined—by income, prestige, and/or level of education. Although the exact relationship is up for debate, there is no dispute that there is a strong relationship between social class and incarceration. The poor and uneducated are the most likely to be in prison.

➤ Race and its relationship to criminal behavior are also of interest to criminologists. Research indicates that in 2006, blacks exhibited the highest official arrest rate, representing 28% of arrests for crime, while they represent only 13% of the U.S. population. American Indians are also disproportionately represented in crime statistics, with a 38% higher incarceration rate than the national rate.

STUDY QUESTIONS

1. What is the difference between primary and secondary data?
2. How did Thomas Malthus contribute to the gathering of crime statistics?
3. What are some of the limitations of the Uniform Crime Reporting program?
4. What are the advantages of the National Incident-Based Reporting System?
5. What are some of the potential inaccuracies with self-report surveys?
6. What are some of the reasons that have been proposed for the reason that males commit significantly more crimes than females?
7. How does underreporting affect crime statistics?

ONLINE@CRIMINOLOGY INTERACTIVE

Crime Analysis

Drag and Drop Exercise

Chapter 9

Crimes Against Property

CHAPTER OUTLINE

KEY IDEAS

➤ Property crimes refer to a wide range of crimes that involve the misappropriation of property or services, larceny-theft, fraud, burglary, and arson.

➤ Larceny is the taking of property without permission and can involve small amounts of money as in petty larceny, or larger amounts, which is called grand larceny and can be considered a felony.

➤ Shoplifting is one of the most common types of larceny and costs consumers significant amounts of money each year.

➤ Motor vehicle theft is the theft or attempted theft of a car, bus, truck, or other motor vehicle.

➤ The acquisition of property through cheating and deception is known as fraud. Check fraud, insurance fraud, confidence games, and identity fraud are common types of fraud.

➤ Burglary is the unlawful entry into a structure to commit a theft or a felony of some kind.

➤ Arson is the burning or the attempt to burn a building, an object, or a piece of property of another.

KEY TERMS

arson
burglary
confidence games
fencing
fraud
hacker
identity fraud
jockeys
joyriding
larceny-theft
motor vehicle theft

9.0   Crimes against property

9.1   Property crime involves the misappropriation of property or services.

- A variety of means can be used in this misappropriation:
  - ❖ Theft or stealing
  - ❖ Fraud
    - ◆ False pretenses
    - ◆ Forgery
    - ◆ Confidence games
    - ◆ Unauthorized use of credit cards
    - ◆ Arson
    - ◆ Some forms of high-tech crimes and some white-collar crimes

For more on property crime, visit Criminology Interactive online > Property Crimes > Crime Explained: Introduction.

9.1.1   Types of property crime:

- **Theft**
- **Fraud**
- **Burglary**
- **Arson**

9.1.2   Varieties of larceny-theft:

- Shoplifting
- Pickpocketing
- Art theft
- **Motor vehicle theft**

9.1.3   Fraud or acts of obtaining property by false pretenses:

- Confidence games
- Check forgery/bad checks
- Credit card crimes
- Embezzlement
- Insurance fraud

9.2   The extent/cost of property crime

9.2.1   UCR statistics

- In 2007, there was an estimated 9.8 million property crime offenses in the United States.

LARCENY-THEFT

The unlawful taking, carrying, leading, or riding away by stealth of property other than a motor vehicle, from the possession or constructive possession of another, including attempts.

FRAUD

The use of trickery and deception to coerce something of value from another.

BURGLARY

The unlawful entry of a structure to commit a felony or a theft.

ARSON

Any willful or malicious burning or attempt to burn, with or without intent to defraud, a dwelling house, public building, motor vehicle or aircraft, personal property of another, and so on.

MOTOR VEHICLE THEFT

The theft or attempted theft of a motor vehicle. This offense category includes the stealing of automobiles, trucks, buses, and motorcycles.

- When comparing 2007 data to that of 2006, the two-year trend showed property crime decreased by 1.4%.

- The rate of property crimes was estimated at 3,235 offenses per 100,000 inhabitants in 2007.

  ❖ This represents a 2.1% decrease when compared to the rate in 2006.

- Larceny-theft offenses accounted for over 66.7% of all property crimes in 2007.

- In 2007, an estimated $17.6 billion in losses resulted from property crimes.

9.2.2   Two groups generally commit property crimes.

- Amateurs thieves

  ❖ Commit one or few crimes primarily because of low-risk opportunities

  ❖ Commit crimes that involve low levels of skill and planning

  ❖ May be motivated by some pressing or immediate need (e.g., gambling debt)

  ❖ Otherwise lead conventional lives

- Professional thieves

  ❖ Make theft a career, making most of their income from stealing

  ❖ Are involved in pickpocketing, burglary, auto theft, and a wide range of fraud and confidence games

  ❖ Work hard at being successful

  ❖ Have altered their techniques as a result of new crime control technologies

9.2.3   **Fencing** is the buying, selling, or dealing of stolen goods.

FENCING

Buying, selling, and distributing stolen goods, usually by an individual who has not been directly involved in the burglary itself.

- Fences acquire goods from burglars, robbers, shoplifters, confidence criminals, art thieves, and so on.

- There are both professional and amateur fences.

- Buying stolen goods is also a crime.

9.2.4   Age and property crime

- Young people are disproportionately involved in criminal activity.

- Involvement in conventional crime increases with age, but peaks in the teenage and early adult years.

- Much of the crime committed by young people is described as amateur property crime.

9.3 Larceny-theft is typically called stealing; it is taking or misappropriating property from another without their express permission for the purpose of personal gain.

- Larceny-theft includes:
  - ❖ Bicycle theft
  - ❖ Stealing motor vehicle parts and accessories
  - ❖ Shoplifting
  - ❖ Pocketpicking
  - ❖ The stealing of any property or article that is not taken by force, violence, or fraud
  - ❖ Attempted larcenies are included
- NCVS divides larceny into two categories: household and personal larceny.
- Crimes of larceny do not involve force and victims are not deliberately put in harm's way.
- Elements of larceny (adapted from Adler et al., 1998):
  - ❖ The offender takes control over property.
  - ❖ The offender takes the property.
  - ❖ The offender carries the property away.
    - ◆ Even slight removal satisfies this element
  - ❖ The property has to be personal property.
  - ❖ The property has to belong to another person.
    - ◆ The person from whom it is taken must have a right to possess the property.
  - ❖ There must be intent to permanently deprive the rightful owner of his property.

9.3.1 Classification of larceny

- Petty larceny is a theft that represents small amounts of money or property and is usually considered a misdemeanor.
- Grand larceny involves great amounts of money or property and can be classified as a felony.

9.3.2 Extent/cost of larceny and theft

- UCR
  - ❖ During 2007, there was an estimated 6.6 million larceny-thefts nationwide.
  - ❖ Among all property crimes, larceny-thefts accounted for an estimated 66.7% in 2007.
  - ❖ There was an estimated rate of 2,177.8 larceny-thefts per 100,000 inhabitants in 2007.

❖ When compared with the 2006 figure, there was a 0.6% decrease in the estimated number of larceny-thefts in 2007.

◆ When compared with the 1998 estimate, the 2007 figure showed a 9% decline.

❖ From 2006 to 2007, the rate of larceny-thefts declined 1.3%, and from 1998 to 2007, the rate declined 20.2%.

❖ In 2007, larceny-theft offenses cost victims an estimated $5.8 billion in lost property.

❖ The average value of property taken during larceny-thefts was $886 per offense.

❖ Larceny-theft by type

◆ Pocket picking

❒ 21,984 reported offenses

❒ A decline of 3.5% from 2006

❒ A $728 average for each offense

◆ Purse snatching

❒ 30,526 reported offenses

❒ A decline of 7.3% from 2006

❒ A $402 average for each offense

◆ Shoplifting

❒ 785,228 reported offenses

❒ An increase of 9.2% from 2006

❒ A $205 average for each offense

◆ Motor vehicles (except accessories)

❒ 1,369,150 reported offenses

❒ A decline of 0.8% from 2006

❒ A $722 average for each offense

◆ Motor vehicle accessories

❒ 480,502 reported offenses

❒ A decline of 7% from 2006

❒ A $554 average for each offense

◆ Bicycles

❒ 179,945 reported offenses

❒ A decline of 3.6% from 2006

❒ A $273 average for each offense

◆ From buildings

❒ 632,947 reported offenses

❒ A decline of 3% from 2006

❒ A $1,263 average for each offense

- ◆ From coin-operated machines
  - ❏ 24,894 reported offenses
  - ❏ A decline of 9.7% from 2006
  - ❏ A $363 average for each offense
- ◆ All others
  - ❏ 1,743,406 reported offenses
  - ❏ A decline of 2% from 2006
  - ❏ A $1,357 average for each offense
- ❖ Larceny-theft by value
  - ◆ Over $200
    - ❏ 2,313,327 offenses
    - ❏ An increase of 1.8% from 2006
    - ❏ A $1,945 average value per offense
  - ◆ $50 to $200
    - ❏ 1,179,936 offenses
    - ❏ A decrease of 0.9% from 2006
    - ❏ A $110 average value per offense
  - ◆ Under $50
    - ❏ 1,775,319 offenses
    - ❏ A decrease of 3.6% from 2006
    - ❏ A $22 average value per offense
- ❖ Larceny-theft by size of city
  - ◆ Population of over 1,000,000
    - ❏ 579,090 offenses reported
    - ❏ A 0.1% decrease from 2006
  - ◆ Population of 500,000 to 999,999
    - ❏ 540,743 offenses reported
    - ❏ A 0.3% increase from 2006
  - ◆ Population of 250,000 to 499,999
    - ❏ 381,782 offenses reported
    - ❏ A 0.3% decrease from 2006
  - ◆ Population of 100,000 to 249,999
    - ❏ 802,535 offenses reported
    - ❏ A 1.4% decrease from 2006
  - ◆ Population of 50,000 to 99,999
    - ❏ 735,297 offenses reported
    - ❏ A 1.3% decrease from 2006

- ◆ Population of 25,000 to 49,999
  - ❐ 612,512 offenses reported
  - ❐ A 0.8% decrease from 2006
- ◆ Population of 10,000 to 24,999
  - ❐ 592,013 offenses reported
  - ❐ A 0.2% increase from 2006

- ■ NCVS
  - ❖ The National Crime Victimization Survey reports that in 2006, there were 11,362,570 thefts, of which 13,791,020 were completed.
  - ❖ Victimizations by value
    - ◆ Less than $50
      - ❐ 3,822,200 thefts completed
      - ❐ Rate of 32.4 per 1,000 households
    - ◆ $50 to $249
      - ❐ 4,940,790 thefts completed
      - ❐ Rate of 41.9 per 1,000 households
    - ◆ $250 or more
      - ❐ 3,718,530 thefts completed
      - ❐ Rate of 31.6 per 1,000 households
    - ◆ Amount not available
      - ❐ 1,309,500 thefts completed
      - ❐ Rate of 9.1 per 1,000 households
  - ❖ Victimization by race
    - ◆ White
      - ❐ 11,159,650 thefts completed
      - ❐ Rate of 116 per 1,000 households
    - ◆ Black
      - ❐ 1,838,530 thefts completed
      - ❐ Rate of 124.1 per 1,000 households
    - ◆ Other races
      - ❐ 552,570 thefts completed
      - ❐ Rate of 99.1 per 1,000 households
  - ❖ Victimization by ethnicity
    - ◆ Hispanic
      - ❐ 1,869,420 completed thefts
      - ❐ Rate of 152.9 per 1,000 households
    - ◆ Non-Hispanic
      - ❐ 11,873,260 completed thefts
      - ❐ Rate of 113.1 per 1,000 households

❖ Victimization by age

◆ 12 to 19

❏ 291.8 completed thefts per 1,000 households

◆ 20 to 34

❏ 151.2 completed thefts per 1,000 households

◆ 35 to 49

❏ 113.6 completed thefts per 1,000 households

◆ 50 to 64

❏ 101.8 completed thefts per 1,000 households

◆ 65 and over

❏ 49 completed thefts per 1,000 households

❖ Victimization by annual income

◆ Less than $7,500

❏ 115.3 completed thefts per 1,000 households

◆ $7,500 to $11, 999

❏ 136.7 completed thefts per 1,000 households

◆ $15,000 to $24,999

❏ 128.0 completed thefts per 1,000 households

◆ $25,000 to $34, 999

❏ 129.2 completed thefts per 1,000 households

◆ $35,000 to $49,999

❏ 119.4 completed thefts per 1,000 households

◆ $50,000 to $74,999

❏ 126.3 completed thefts per 1,000 households

◆ $75,000 or more

❏ 127.8 completed thefts per 1,000 households

For more on motor vehicle theft, visit Criminology Interactive online > Property Crimes > Crime Explained: Motor Vehicle Theft.

9.4   Types of larceny-theft

9.4.1   Shoplifting

■ Stealing goods from retail merchants

❖ One of the most common forms of larceny; studies indicate that as many as 9% of shoppers steal from retailers.

❖ In 2007, there were 786,228 apprehensions of shoplifters, representing a 9.2% increase over 2006.

- ❖ Shoplifting is expensive to society.
  - ◆ In 2007, shoplifting is estimated to have cost retailers $160,971,740, or an average of $205 per offense for those apprehended.
  - ◆ The cost of shoplifting is ultimately passed on to the consumer in the form of increased costs of goods and services.

- ■ Mary Cameron (1964) identified two general types of shoplifters:
  - ❖ Professionals
    - ◆ Professionals constitute about 10% of all shoplifters.
    - ◆ They steal as their livelihood.
    - ◆ They steal with the intent to resell the items.
  - ❖ Amateurs
    - ◆ Steal for a wide range of reasons: out of need or greed, because of opportunity, as the result of peer pressure, because of emotional or psychological problems

- ■ Characteristics of shoplifters
  - ❖ Juveniles are overrepresented.
  - ❖ Females are more likely than males to shoplift.
  - ❖ Petty theft is the primary pattern.
  - ❖ Lower-class youths are more likely to shoplift than higher-income youths.
  - ❖ Youths as shoplifters
    - ◆ A majority of youths report shoplifting activity.
    - ◆ Shoplifting may be part of adolescence behavior for the following reasons:
      - ❏ High prevalence
      - ❏ Adolescents loosen their ties to social control.
      - ❏ Periodical crises and phases, such as those that occur with episodic shoplifting, are accepted behavior during adolescence.
  - ❖ Shoplifting in adolescence can be predicted in terms of the period of time it occurs and when the behavior will cease.
    - ◆ Jane Kivivouri in "The Case of Temporarily Intensified Shoplifting," published by *British Journal of Criminology*, Vol. 38, No. 4 (1998), studied a group of Finnish adolescents.
      - ❏ Looked for the period of time that shoplifting occurred, especially for periods of intense activity
      - ❏ Twenty-six percent of adolescents reported a lack of money as the primary reason for shoplifting.

□ Twenty-six percent reported excitement as their motivations.

□ Adolescents ceased to shoplift as they became adults because:

  • Almost one-third reported boredom as the reason for stopping shoplifting and this boredom dissipated with the challenges of adulthood.

  • Twenty-one percent of those who were caught stopped shoplifting.

  • Nine percent claimed that maturity and wisdom were the reasons they ceased to shoplift.

9.4.2   Employee theft

■ In 2002, 47% of all retail theft was committed by employees.

■ Most of the employees engaging in theft of either cash or merchandise are short-term workers.

  ❖ Typically found in stores with higher-than-average sales and a large degree of management turnover

■ Technology, including computerized inventory counters, cameras, and merchandise-tagging systems, is one of the best ways to discourage shoplifting and employee theft.

9.4.3   Motor vehicle theft is the theft or attempted theft of a motor vehicle, and is one of the most common forms of larceny.

■ In the UCR program, a motor vehicle is a self-propelled vehicle that runs on land surfaces and not on rails, and includes automobiles, sport utility vehicles, trucks, buses, motorcycles and motor scooters, all-terrain vehicles, and snow mobiles.

■ Motor vehicle theft does not include farm equipment, bull dozers or other construction vehicles, airplanes, or watercraft.

■ In 2007, there were 1,095,768 thefts of motor vehicles reported in the United States, a rate of 363.3 for every 100,000 vehicles.

■ The number of motor vehicles reported stolen represents the lowest number reported in the last 20 years.

■ The decline in the number of stolen motor vehicles represents an 8.1% drop from 2006.

■ The total estimated value of motor vehicles stolen in 2007 was $7.4 billion, averaging $6,755 per stolen vehicle.

- Among vehicle types, automobiles accounted for 73.4% of the motor vehicles reported stolen in 2007.
- Motor vehicle theft by region
  - Northeast
    - 18.1% of the population, 9.8% of the motor vehicle thefts
  - Midwest
    - 22% of the population, 18.2% of the motor vehicle thefts
  - South
    - 36.6% of the population, 36.4% of the motor vehicle thefts
  - West
    - 23.2% of the population, 35.7% of the motor vehicle thefts
- Motor vehicle theft by city size
  - Population of 1,000,000 and over
    - 156,996 motor vehicle thefts
    - A decrease of 9.5% from 2006
  - Population of 500,000 to 999,999
    - 138,689 motor vehicle thefts
    - A decrease of 10.5% from 2006
  - Population of 250,000 to 499,999
    - 104,019 motor vehicle thefts
    - A decrease of 9.9% from 2006
  - Population of 100,000 to 249,999
    - 114,292 motor vehicle thefts
    - A decrease of 7.8% from 2006
  - Population of 50,000 to 99,999
    - 112,188 motor vehicle thefts
    - A decrease of 9.3% from 2006
  - Population of 25,000 to 49,999
    - 68,600 motor vehicle thefts
    - A decrease of 8.7% from 2006
  - Population of 10,000 to 24,999
    - 54,759 motor vehicle thefts
    - A decrease of 7.4% from 2006

JOYRIDING
The opportunistic theft of a car for the purpose of a short-term ride, often by teenagers seeking fun and thrills.

JOCKEYS
Professional car thieves who have an organized and consistent pattern of car theft.

- Types of motor vehicle theft
  - ❖ **Joyriding** involves the temporary appropriation of a motor vehicle to seek fun or thrills, typically committed by teenagers.
    - ◆ Most vehicles are recovered, usually found abandoned, often after they have been crashed.
    - ◆ While adolescents may select a vehicle that belongs to a stranger, they are more likely to select a car of a known owner.
  - ❖ The typical auto theft involves a car left unlocked on a public street or in a public parking lot, often with keys in the ignition or in plain view.
  - ❖ Short-term transportation is theft that is designed to supply transportation from one location to another.
    - ◆ Similar to joyriding, but not committed by a minor
    - ◆ Once the person gets to the location they seek, they leave the vehicle.
  - ❖ Long-term transportation occurs when a vehicle is stolen for personal use.
    - ◆ Offenders are usually older than joyriders.
  - ❖ **Jockeys** are professional car thieves involved in systematic and calculated car thefts.
    - ◆ Vehicles are stolen for profit
      - ❐ Some cars are sold overseas and shipped to third-world countries.
      - ❐ Some are stolen and sold for parts
    - ◆ Offenders range from very organized professional theft rings to amateur auto strippers.
    - ◆ Involves a great deal more planning and calculation in selecting a target
    - ◆ Cars stolen are often luxury cars that may be driven across national borders or shipped overseas.
    - ◆ Have the lowest recovery rates
  - ❖ Commission of another crime
    - ◆ Vehicles are stolen to be used in another crime, such as a get-away car in a robbery.
- Carjacking is the stealing of a car while it is occupied.
  - ❖ Carjacking is classified as robbery rather than a motor vehicle theft.
  - ❖ Twenty-four percent of the victims suffer injuries when their car is taken by force from them, and 4% of these injuries are serious.

❖ About 60% of carjackers use a handgun in the commission of the crime.

❖ Approximately 2% of auto thefts are carjackings.

For more on larceny-theft, visit Criminology Interactive online > Property Crimes > Crime Explained: Larceny-Theft.

9.5 Fraud is the acquisition of the property of another through cheating or deception and includes such crimes as:

❖ False pretenses and confidence games

❖ Check fraud

❖ Credit card fraud

❖ Insurance fraud

■ Occupational and corporate frauds are discussed in detail in Chapter 11: White-Collar and Organized Crime.

9.5.1 False pretenses and confidence games

■ False pretenses

❖ The victim is convinced to part with money when presented with convincing information that turns out to be false. Examples:

◆ A person wearing a shirt and hat with the logo of a soccer team sells raffle tickets door-to-door, supposedly as a soccer team fundraiser.

◆ The person has no association with the soccer team and the tickets are fake.

◆ Those who bought soccer tickets willingly did so because the individual lied and tricked them into buying the tickets.

❖ Obtaining property or money by false pretenses is a crime in all 50 states.

■ **Confidence games**

❖ Confidence games are crimes that gain the victim's confidence and then scams them.

❖ Those who commit confidence crimes prey on people's own greed or desire to get rich quick. Examples:

◆ The Nigerian "419" fraud relied on a letter mailed from Nigeria that claims the receiver has the opportunity to share the millions of dollars that the sender is attempting to transfer out of Nigeria.

◆ The scheme then convinces a willing victim to send money to the author of the letter in Nigeria in several installments of increasing amounts.

CONFIDENCE GAMES

Crimes in which the offender gains a victim's confidence and then cheats them.

- ◆ The receiver of the letter is asked to send personal information as well, including bank name and account numbers.
- ◆ According to the sender, the money will be used to pay for taxes, bribes to government officials, and legal fees that will all be reimbursed as soon as the funds are transferred out of Nigeria.
- ◆ Once the victim stops sending money, the personal information is sometimes used to drain bank accounts.

- ■ Telemarketer schemes
    - ❖ Individuals are contacted by phone and told they have won a free gift and that they must act immediately.
    - ❖ Individuals are told they need to send money for the handling charge, which they can do with a credit card number.
    - ❖ The individual has actually not won anything and the caller has duped the individual out of the handling charge, as well as stolen his credit card information.

9.5.2 Check fraud

- ■ The most common form of check fraud is passing bad checks.
    - ❖ Money is received by drawing checks against nonexistent or underfunded accounts.
    - ❖ This crime is difficult to detect at the time it is committed; it is only after the bank issues a nonsufficient fund or a check overdraft notice that the crime is revealed.

- ■ Other types of check fraud
    - ❖ Changing the amount on a check
    - ❖ Forging someone else's signature on the checks
    - ❖ Producing counterfeit personal or payroll checks
    - ❖ Stealing government checks and forging signatures

- ■ Amateur check forgers
    - ❖ Do not consider themselves criminals
    - ❖ Act during times of stress or immediate financial need
    - ❖ Tend to view the act as relatively harmless

- ■ Professional check forgers
    - ❖ Make a living committing various forms of check fraud
    - ❖ Assume fictitious roles (i.e., impersonate another)

- ■ The number of check forgeries and the amounts involved are hard to estimate.
    - ❖ Stores may choose not to press charges because the effort and expense may not be worth it.
    - ❖ It is sometimes difficult to distinguish between a forger and someone who has made an honest mistake.

9.5.3   Credit card fraud

- The rapid rise in the use of credit cards as a preferred method of payment has created a wealth of opportunities for fraud.

  - In 1994, there were 124 million credit cards in circulation in the United States.

  - In 2006, there were 984 million bank-issued Visa and MasterCard credit card and debit card accounts in the United States.

  - In the United States, each adult owns an average of four credit cards.

- According to the U.S. Department of Homeland Security, credit card and debit card fraud may be as high as $500 million per year.

- Types of credit card fraud:

  - Stolen/lost cards

    - The unauthorized use of another's credit card that has been found or acquired via theft

    - Most such acts are attributable to amateurs

      - Acquire the card and use it for two or three days

      - May use it to purchase material goods and services or to obtain cash from banks

  - Counterfeit and modified cards

    - Technological advances have increased opportunities for credit card fraud.

    - Computers can modify stolen, lost, or expired cards so that they appear to be valid.

    - Computer graphic programs can also produce extremely sophisticated counterfeit cards.

  - Stolen credit card accounts

    - **Hackers** get into e-company accounts and steal credit card numbers of those who have made purchases.

    - Fictitious Internet companies are started to acquire credit card numbers.

    - Numbers are stolen by retail employees from customer purchase records and sold to individuals who then use the numbers.

HACKER

A person who views and uses the computer for exploration and exploitation.

9.5.4   Insurance fraud

- In the United States, insurance is big business.

  - Two major kinds of insurance are auto and health care.

  - Both are paid billions of dollars per year in premiums by individuals and companies.

❖ Both forms of insurance are also involved in large numbers of payouts for claims.

❖ The very nature of the two products and processes make them vulnerable to fraud.

■ Automobile insurance fraud

❖ It is estimated that over $80 million per year are paid in auto claims, and that 10% of these claims are fraudulent.

❖ In 2007, the average auto injury claim was $5,554.

❖ Types of auto insurance fraud (Adler et al., 1998):

◆ Staged claims

❏ The owner removes/steals parts or contents and files a loss claim.

◆ Abandoned vehicles

❏ A car is left in a vulnerable location for theft and reported stolen.

◆ Staged accidents

❏ There is no real accident but a bogus accident scene is prepared as the basis for a claim.

◆ Intended accidents

❏ Parties conspire to have an accident.

◆ Caused accident

❏ The defrauder purposely causes an innocent person to crash into his car, often in the presence of a friendly witness.

◆ Auto repair shop

❏ Billing for unperformed work or charging to replace parts that were merely repaired

◆ Faked accidents

❏ Accidents that never occurred are reported and a claim is filed.

◆ Added damage

❏ After a staged accident, the person trying to defraud the insurance company will take the vehicle to another location and cause extensive additional damage claiming all the damage occurred during the original accident.

■ Health insurance fraud

❖ Occupational health insurance fraud

◆ This is a kind of white-collar crime; health care providers file false or modified claims for services. Examples:

❏ Charging for services that were not performed

❏ Unbundling of claims, or billing for procedures or tests individually so the amount is greater than the actual tests

  ❑ Double billing
  - Billing twice for the same test or procedure

  ❑ Upcoming
  - Charging for a more complex service than was performed

  ❑ Miscoding
  - Using a code number when filing for insurance payments that does not apply to the procedure

  ❑ Kickbacks
  - Receiving payments for making referrals

  ❑ Medical equipment fraud
  - Equipment manufacturers offer products to individuals at no cost.
  - Insurance companies are then charged for products that were not needed and/or may not have been delivered.

  ❑ Rolling lab schemes
  - Unnecessary and sometimes bogus tests are given to individuals at health clubs, retirement homes, or shopping malls, and billed to insurance companies or Medicare.

  ❑ Medicare fraud
  - Can take the form of any of the health insurance frauds mentioned
  - Senior citizens are the targets, especially by medical equipment manufacturers who offer seniors free medical products in exchange for their Medicare numbers.
  - Because a physician has to sign a form certifying that the equipment or testing is needed before Medicare pays for it, con artists fake signatures or bribe corrupt doctors to sign the forms and then Medicare is billed.

❖ Nonoccupational health insurance fraud
  ◆ When a policyholder files a false claim or when a person sues another's insurance for bogus injuries

9.5.5 Identity fraud

- Occurs when one assumes the identity of another to perform a fraud or other criminal act

- The Federal Trade Commission estimates that as many as 9 million Americans have their identities stolen each year.

- Identity theft starts with the misuse of personal information such as someone else's name, social security number, credit card number, or financial account information.

IDENTITY FRAUD

The unauthorized use of another individual's identity to gain money or goods to avoid the payment of a debt of criminal prosecution.

■ Examples of methods used to steal identities:
  ❖ Dumpster diving
  ❖ Rummaging through trash looking for bills or other paper with personal information
  ❖ Skimming
    ◆ Stealing credit/debit card numbers by using a special storage device when processing your card
  ❖ Phishing
    ◆ Pretending to be a financial institution or a company and sending spam or pop-up messages to get a person to reveal his personal information
  ❖ Changing your address
    ◆ Diverting an unsuspecting person's billing statements to another location by completing a change of address form
  ❖ Old-fashioned stealing
    ◆ Stealing wallets, mail, tax information, or personal records
  ❖ Pretexting
    ◆ Using false pretenses to obtain another person's personal information from financial institutions, telephone companies, and other sources

9.6 Burglary is the unlawful entry into a building to commit a felony or theft.

■ Burglary does not have to involve forceful entry.

■ The UCR has three subclassifications for burglary:
  ❖ Forcible entry
    ◆ Breaking, prying, or evidence of other method of forceful entry is found
  ❖ Unlawful entry where no force is used
    ◆ A burglar enters an unlocked residence uninvited, stealing items found there.
  ❖ Attempted forcible entry
    ◆ Shows evidence of force, although the perpetrator may not have achieved actual entry

■ Nighttime burglary
  ❖ More severely punished in some jurisdictions than daytime burglaries because there is the possibility of a violent confrontation between offender and resident

9.6.1   Nature and extent/costs of burglary

- ■ UCR

    - ❖ In 2007, it was estimated that there were over 2 million burglaries—a decrease of 0.2% when compared with 2006 data.

    - ❖ An examination of five- and 10-year trends revealed an increase of 1.1% in the number of burglaries when compared with the 2003 estimate, and a decline of 6.6% when compared with the 1998 estimate.

    - ❖ Burglary accounted for 22.1% of the estimated number of property crimes committed in 2007.

    - ❖ Of all burglaries, 61.1% involved forcible entry, 32.4% were unlawful entries (without force), and the remainder (6.5%) were forcible entry attempts.

    - ❖ In 2007, burglary offenses cost victims an estimated $4.3 billion in lost property; overall, the average dollar loss per burglary offense was $1,991.

    - ❖ Burglary of residential properties accounted for 67.9% of all burglary offenses.

    - ❖ Offenses for which time of occurrence was known showed that 57.4% of burglaries took place during the day and 42.6% at night.

    - ❖ Offenses for which time of occurrence was known showed that more residential burglaries (63.6%) occurred during the daytime, while 56.4% of nonresidential burglaries occurred during nighttime hours.

    - ❖ Burglaries by region

        - ◆ Northeast

            - ❏ 18.1% of the population
            - ❏ 10.5% of the burglaries

        - ◆ Midwest

            - ❏ 22% of the population
            - ❏ 20.6% of the burglaries

        - ◆ South

            - ❏ 36.6% of the population
            - ❏ 46.7% of the burglaries

        - ◆ West

            - ❏ 23.2% of the population
            - ❏ 22.2% of the burglaries

- ❖ Burglary by location
  - ◆ Residence (dwelling)—1.5 million
    - ❑ Night—400,000
    - ❑ Day—735,000
    - ❑ Unknown—318,000
  - ◆ Nonresidence (store, office, etc.)—700,000
    - ❑ Night—293,000
    - ❑ Day—227,000
    - ❑ Unknown—180,000
- ❖ Burglary by city size
  - ◆ Population of 1 million or more
    - ❑ 187,272 burglaries
    - ❑ 4% increase from 2006
  - ◆ Population of 500,000 to 999,999
    - ❑ 188,743 burglaries
    - ❑ 3.2% decrease from 2006
  - ◆ Population of 250,000 to 499,999
    - ❑ 113,233 burglaries
    - ❑ 2.4% decrease from 2006
  - ◆ Population of 100,000 to 249,999
    - ❑ 254,933 burglaries
    - ❑ 0.1% increase from 2006
  - ◆ Population of 50,000 to 99,999
    - ❑ 229,805 burglaries
    - ❑ 0.7% decrease from 2006
  - ◆ Population of 25,000 to 49,999
    - ❑ 166,475 burglaries
    - ❑ 1.1% decrease from 2006
  - ◆ Population of 10,000 to 24,999
    - ❑ 156,745 burglaries
    - ❑ 0.4% decrease from 2006
- ■ NCVS
  - ❖ For 2006, the NCVS reported 3.5 million household burglaries in the following categories:
    - ◆ Completed—2.9 million household burglaries
      - ❑ Forcible entry—1 million household burglaries
      - ❑ Unlawful entry without force—1.82 million household burglaries
    - ◆ Attempted with forcible entry—712,710 household burglaries

❖ Household burglaries by race (all show total burglaries)
  ◆ White
    ❏ 2,747,200
  ◆ Black
    ❏ 628,630
  ◆ Other race
    ❏ 121,790
❖ Household burglaries by ethnicity
  ◆ Hispanic
    ❏ 491,600 (rate of 40.2 per 1,000 households)
  ◆ Non-Hispanic
    ❏ 3,051,390 (rate of 29.1 per 1,000 households)
❖ Household burglaries per 1,000 households by age of head of household
  ◆ 12 to 19
    ❏ Household burglary rate of 44.9
  ◆ 20 to 34
    ❏ Household burglary rate of 41.8
  ◆ 35 to 49
    ❏ Household burglary rate of 32.7
  ◆ 50 to 64
    ❏ Household burglary rate of 27.3
  ◆ 65 and over
    ❏ Household burglary rate of 16.4
❖ Household burglaries by annual family income by rate per 1,000 inhabitants
  ◆ Less than $7,500
    ❏ 55.7
  ◆ $7,500 to $11, 999
    ❏ 45.8
  ◆ $15,000 to $24,999
    ❏ 35.6
  ◆ $25,000 to $34,999
    ❏ 30.3
  ◆ $35,000 to $49,999
    ❏ 32.2
  ◆ $50,000 to $74,999
    ❏ 28.2
  ◆ $75,000 or more
    ❏ 22.4

9.6.2   Types of burglars

- As with other types of property offenders, burglars can generally be divided into amateur and professional.
    - ❖ Similarities between amateurs and professionals:
        - ◆ Both may burglarize homes and/or commercial establishments.
        - ◆ Both may work alone or as part of a team.
- Amateurs
    - ❖ Motivated by need
    - ❖ Style of entry is unsophisticated
    - ❖ Work is based on quantity than on quality
    - ❖ Very little planning
    - ❖ Rarely specialize in theft of specific items
    - ❖ Likely to engage in opportunistic burglarizing
    - ❖ Commit burglary part time as a small part of a general lifestyle of crime
- Professionals
    - ❖ Career burglars; seek to make a living at it
    - ❖ Specialists who use a good deal of skill and planning
    - ❖ Requires training/apprenticeship
    - ❖ May rely on contacts with persons who tip them off about possible targets
    - ❖ In *Burglary in a Dwelling* (1982), Mike McGuire identified three basic categories of burglars:
        - ◆ Low-level burglars
            - ❏ Primarily juveniles
            - ❏ Often commit crimes on impulse
            - ❏ Usually work with others
            - ❏ Easily turned away by security devices
            - ❏ Rewards gained are usually not significant
            - ❏ Many stop committing burglaries as they become older and anticipate more severe adult sanctions
            - ❏ Do not develop connections that allow them to move large volumes of stolen goods
        - ◆ Mid-level burglars
            - ❏ Generally a bit older
            - ❏ May have begun burglary activities as juveniles
            - ❏ Often go back and forth between legitimate and criminal activities
            - ❏ Use alcohol and other drugs

◻ Select targets that offer good potential payoff and are low risk

◻ Not easily turned away by security devices

◻ Burglaries may be substantial

◻ Lack the connections that would permit dealing of stolen goods on a large scale

♦ High-level burglars

◻ Are professionals

◻ Work in organized crews

◻ Have reliable networks of information about targets

◻ Earn a good living from the proceeds

◻ Crimes are carefully planned

◻ Value autonomy to structure life and work

◻ May be known to the police, but due to their high level or organization, their specific activities are not detected

9.6.3   Motivation of burglars

■ Economic gain

❖ The need for fast cash is the most common reason for residential burglaries.

■ The need for cash is not necessarily to satisfy the basic necessities of life.

■ Active burglars usually do not have conventional lifestyles.

❖ Most of their everyday concerns revolve around maintaining their street status and supporting their lifestyles, which may involve drugs.

■ Burglaries of commercial establishments can net more economic gain than residential burglaries.

9.6.4   Target selection

■ Retail establishments are four times more likely to be burglarized than other types of establishments, such as wholesale or service businesses.

■ Reasons that retail stores are more common targets:

❖ The merchandise is exposed.

❖ The merchandise is new and has a high resale value.

❖ Burglars do not need to spend much time in the establishment to steal items.

■ Because burglars can survey the facility while legitimately visiting the store, retail establishments, especially those located in areas where police do not have adequate response time, are prime targets.

- Most residential burglars already have potential targets in mind before committing their offenses. (Wright and Decker, 1994)
    - ❖ Only very rarely is a burglary target chosen at the spur of the moment.
- Signs of occupancy usually discourage offenders because of potential injury to their victims and to themselves.
- To ensure that a residence is unoccupied, offenders knock on doors and offer an excuse if someone answers.
- Homes with alarm systems and dogs tend to be avoided by burglars.

9.6.5   The burglary-drug connection

- During the 1980s, robberies increased, while burglaries decreased.
- The increased demand for crack cocaine has changed the nature of burglary.
    - ❖ Offenses like robbery, which can result in fast cash, work better for crack users than burglar.
    - ❖ The market for crack drove down the value of stolen property, enhancing the need for cash.

9.6.6   Stolen property

- Prototype of American law is the 1827 English statute:
    - ❖ A person receiving stolen property knowing the same to be stolen is deemed guilty of a felony. (Darrell J. Steffensmeier, 1986)
    - ❖ The exact wording may vary from one state to another, but the basic elements of the crime—buying and receiving stolen property known to be stolen—have remained essentially intact.
        - ◆ Individuals receive stolen property from individuals and groups who have committed burglaries. Some burglars commit their offenses specifically to get something they know others want.
            - ❏ Burglars sell the merchandise directly to waiting customers.
        - ◆ Burglars also may sell to people who sell stolen goods at flea markets or auctions.
        - ◆ Burglars may sell stolen goods to a middleman who buys and sells stolen goods using a legitimate business such as a bar or a restaurant to conceal their activities. Some burglars sell their merchandise to merchants, who represent the items as legal goods.
        - ◆ Fence
            - ❏ Use of a professional fence is the least common method of disposing stolen goods for the majority of thieves.

9.6.7   The role of criminal receivers

- In *Breaking and Entering* (1991), Paul F. Cromwell, Olson, and Avary offer a three-part typology of criminal receivers:
  - ❖ Professional receivers
    - ◆ Uncommon among the majority of residential burglars who lack the connections needed to identify receivers.
    - ◆ Offers a safe and quick means of disposing of goods
      - ❒ Essentially the case with burglars who have committed a high-visibility crime—stealing goods that are easily recognizable.
    - ◆ Types of professional fences:
      - ❒ Generalists
        - • Deal in a wide variety of stolen goods
      - ❒ Specialists
        - • Deal in only certain types of goods
    - ◆ Vast majority of professional fences are involved in a legitimate business that serves as a cover for their criminal activity.
      - ❒ Fully covered fences
        - • Do not deal in stolen goods that are outside their inventory in the legitimate business
      - ❒ Partially covered fences
        - • Inventory partially matches stolen goods received
      - ❒ Noncovered fences
        - • Fences whose illicit lines of goods are distinct from the legitimate commerce
    - ◆ The more the fence is able to incorporate his activities into the guise of a legitimate enterprise, the safer the fence is from detection.
  - ❖ Avocational receivers
    - ◆ Buying stolen property is a part-time endeavor, secondary to, but usually associated with, their primary business activity
    - ◆ A fairly diverse group that can include individuals involved in respectable occupations such as attorneys or bail bondsmen
      - ❒ Provide professional services to property offenders who pay them in stolen goods
      - ❒ Those in illegitimate occupations, such as drug dealers, may also accept stolen goods.
  - ❖ Amateur receivers
    - ◆ Otherwise honest citizens who buy stolen property on a relatively small scale for personal use

◆ Crime is peripheral to their lives

❐ Involvement in activities that produce stolen goods is occasional

9.6.8 The social ecology of burglary

■ Burglary rates are higher in large metropolitan areas and in particular regions of the country such as the South.

❖ Lifestyle theory and routine activities theory have been used to explain how the nature and level of property crime is affected by response to changes in routine activities.

❖ Routine activities theory claims that three ingredients are necessary for the crime of burglary to occur:

◆ A person who desires something (a motivated offender)

◆ That person comes in contact with another who has what the motivated offender wants (a suitable target).

◆ There is nothing and no one to stop the crime (lack of a capable guardian).

❖ Individuals, families, and communities all change in response to technology, production and distribution of services and goods, and change in social structure of the population.

❖ Both lifestyle theory and routine activities theory claim that the following influence the risk of criminal victimization:

◆ What people do

◆ Where they do it

◆ How often they do it

◆ With whom they do it

❖ Concern is to explore how the social structure supports the inclination to commit crimes, not why people commit crimes.

❖ Routine activities offer choices to individuals, including criminals, and create the opportunity for subsequent events that determine the success of the offender or the success of the victim in avoiding the crime.

For more on burglary, visit Criminology Interactive online > Property Crimes > Crime Explained: Burglary.

9.7 Arson is any willful or malicious burning of a house, public building, motor vehicle, aircraft, or personal property of another and covers only fires that have been willfully or maliciously set.

9.7.1 The nature of arson

■ In 2007, 11,197 law enforcement agencies (providing 1 to 12 months of arson data) reported 64,332 arsons.

❖ Of those agencies, 11,131 provided expanded offense data of about 57,224 arsons

- Arsons involving:
  - ❖ Structures (residential, storage, public, etc.) accounted for 42.9% of the total number of arson offenses.
  - ❖ Mobile property was involved in 27.9% of arsons.
  - ❖ Other types of property (crops, timber, fences, etc.) accounted for 29.2% of reported arsons.

- The average dollar loss due to arson was $17,289.

- Arsons of industrial/manufacturing structures resulted in the highest average dollar losses (an average of $111,699 per arson).

- In 2007, arson offenses decreased 6.7% compared with arson data reported in 2006.

- Nationwide, the rate of arson was 24.7 offenses for every 100,000 inhabitants.

9.7.2   Arson offenders

- Examples of arson offenders are:
  - ❖ Thrill seekers who set fires for excitement
  - ❖ Vandals who set fires for destruction (pyromaniacs)
  - ❖ Those seeking vengeance
  - ❖ Vanity pyromaniacs: people often in official roles who take credit for putting out fires that they secretly started (security guards and firefighters may fall into this category)
  - ❖ Those who want to disguise other crimes
  - ❖ Those who are seeking to defraud insurance companies

- Motives for arson
  - ❖ Arson for profit
    - ◆ These types of fires may be set by professionals.
    - ◆ The main motive is to collect insurance money.
    - ◆ In addition to insurance money, individuals may also benefit by:
      - ❑ Clearing out old inventory
      - ❑ Destroying outmoded equipment
      - ❑ Eliminating competition by burning out a rival
      - ❑ Concealing other crimes
  - ❖ Emotional/psychological disturbance
    - ◆ Some adult and juvenile arsonists suffer from emotional or psychological disturbances.
    - ◆ Such cases are relatively rare.
  - ❖ Other emotional factors may also serve as motives, such as anger against a property owner.

❖ Juvenile arson

◆ In 2003, persons under 18 accounted for 49% of arson arrests (the highest of all index crimes).

◆ Juveniles may start fires for a variety of reasons:

❐ Vandalism/excitement

❐ An expression of psychological pain

❐ Out of anger or revenge

❐ Out of a need for attention

❐ Juvenile fire starters can be classified into three groups, according to Eileen M. Garry in *Juvenile Firesetting and Arson* (1997):

• Children younger than 7

• Generally start fires either accidentally or out of curiosity

• Children between the ages of 8 and 12

• May start fires out of curiosity, but a greater proportion of their fire setting represents underlying psychosocial conflicts

• Youths between the ages of 13 and 18

• Has a history of fire setting, usually undetected

9.7.3   Extent and costs of arson

■ Arson rate by city size by rate per 100,000 inhabitants:

❖ 1,000,000 or more, rate of 40.8

❖ 500,000 to 999,999, rate of 40.4

❖ 250,000 to 449,999, rate of 40.9

❖ 100,000 to 249,999, rate of 28.9

❖ 50,000 to 99,999, rate of 23.9

❖ 25,000 to 49,999, rate of 20.5

❖ 10,000 to 24,999, rate of 17.9

■ Arson by type of property, average damage per occurrence, and percent cleared

❖ Single occupancy residential

◆ 10,995 arsons

◆ $26,729 average damage

◆ 22.8% cleared

❖ Other residential

◆ 4,119 arsons

◆ $31,642 average damage

◆ 26.6% cleared

- ❖ Storage
    - ◆ 1,678 arsons
    - ◆ $20,237 average damage
    - ◆ 19.8% cleared
- ❖ Industrial/manufacturing
    - ◆ 269 arsons
    - ◆ $111,699 average damage
    - ◆ 21.6% cleared
- ❖ Other commercial
    - ◆ 2,260 arsons
    - ◆ $58,610 average damage
    - ◆ 20.8% cleared
- ❖ Community/public
    - ◆ 2,850 arsons
    - ◆ $41,632 average damage
    - ◆ 31.4% cleared
- ❖ Other structures
    - ◆ 2,371 arsons
    - ◆ $22,832 average damage
    - ◆ 19.9% cleared
- ❖ Motor vehicles
    - ◆ 15,105 arsons
    - ◆ $7,890 average damage
    - ◆ 8.4% cleared
- ❖ Other mobile vehicles
    - ◆ 879 arsons
    - ◆ $11,929 average damage
    - ◆ 15.7% cleared
- ❖ Other
    - ◆ 16,698 arsons
    - ◆ $3,918 average damage
    - ◆ 20.9% cleared

For more on arson, visit Criminology Interactive online > Property Crimes > Crime Explained: Arson.

CHAPTER SUMMARY

➤ Property crime describes a wide range of crimes that involve the misappropriation of property or services. Property crimes include larceny-theft, fraud, burglary, and arson. The category of larceny and theft includes shoplifting, pick pocketing, art theft, and motor vehicle theft. Fraud includes check forging, credit card crimes, embezzlement, insurance fraud, and confidence games. Property crimes are committed both by amateur thieves, who are occasional offenders, and professional thieves, who make theft a career.

➤ Larceny is the taking or misappropriation of the property of another without express permission. NCVS describes two categories of larceny: household larceny and personal larceny. Larceny is also classified based on the amount stolen. Petty larceny occurs when small amounts of money or property are taken. Grand larceny involves significantly great amounts of money and property and can sometimes be considered a felony.

➤ One of the most common types of larceny is shoplifting or stealing goods from retailers. All the costs of shoplifting are ultimately passed on to the consumer as higher costs for goods and services. Youths are disproportionately represented as shoplifting offenders. Shoplifting among youths can be a gateway offense to more serious property crimes. Employee theft is one of the most common forms of shoplifting and is often found in stores with higher-than-average sales and large turnover in management.

➤ Motor vehicle theft is the theft or attempted theft of a motor vehicle, and is one of the most common forms of larceny. Joyriding is an opportunistic car theft often committed by a teenager seeking fun and thrills. Typically, the teen temporarily appropriates a vehicle and then abandons it, often after it has been crashed. Short-term transportation refers to theft of a vehicle for transportation from one place to another. Long-term transportation refers to a vehicle that is stolen for long-term use.

➤ Fraud, the acquisition of property through cheating and deception, has been categorized into four basic types: false pretenses or confidence games, check fraud, credit card fraud, and insurance fraud. When an offender uses false pretenses or confidence games, he fools the victims into parting with their property by providing untrue information. Confidence games are crimes that occur when an offender gains a victim's confidence and then scams them. Check fraud takes a variety of forms—passing bad checks, altering checks, and forging checks. Incidence of credit card fraud has risen as the use of credit cards has increased. Stolen/lost cards involve the unauthorized use of another person's credit card, which has most likely been stolen from the owners. Counterfeit or modified cards rely on the use of computers to alter stolen, lost, or expired cards.

➤ Insurance fraud is a serious form of larceny in the United States. Automobile insurance fraud includes staged claims, staged accidents, faked accidents, or damage added to what has already occurred. Health insurance fraud occurs when health care providers file false or modified claims for services, a policyholder files a false claim, or a person sues another's insurance company for false injuries.

➤ Identity fraud occurs when an individual assumes an identity that is not his or her own. An offender appropriates a name, social security number, credit card numbers, or other information. The offender of identity fraud can use both the traditional way of stealing information, such as theft or dumpster diving, or more sophisticated methods, such as phishing.

➤ Burglary is the unlawful entry into a structure to commit a theft or felony. Unlawful entry can occur through forcible entry, such as breaking a window, or entry that does not involve force, such as through an unlocked door. Like other offenders, burglars can be amateurs or professionals. As a whole, active burglars do not have a conventional lifestyle and are motivated by the need for fast cash.

➤ Arson is any willful or malicious burning or attempt to burn a house, public building, motor vehicle, aircraft, or personal property of another. Arson is committed by thrill seekers, vandals, and those seeking vengeance. It can also be perpetrated by vanity pyromaniacs who often have a responsible role, such as a security guard, who take credit for putting out the fires they secretly started. Arson is also used to disguise other felonies and to defraud insurance companies.

STUDY QUESTIONS

1. What are the various crimes that are classified as property crimes?
2. How is shoplifting harmful to society as a whole?
3. What is a fence?
4. What is joyriding? At what age is joyriding likely to occur?
5. What is a confidence game?
6. How does burglary differ from robbery?
7. What are some of the motivations for arson?

ONLINE@CRIMINOLOGY INTERACTIVE

Identifying Crimes

Drag and Drop Exercise

Review

Vocabulary Shootout
Section Test

Chapter 10

Crimes Against Persons

CHAPTER OUTLINE

KEY IDEAS

➤ In spite of the fact that violent crime is decreasing in the United States, it still has a major impact on day-to-day lives.

➤ The FBI defines four offenses as violent crime: homicide, rape, robbery, and assault.

➤ Homicide is the willful killing of a human being by another that involves some degree of reflection or premeditation. First-degree murder implies that there is planning before the murder takes place. Second-degree murder occurs in the heat of the moment, when the plan to commit murder and the murder itself happen almost at the same time.

➤ Manslaughter is the unlawful killing of another without malice of forethought.

➤ Serial murder is criminal homicide that involves the murder of several victims in three or more separate events. When three or more individuals are killed at the same time serial murder has occurred.

➤ Forcible rape is nonconsensual intercourse performed by a male on a female, although it can also involve a male offender and a male victim, as well as a female offender and male victim.

➤ Robbery is the taking or the attempt to take something from an individual. Because it is a personal crime and is committed in the presence of a victim, robbery is considered a crime against persons.

➤ Aggravated assault refers to the unlawful attack of one individual on another with the intent of creating bodily harm.

➤ The taking of a person or persons against his will and transporting him to another location is called kidnapping.

➤ Terrorism is the commission of violence or the threat of violence in order to change a system of politics, power, or wealth.

➤ Child abuse can be any kind of abuse—sexual, psychological, and physical—against children. Medical, nutritional, and neglect also constitute child abuse.

➤ Elder abuse occurs when older people are abused, usually by the people who care for them.

➤ Hate crimes are crimes that are motivated by a bias against persons, property, or society, most commonly against race, religion, sexual orientation, or ethnicity.

KEY TERMS

aggravated assault
child abuse
domestic violence
elder abuse
hate crimes
homicide
kidnapping
rape
robbery
terrorism

10.0   Crimes against persons

10.1   Introduction

    10.1.1   Overview of violent crime

- In 2007, more than 17,700 police agencies voluntarily submitted data to the UCR program.

  ❖ Types of police agencies that submitted crime data include:

  - ◆ City police departments
  - ◆ County police departments (sheriff's departments)
  - ◆ College and university police departments
  - ◆ State police agencies
  - ◆ Tribal law enforcement agencies
  - ◆ Federal agencies

- In 2007, there was an estimated 1,408,337 violent crimes reported nationwide.

- The FBI Uniform Crime Report reported a 1.8% drop in violent crime for the first six months of 2007 compared to 2006.

  ❖ This decrease in crime can be categorized this way:

  - ◆ Murder and non-negligent manslaughter dropped 0.6%.
  - ◆ Forcible rapes declined 2.5%.
  - ◆ Aggravated assaults decreased by 0.6%.
  - ◆ Robbery decreased by 0.5%.

  ❖ In 2007, violent crimes fell from those reported in 2006 in each of the four regions of the country.

  - ◆ Percent of decline in violent crime by region for 2007
    - ❐ Northeast—5%
    - ❐ South—0.1%
    - ❐ Midwest—2.6%
    - ❐ West—1.6%

  ❖ Violent crimes fell in all four regions of the country and for each of the four offense categories. Nationally for the first six months of 2007:

  - ◆ Murder and non-negligent murder dropped 1.1%.
  - ◆ Forcible rape fell 6.1 %.
  - ◆ Robbery was down 1.2%.
  - ◆ Aggravated assault saw a decline of 1.7%.

  ❖ Among population groups, decreases in violent crimes were the largest.

  - ◆ Cities with a population of 250,000 to 499,999 reported a decline of 5.1%

- ◆ For cities with 1,000,000 or more people, decrease in violent crimes was:
  - ❐ 6.5% for murder
  - ❐ 14.2% for forcible rape
  - ❐ 4.3% for robbery
  - ❐ 3.3% for aggravated assault
- ❖ Among increases in crime rates:
  - ◆ Violent crime rose:
    - ❐ 1.1% in nonmetropolitan counties and in cities with populations between 10,000 and 24,999
  - ◆ Homicide rates jumped:
    - ❐ 4.9% in metropolitan counties
    - ❐ 3.2% in cities with 50,000 to 99,999 inhabitants
    - ❐ 1.3% in nonmetropolitan counties

- ■ Violent crimes have generally been decreasing nationally for the last 15 years.

- ■ Teens still experience the highest overall rates of violent crime victimization.

10.2   Social perceptions

10.2.1   Violence plays a dominant role in culture/society.

- ■ Movies and music are full of violent images.

- ■ Television news and newspapers carry stories of violence, both at home and abroad.

- ■ Violence and the fear that accompanies it have pervaded many facets of our lives.

10.2.2   Fear of violent crime

- ■ Many Americans are afraid of being victimized.
  - ❖ These perceptions have great impact on our behavior.
  - ❖ Violence affects everyone, directly and indirectly.

- ■ In response to fear, people alter their lifestyles in many ways.
  - ❖ Families have left cities to the perceived safety of suburban life.
  - ❖ Large segments of the population will not venture out onto the streets after dark.
  - ❖ People have installed a wide range of home security devices/systems and carry firearms.

HOMICIDE

The causing of death of another person without legal justification or excuse. Also, the illegal killing of one human being by another.

RAPE

Carnal knowledge through the use of force or the threat of force, including attempts. Statutory rape (without force) is excluded. Both heterosexual and homosexual rapes are included.

ROBBERY

The unlawful taking or attempted taking of property that is in the immediate possession of another by force or threat of force or violence and/or by putting the victim in fear.

AGGRAVATED ASSAULT

The unlawful attack by one person upon another for the purpose of inflicting severe or aggravated bodily injury.

KIDNAPPING

The taking of a person against his will, usually involving the transport of that person to another location.

TERRORISM

Violence that is carried out with the purpose of changing a political system or a power structure.

DOMESTIC VIOLENCE

Violence that occurs within the context of the family.

HATE CRIMES

Crimes that are motivated by a bias against a person, property, or society.

10.3 What is violent crime?

    10.3.1 There are many and varied definitions of violence.

    10.3.2 FBI's categories of violent crime:

- Murder and non-negligent manslaughter, forcible rape, robbery, and aggravated assault

    10.3.3 Penal code distinctions

- According to the penal code, there are many types of violent crime, each defined/distinguished by a specific set of elements.

- The following different types of violent crimes are discussed in this chapter:
  - ❖ **Homicide**
  - ❖ **Rape** and sexual assault
  - ❖ **Robbery**
  - ❖ **Aggravated assault**
  - ❖ **Kidnapping** and **terrorism**
  - ❖ **Domestic abuse**
  - ❖ **Hate crimes**

For more on violent crime, visit Criminology Interactive online > Violent Crime > Crimes Explained: Types of Violent Crime.

10.4 Homicide is the willful non-negligent killing of one human being by another (UCR, 2007).

- Some murders are not violations of law.
  - ❖ Justifiable homicide includes homicides by police in the line of duty, the killing of other human beings by soldiers in combat, homicides committed in self-defense.

- Two key elements distinguish murder.
  - ❖ Prior intent
    - ◆ The act was planned before it was committed.
    - ◆ The act was not motivated by violence.
  - ❖ Malice
    - ◆ An awareness by the perpetrator that killing is wrong, but he kills anyway
    - ◆ Often referred to as premeditation

For more on homicide, visit Criminology Interactive online > Violent Crime > Crimes Explained: Homicide.

10.4.1   Degrees of murder

- The time frame for premeditation (the period of time before the murder occurs) has shifted and this has led to a distinction between first- and second-degree murder.

- First-degree murder
  - ❖ Killing with deliberation and premeditation
  - ❖ Involves malice aforethought
    - ◆ Any activity that suggests that the perpetrator formed an intent to kill some time before the act of killing itself
    - ◆ To kill deliberately and intentionally
    - ◆ To kill recklessly with extreme disregard for human life
  - ❖ Some states have passed laws that automatically charge the individual with first-degree murder when the victim is a police officer, a judge, a firefighter, or a witness to a crime.
  - ❖ Felony murder
    - ◆ A special category of first-degree murder
    - ◆ Involves the murder of an individual during the commission of another felony such as robbery or rape, even if the victim dies accidentally
      - ❏ The offender can be found guilty of first-degree murder even though the person committing the crime had no intention of killing anyone.
      - ❏ All individuals involved in the initial felony are charged with the murder under the felony murder rule.

- Second-degree murder
  - ❖ An unlawful killing in which the intent to kill and the killing itself arise almost simultaneously, often in the heat of passion

- Manslaughter
  - ❖ Meaning varies depending on the jurisdiction, but generally means the unlawful killing of another person without malice
  - ❖ Often refers to homicides that are the result of some other action that is unlawful or negligent
  - ❖ Commonly referred to as negligent homicide, negligent manslaughter, manslaughter, or involuntary manslaughter
  - ❖ Types of manslaughter:
    - ◆ Voluntary (non-negligent)
      - ❏ The killing is intentional, but not with malice
      - ❏ Can occur as the result of a heated disturbance or argument

♦ Involuntary (negligent)

  ❐ Unintentional, but reckless action that causes the death of another

  ❐ The act is negligent and without regard for potential harm

  ❐ Can occur as the result of the commission of some unlawful behavior

❖ Some states identify a special category of involuntary manslaughter, which refers to negligence while operating a vehicle that results in the death of another.

❖ Generally considered a lesser charge than manslaughter

10.4.2   Extent and characteristics of murder

■ The murder rate has fluctuated over the past 30 years.

■ For the year 2007 nationwide, 14,831 persons were murdered, a slight decline from the 2006 estimate.

■ The murder rate for 2007 was at 5.6 per 100,000, down from a peak of 102 per 100,00 in 1980.

■ Of single victim/single offender incidents, 91.9% of black victims were murdered by black offenders, and 82.5% of white victims were murdered by white offenders.

■ Among the single victim/single offender incidents, 91.1% of female victims were killed by male offenders.

■ Twenty-two percent of victims were killed by family members, 24.1% were murdered by strangers, and 53.7% were slain by acquaintances (neighbor, friend, boyfriend, etc.).

❖ Among female victims for whom their relationships with their murderers were known, 32.9% were murdered by their husbands or boyfriends.

■ Victims

❖ Age of victims

♦ The largest percentage of victims (87.7%) were 18 and over.

❖ Race of victims

♦ Whites accounted for 46.8% of victims, while blacks accounted for 49.3%. The remaining victims belonged to other races or were of unknown race.

❖ Sex of victims

♦ 78.3% of the victims were male, compared to 21.4% who were female

❖ Weapon used on victim

♦ 68% of weapons used were firearms, with 49.6% being handguns

- Offenders
  - ❖ There was a total of 17,040 offenders who murdered in 2007.
  - ❖ Age of offenders
    - ◆ 59.5% of offenders were 18 and over
  - ❖ Justifiable homicide
    - ◆ 254 justifiable homicides by private citizens, of which 198 were by firearms
    - ◆ 391 justifiable homicides by law enforcement officers, of which 388 were by firearms

10.4.3   Serial murder

- Serial murder is criminal homicide that involves the killing of several victims in three or more separate events.

- In *Serial Murder: Popular Myths and Empirical Realities* (2008), James Alan Fox and Jack Levin offer 10 myths of serial murder:
  - ❖ Serial murder is at epidemic proportions.
  - ❖ Serial killers have a distinct appearance.
  - ❖ All serial killers are insane.
  - ❖ All serial killers are sociopaths.
  - ❖ Serial killers are primarily motivated by pornography.
  - ❖ Traumatic childhoods are the root of most serial killers' problems.
  - ❖ Identification of serial killers prior to killing occurs is a straightforward task.
  - ❖ Serial killers are primarily sexual sadists.
  - ❖ The victim's resemblance to a family member (usually the killer's mother) is the primary source of victim selection.
  - ❖ Serial killers want to be apprehended.

- Reasonable estimates suggest that perhaps 100 murders each year are the result of serial killings.

- The typical serial murderer is a white male, in his late 20s or 30s, who targets strangers near where he lives of works.

- The vast majority of serial killers are not legally insane or medically psychotic, although many serial killers are sociopaths.

- Serial murder is likely to involve strangers and rarely involves the use of guns.

- Ronald Homes and J. DeBurger, in *Murder in America* (1988), identified four types of serial killers:
  - ❖ Visionary serial killers
    - ◆ Hear voices and have visions that are the basis for a compulsion to murder

- ❖ Comfort serial killers
  - ◆ Motivated by financial or material gain
- ❖ Hedonistic serial killers
  - ◆ Murder because they find it enjoyable and derive psychological pleasure from killing
- ❖ Power seekers
  - ◆ Operate from some position of authority over others
  - ◆ Their killings usually involve a period where the killer plays a kind of cat-and-mouse game with the victim
- ■ James Alan Fox and Jack Levin (2008) offer a three-part typology:
  - ❖ Thrill-motivated serial killers
    - ◆ The most common type of serial killer
    - ◆ May be two types: the sexual sadist and the dominance killer
  - ❖ Mission-oriented serial killers
    - ◆ Generally two types:
      - ❏ Reformist orientation
        - • Want to rid the world of evil
      - ❏ Visionary orientation
        - • Hear voices commanding them to do certain activities
  - ❖ Expedience-directed serial killers
    - ◆ Two types:
      - ❏ Those driven by profit
        - • May kill for financial or material gain
      - ❏ Those driven by protection
        - • Commit murder to mask other crimes, such as robbery
- ■ Female serial killers
  - ❖ Patterns and activities of female serial killers are very different from those of males.
  - ❖ Female serial killers typically select their victims from among people who are known to them.
  - ❖ Disciple killer
    - ◆ A person who murders as the result of the influence of a charismatic personality
  - ❖ Geographic stability
    - ◆ The area in which serial killers operate
    - ◆ Geographic stability characterizes almost all of the known female serial killers.

❖ Michael D. Kelleher and C.L. Kelleher, in *Murder Most Rare: The Female Serial Killer* (1999), developed a typology of female serial killers based on motivation.

◆ Category includes two types:

❑ Black widow

- Female who generally kills spouses and usually for economic profit

❑ Angel of death

- Female who generally kills those in her care or who rely on her for some form of medical attention or similar support

❖ The career of female serial killers is typically longer than that of males.

10.4.4 Mass murder

■ Mass murder refers to the killing of more than three individuals at a single time.

❖ In *Extreme Killing: Understanding Serial and Mass Murder* (2005), Jack Levin and James Alan Fox offer a four-part typology of mass murder differentiated by motive:

◆ Motive categories

❑ Revenge

- Represents the largest category of mass murders

- May be against either particular individuals or groups of individuals

❑ Love

❑ Profit

- May result when killer wants to eliminate witnesses to a crime

❑ Terror

◆ Contributing factors

❑ Predisposers

- Long-term and stable preconditions that become incorporated into the personality of the killer

- These preconditions are nearly always present in the personal history of the killer.

❑ Precipitants

- Short-term and acute triggers

◻ Facilitators

- Conditions, usually situational, that increase the likelihood of a violent outburst but are not necessary to produce that response

◻ Victim-offender relationship

◻ Degree of planning and randomness

◻ State of mind of perpetrator

❖ Most mass killers choose their victims.

❖ Mass murderers are easy to apprehend because they typically do not leave the scene of the crime—they commit suicide after the killings or they stay long enough to be detected.

10.5 Forcible rape is defined as nonconsensual intercourse performed by a male on a female.

10.5.1 UCR and NIBRS distinctions

■ Uniform Crime Report defines three categories of rape: forcible rape, statutory rape, and attempted forcible rape.

■ National Incident-Based Reporting System distinguishes between forcible rape with and without the use of a weapon.

10.5.2 Common law definition of rape

■ Until the 1970s in the United States, rape was an offense that involved sexual intercourse with a woman who was not one's wife by force or against her will.

■ The definition of rape was quite narrow.

❖ Men were not recognized as victims.

❖ Rape within marriage was not recognized.

❖ Only vaginal penetration by a penis was recognized, ignoring other acts of sexual penetration.

■ Rules of evidence required that the victim who brought the charge of rape had physically resisted the attack and could provide corroboration that the rape occurred.

■ The victim's previous sexual history could be brought forth as relevant at trial.

■ The victim was often forced to experience further trauma during trial.

10.5.3 Rape law reform

■ Cassia Spohn and Julie Horney, in *Rape Law Reform: A Grassroots Revolution and Its Impact* (1992), suggested these categories of rape reform:

❖ Replacing the single crime of rape with a series of graded offenses

❖ Eliminating the requirement that the victim physically resist the attacker and that the victim's testimony be corroborated

10.5.4   Other types of rape

■ Stranger vs. acquaintance rape

❖ Stranger rape is where there is no prior relationship between the victim and the offender.

◆ These types of rape are more likely to involve violence and physical harm.

❖ Acquaintance rape occurs when the victim and offender know each other.

◆ Rapes are less likely to be reported.

◆ Acquaintance rapes are often date rape and occurs within the context of a dating relationship.

■ Marital rape, also called spousal rape

❖ Wives may prosecute their spouses if their husbands force them to have intercourse.

❖ Marital rape is generally part of a pattern of abuse.

■ Nonstranger/general acquaintance rape

■ Gang rape

■ Same-sex rape

❖ Many states now prosecute men who rape other men.

10.5.5   Rape statistics

■ Uniform Crime Reports

❖ In 2007, the estimated number of forcible rapes (90,427) decreased 2.5% from the 2006 estimate.

❖ The rate of forcible rapes in 2007 was estimated at 30 offenses per 100,00 inhabitants (male and female), a 3.2% decrease when compared with the 2006 estimated rate of 31%.

❖ Based on data reported to the UCR program in 2007, rapes by force comprised 92.2% of reported rape offenses.

■ National Crime Victimization Survey

❖ Reports only on victimization of household residents who are 12 years of age or older

❖ Reported approximately 192,320 rapes/attempted rapes for 2006, of which only 41.4% were reported to the police

❖ Rape and gender

◆ Males experienced 27,970 victimizations (14.5%).

◆ Females experienced 164,340 victimizations (85.5%).

❖ Rape/attempted rape by race
  ◆ Whites had 160,440 victimizations (80 per 100,000)
  ◆ Blacks had 28,690 victimizations (100 per 100,000)
❖ Rape/attempted rape by ethnicity
  ◆ Hispanics were victimized 24,490 (80 per 100,000)
  ◆ Non-Hispanics were victimized 163,180 (80 per 100,000)
❖ Rapes by strangers occur at almost twice the amount as those by nonstrangers.
❖ Rapes occur between 6:00 P.M. and midnight.
  ◆ Rapes involving strangers: 50%
  ◆ Rapes involving nonstrangers: 38%
❖ Location of reported rapes
  ◆ Rapes described as occurring on the street not near own or friend's home: 17.9%
  ◆ Rapes involving nonstranger rape occurring within the victim's home: 50%
❖ Use of weapons
  ◆ All reported rapes involving the use of weapons: 17.2%
  ◆ Rapes committed by strangers employing the use of a weapon: 34.6%
❖ Use of self-protection
  ◆ Eighty percent of rape victims reported using some type of self-protective measure.
  ◆ Perceived effectiveness of self-protection measures
    ❑ Fifty-one percent of rape victims reported self-protection measures taken helped the situation.
    ❑ Seventeen percent of rape victims believed self-protective measures made their situation worse.
    ❑ Fourteen percent of the rape victims said self-protective measures had no effect on the situation.
❖ National Violence Against Women (NVAW) Survey
  ◆ According to the survey, 17.6% of women reported either a completed or an attempted rape at some point in their lifetime.
    ❑ This translates to slightly more than 300,000 rape victims and 876,064 rape incidents annually in the population.

10.5.6   Motives of rape offenders
  ■ General explanations as to the cause of rape
    ❖ There are a variety of potential theories/explanations of rape, including biological, psychological, socialization, sexual motivation.

- There are a number of specific motives:
  - ❖ Stranger rapes are more likely to be motivated by things like anger, power, or sadistic tendencies.
  - ❖ The dominant drive in acquaintance date rape may be sex.

10.5.7   Rape myths

- False assumptions about rape include women bringing rape charges as a way of retribution against men, women invite rape by the clothes they wear, or women who go to bars or other places of entertainment are asking to be raped.

- Rape myths exacerbate the trauma of the event

10.5.8   Typologies of rapists

- In *Practical Aspects of Rape Investigation: A Multidisciplinary Approach* (1995), Robert R. Hazelwood and Ann Burgess proposed four types of rapists based on the offender's motivation:
  - ❖ Power-assertive: plans crime, uses force, may use seduction initially, and usually attacks victims several times during the same rape event
  - ❖ Power-reassurance (most common among rapists who participate in stranger rape): acts out of sexual inadequacy, stalks victims, does not deliberately degrade victims, usually targets victims of own age
  - ❖ Anger retaliatory: expresses anger through rape, subdues victim with immediate physical force
  - ❖ Anger-excitation: receives gratification by inflicting pain, usually involves the most planning

- In *Understanding Sexual Violence: A Study of Convicted Rapists* (1990), Diana Scully reported on interviews with 114 convicted rapists in seven prisons; rejects psychopathological explanation of rape.
  - ❖ Employs a feminist perspective based on the premise that rape is a socially learned behavior and not a reflection of pathology
  - ❖ Identified two broad types of rapists:
    - ◆ Admitters (largest category) acknowledge that they have committed rape but downplay the amount of force used
    - ◆ Deniers: claim that sexual relations were consensual
    - ◆ Both admitters and deniers expressed little guilt or empathy for their victims.

For more on forcible rape, visit Criminology Interactive online > Violent Crime > Crimes Explained: Forcible Rape.

10.6   Robbery is the taking or attempt to take items of value from a person by threat or force.

- Robbery is considered violent because of the means that are used.

- Considered a personal crime because it is committed in the presence of the victim

- The terms robbery and burglary are often incorrectly used interchangeably.
    - ❖ Robbery is a personal crime where individuals are robbed; houses are burglarized.

10.6.1   Subtypes of robbery

- Highway robbery or street robbery
    - ❖ Any robbery that occurs in a public place; generally outdoors

- Strong-arm robbery
    - ❖ Robber or a group of robbers who are unarmed take a victim's possessions through intimidation or brute physical force

- Armed robbery
    - ❖ Weapon is used, usually a gun
    - ❖ Banks, service stations, convenience stores, and other commercial establishments are usually the institutions that are robbed.

10.6.2   Characteristics and motives of robbers

- John Conklin (1972) identified four types of robbers:
    - ❖ Professional
        - ◆ Robbing is a long-term enterprise.
        - ◆ The robber carefully plans and executes robberies and often uses accomplices.
        - ◆ Robberies often involve large sums of money.
        - ◆ Robbers base their choice of targets on potential yield of robbery.
    - ❖ Opportunistic
        - ◆ Most common type of robber
        - ◆ Robbing is a part of a general criminal lifestyle rather than a career.
        - ◆ Robberies usually involve smaller amounts of money.
        - ◆ Targets are selected based primarily on vulnerability and may include the elderly, cab drivers, drunks, or others who put up little resistance.
    - ❖ Addict
        - ◆ Robs to support addiction.
        - ◆ These robbers plan less than professionals, but more than opportunistic robbers.
        - ◆ May target drug dealers, pimps, or others who cannot go to the police

❖ Alcoholic

◆ Robbing usually occurs after an assault.

■ Motivation of robbers

❖ Usually involves little planning on the part of the offender

◆ Floyd Feeney in "Robbers as Decision Makers," Derek B. Cornish and Ronald V. Clarke (eds.), *The Reasoning Criminal* (1986) determined that the majority of bank robbers do not plan their robberies.

◆ In "Stick-Up, Street Culture and Offender Motivation," *Criminology*, Vol. 37, No. 1 (1999), Bruce A. Jacobs and Richard Wright found that "fast cash" was the motivation for most robbers.

◆ The majority of robbers gave little thought to planning robberies until they found themselves needing money.

◆ Over half the robbers committed robbery because they needed basic necessities.

◆ For most robbers, the financial need was connected to a fairly hedonistic lifestyle.

◆ Legitimate employment was not a viable option for these types of robbers because:

❐ Most robbers had neither the skills nor the education to obtain decent-wage jobs.

❐ Even if they had the skills/education, their perceived need for cash was too immediate for legitimate work to satisfy.

❐ Legitimate work was viewed as an impediment to their party-oriented lifestyle.

◆ Borrowing money was not viable because:

❐ Many had no one to turn to for a loan

❐ For those who had someone to borrow from, borrowing is not part of the self-sufficient code of the streets.

◆ Robbery is perceived to be safer than other crimes, like burglary.

◆ The economic motivation behind robbery is generally a constant, ongoing crisis situation experienced as result of the offender's life on the street.

❖ Drug robberies

◆ In *Armed Robbers in Action: Stickups and Street Culture* (1997), the research of Richard T. Wright and Scott H. Decker revealed that:

❐ Six out of every ten offenders who specialized in street robbery said they usually preyed on individuals who themselves were involved in lawbreaking.

❐ Since motivation for many of the offenders was to get high, drug dealers were obvious robbery targets.

- In "Managing Retaliation: Drug Robbery and Informal Sanction Threats," *Criminology*, Vol. 38, No. 1 (2000), Bruce A. Jacobs, Volkan Topalli, and Richard Wright presented their research on those who rob to support their drug habits.

- Drug robbers interviewed in a St. Louis study were completely aware of the risk in targeting drug dealers.

  - They sought to minimize this risk through intimidation, vigilance, or by remaining anonymous.

  - As a general guideline, drug robbers primarily targeted dealers whose ability to retaliate was weak.

- ❖ Gendered nature of robbery

  - Women represent only 10% of robbery offenders.

    - Economic incentives were the primary motivation among both men and women.

    - Men and women carried out street robberies differently:

      - Men exhibited a uniform pattern of crime that included violence and/or a gun.

      - Women did not exhibit one clear style although they did tend to use sexuality to attract male victims and/or acted as accomplices to male robbers in robberies that involved men.

10.6.3   Lethal potential of robbery

- Based on National Incident-Based Reporting System (NIBRS) data:

  - ❖ One of every three robbery victims receives an injury of at least a minor nature.

  - ❖ Sixteen percent of all homicides occurred during the commission of another felony.

    - Robbery was the most likely felony to result in homicide, accounting for 45% of all felony murders.

    - The firearm is the weapon most often used in robbery homicides, accounting for 42% of all cases.

      - In 85% of those cases, the firearm was a handgun.

10.6.4   Robbery statistics

- Uniform Crime Report

  - ❖ In 2007, the estimated number of robberies (445,125) decreased .5% from the 2006 estimate.

    - However, the five-year robbery trend (2003 data compared with 2007) showed an increase of 7.5%.

- ❖ The average dollar loss per robbery offense was $1,321.

  - ◆ The highest average dollar loss was for banks, which lost $4,201 per offense.

- ❖ Robberies cost victims a total of $588 million.

- ❖ Firearms were used in 42.8% of robberies.

- ❖ For 2007, the robbery rate of 146.7 robberies per 100,000 was a 1.2% decline from 2006.

- ❖ Robberies by location

  - ◆ Street/highway—194,772

  - ◆ Commercial house—62,026

  - ◆ Gas or service station—11,766

  - ◆ Convenience store—24,933

  - ◆ Residence—67,508

  - ◆ Bank—9,252

  - ◆ Miscellaneous—74,868

- ■ National Crime Victimization Survey

  - ❖ In 2006, 712,610 robberies were identified (the most recent year for which data is available).

    - ◆ 482,290 completed robberies/property taken

    - ◆ 230,320 attempts to take property

  - ❖ Robbery/attempted robbery victims by gender (for those age 12 and older)

    - ◆ Males

      - ❏ 465,130 males (rate of 390 per 100,000 individuals).

    - ◆ Females

      - ❏ 165,700 females (rate of 130 per 100,000 individuals).

  - ❖ Robbery/attempted robbery by age of victim

    - ◆ 12 to 15

      - ❏ Robbery rate of 400 per 100,000 individuals

    - ◆ 16 to 19

      - ❏ Robbery rate of 460 per 100,000 individuals

    - ◆ 20 to 24

      - ❏ Robbery rate of 730 per 100,000 individuals

    - ◆ 25 to 34

      - ❏ Robbery rate of 460 per 100,000 individuals

    - ◆ 35 to 49

      - ❏ Robbery rate of 200 per 100,000 individuals

- ◆ 50 to 64
  - ❒ Robbery rate of 130 per 100,000 individuals
- ◆ 65 and over
  - ❒ Robbery rate of 110 per 100,000 individuals
- ❖ Robbery/attempted robbery by race of victims
  - ◆ White
    - ❒ 556,860 robberies for a rate of 280 per 100,000 individuals
  - ◆ Black
    - ❒ 112,860 robberies for a rate of 380 per 100,000 individuals
  - ◆ Other race
    - ❒ 35,370 robberies for a rate of 270 per 100,000 individuals
- ❖ Robbery/attempted robbery by ethnicity
  - ◆ Hispanic
    - ❒ 151,540 robberies for a rate of 490 per 100,000 individuals
  - ◆ Non-Hispanic
    - ❒ 554,960 robberies for a rate of 260 per 100,000 individuals
- ❖ Robbery/attempted robbery by marital status
  - ◆ Never married
    - ❒ 560 per 100,000 individuals
  - ◆ Married
    - ❒ 110 per 100,000 individuals
      - • 70 completed robberies/property taken per 100,000 individuals
  - ◆ Widowed
    - ❒ 100 per 100,000 individuals
  - ◆ Divorced or separated
    - ❒ 410 per 100,000 individuals
- ❖ Completed robbery/attempted robbery by family income
  - ◆ Less than $7,500
    - ❒ 540 per 100,000 individuals
  - ◆ $7,500 to $14, 999
    - ❒ 420 per 100,000 individuals
  - ◆ $15,000 to $24,999
    - ❒ 280 per 100,000 individuals
  - ◆ $25,000 to $34,999
    - ❒ 380 per 100,000 individuals

◆ $35,000 to $49,999

    ❏ 80 per 100,000 individuals

◆ $50,000 to $74,999

    ❏ 150 per 100,000 individuals

◆ $75,000 or more

    ❏ 130 per 100,000 individuals

For more on robbery, visit Criminology Interactive online > Violent Crime > Crimes Explained: Robbery.

10.7 Aggravated assault is the unlawful attack by one person upon another for the purpose of causing severe or aggravated bodily injury, especially with the use of a deadly weapon.

- ■ If an assault results in serious bodily injury, it is categorized as an aggravated assault even if no weapon was used. If it results in death, the offense is a homicide.

10.7.1 Aggravated assault statistics

- ■ UCR
  - ❖ For 2007, there were 855,856 reported aggravated assaults, a decline of 0.6% from 2006, and a decrease in the rate per 100,000 of 1.3%.
  - ❖ In 2007, 21.4% of the assaults involved a firearm.
    - ◆ The use of firearms during aggravated assaults decreased 2.8% when 2007 data were compared with 2006 data.
  - ❖ Aggravated assault rate for the past five years has been steadily declining each year except in 2005 when there was a slight increase in the number of aggravated assaults.
  - ❖ Aggravated assaults by region
    - ◆ Northeast had 18.1% of the population and 13.5% of the reported aggravated assaults.
    - ◆ Midwest had 22% of the population and 19% of the reported aggravated assaults.
    - ◆ South had 36.6% of the population and 44.9% of the reported aggravated assaults.
    - ◆ West had 23.2% of the population and 22.7% of the reported aggravated assaults.
  - ❖ Aggravated assaults by population
    - ◆ Cities with a population of 1 million or more and cities between 250,000 to 499,999 saw the largest decline in the number of aggravated assault at around 4%. (NCVS)

❖ For 2006, the NCVS reported that 1,344,280 aggravated assaults took place, with 466,610 resulting in injury.

❖ The NCVS also reports on the number of simple assaults, which for 2006 amounted to 3,776,550, of which 900,850 occurred with minor injury.

❖ Aggravated assault victims by gender

  ◆ Males

    ❑ 757,500 males; a rate of 630 per 100,000

  ◆ Females

    ❑ 586,780 females; a rate of 460 per 100,000

❖ Aggravated assault by race

  ◆ White

    ❑ 933,960 aggravated assaults; a rate of 460 per 100,000 individuals

  ◆ Black

    ❑ 289,100 aggravated assaults; a rate of 960 per 100,000 individuals

  ◆ Other race

    ❑ 45,050 aggravated assaults; a rate of 1530 per 100,000 individuals

❖ Aggravated assault by ethnicity

  ◆ Hispanic

    ❑ 195,880 aggravated assaults; a rate of 630 per 100,000

  ◆ Non-Hispanic

    ❑ 1,144,660 aggravated assaults; a rate of 530 per 100,000

❖ Aggravated assault by marital status

  ◆ Never married

    ❑ Had a victimization rate of 920 per 100,000

  ◆ Married

    ❑ Had a victimization rate of 290 per 100,000

  ◆ Widowed

    ❑ Had a victimization rate of 60 per 100,000

  ◆ Divorced or separated

    ❑ Had a victimization rate of 88 per 100,000

❖ Aggravated assault by income

  ◆ Less than $7,500

    ❑ Had a victimization rate of 1330 per 100,000

  ◆ $7,500 to $14, 999

    ❑ Had a victimization rate of 830 per 100,000

- ◆ $15,000 to $24,999
    - ❏ Had a victimization rate of 830 per 100,000
- ◆ $25,000 to $34, 999
    - ❏ Had a victimization rate of 760 per 100,000
- ◆ $35,000 to $49,999
    - ❏ Had a victimization rate of 480 per 100,000
- ◆ $50,000 to $74,999
    - ❏ Had a victimization rate of 560 per 100,000
- ◆ $75,000 or more
    - ❏ Had a victimization rate of 290 per 100,000

For more on aggravated assault, visit Criminology Interactive online > Violent Crime > Crimes Explained: Aggravated Assault.

10.8   Kidnapping refers to any situation in which a person unlawfully and nonconsensually transports a person away or holds a person for certain purposes. These purposes include gaining a ransom or reward, facilitating the commission of a felony or a flight after the commission of a felony, terrorizing or inflicting bodily injury on the victim or a third person, and interfering with a governmental or political function. (Model Penal Code § 212.1)

10.8.1   Motives for kidnapping

- Ransom/reward
    - ❖ Involves the use or threat of force in an attempt to acquire property (e.g., money)
    - ❖ A person is held against his will to force another to pay for his safe return.
- To sell others into servitude
    - ❖ The most dramatic and disturbing cases are those in which women and children are forced to work in the sex industry.
    - ❖ There are also individuals serving in forced servitude in other capacities, including labor situations.
- Hostage taking
    - ❖ Done to secure some benefit other than financial, such as political gain
    - ❖ Hostage taking occurs as a result of domestic violence situations, as an element of another crime such as robbery, or as part of a political struggle.

10.8.2   Federal statutes

- Lindbergh Act (1932) passed to prohibit interstate kidnapping
    - ❖ Named after Charles A. Lindbergh, famous aviator whose son was allegedly kidnapped and killed by Bruno Hauptmann.

❖ Provides that if the victim is not released within 24 hours after abduction, the courts may presume the victim was transported across state lines, making the crime a federal offense

■ Federal government has also passed legislation prohibiting kidnapping.

10.9   Terrorism is the unlawful use of violence or threat of violence to cause fear in an attempt to alter a government's political, religious, or ideological position.

■ Generally, terrorism is the commission of violence or the threat of violence by an individual or group seeking to bring about change in an existing political system or to the distribution of power and wealth.

■ Terrorist acts include assassinations, bombings, the taking of hostages, bioterrorism, or the disruption of government, business, or transportation processes.

■ Terrorists may also engage in other criminal acts to fund their activities, including robberies, drug dealing, or weapons smuggling.

■ Terrorism is usually classified as a political crime against state, domestic, or international entities as well as crimes committed by a state.

10.9.1   Types of terrorism

■ Revolutionary terrorism
  ❖ Goal is to replace existing government

■ Narcoterrorism
  ❖ Refers to violence that drug traffickers use to influence governments or prevent government efforts to stop the drug trade

■ Political terrorism
  ❖ Directed at groups or individuals who oppose the political ideology espoused by the terrorists

■ Nationalist terrorism
  ❖ Promotes the interests of ethnic or religious groups that have been persecuted

■ Cause-based terrorism
  ❖ Not aligned with a particular minority group, but united and motivated by a common cause
    ◆ Anti-abortion groups fit in this category.

■ Environmental terrorism

❖ Relies on various violent/destructive/disruptive means to protect the environment and to bring attention to environmental causes

◆ Examples include tree spiking to prevent logging, destruction of construction equipment, and raids on animal research labs.

■ State-sponsored terrorism

❖ Used by repressive governments to force obedience (domestic)

◆ Examples include death squads and the use of the military to intimidate or destroy opposition.

❖ May also take a more international form

■ Bioterrorism

❖ The intentional release of toxic biological agents to harm and terrorize civilians

❖ U.S. Centers for Disease Control and Prevention has classified the following as Category A Biological Diseases because of the damage they can do:

◆ Botulism (*Clostridium botulinum* toxin)

◆ Plague (*Yersinia pestis*)

◆ Anthrax (*Bacillus anthracis*)

◆ Tularemia (*Francisella tularensis*)

◆ Viral hemorrhagic fevers, due to Ebola or Marburg virus

◆ Smallpox (variola major)

■ Nuclear terrorism

❖ Refers to the variety of ways nuclear materials might be used as a terrorist tactic, including attacking nuclear facilities, purchasing nuclear weapons, building nuclear weapons, and dispersing radioactive materials

10.10 Violent crimes within the family or domestic violence

■ Violence within the family, or domestic violence, occurs in a safe and loving environment, happens between people who are supposed to love and care for each other, involves a person(s) being victimized by someone whom they should be able to trust and upon whom they should be able to depend.

■ It is less visible and less likely to be reported than any other type of violence.

■ Violence within the family is as old as the nature of the family itself.

■ Domestic violence is a problem that has received far less attention and concern than other crimes.

■ In the United States, the level of attention and concern changed in the early 1960s with the publication of an article on battered child syndrome. (Kempe et al., 1962)

■ Since the early 1960s, a wide range of professionals and activist groups forced the public and the government to take action to address not only child abuse, but also spousal abuse.

10.10.1 Spousal abuse

■ Takes a variety of forms

❖ In a significant majority of the cases, the wife or female partner is the victim and the husband or male partner is the offender.

■ Spousal abuse includes a wide range of behaviors, including physical abuse, sexual abuse or rape, or psychological or emotional abuse.

■ Causes of spousal abuse (adapted from Adler et al., 1998)

❖ Individual level

◆ Violence causes more violence.

❒ Intrafamilial violence can be cyclical and is related to socialization, especially the exposure to role models.

◆ Stress and frustration

❒ Increased levels of stress and frustration can negatively impact a person's ability to cope.

❒ Aggressive and violent behaviors have been linked with stress and frustration.

◆ Drug/alcohol abuse

❒ Alcohol and other substance abuse have been found to be a factor in spousal abuse.

◆ Psychopathology

❒ In some cases, psychopathology may be a factor in spousal abuse (and other forms of violence).

❖ Cultural level

◆ There is evidence that levels of and perceptions about spousal abuse vary by culture.

❒ In a study of 90 cultures, spouse beating was found to be common in all but 15. (Adler et al., 1998)

❒ In some cultures, abuse of wives by their husbands is expected, tolerated, and may even be encouraged.

◆ A cultural factor that has been associated with spousal abuse is unequal distribution of power by gender.

  ❑ In some cultures, wives are viewed as the property of their husbands.

  ❑ Spousal abuse is more likely to be perceived as a social problem rather than a criminal act.

■ Characteristics and extent of spousal abuse

  ❖ National Violence Against Women Study (2000)

    ◆ Nearly 25% of the women surveyed (8,000 women in study) said they were raped and/or physically assaulted by a current or former spouse, cohabitating partner, or date.

    ◆ According to the survey, 1.5% of the women said they were raped and/or physically assaulted by a partner in the previous 12 months.

    ◆ According to these estimates, approximately 1.5 million women are raped and/or physically assaulted by an intimate partner annually in the United States.

    ◆ Stalking by intimates is more prevalent than previously thought.

      ❑ Almost 5% of surveyed women reported being stalked by a current or former spouse, cohabitating partner, or date at some time in their life.

      ❑ Of the surveyed women, .5% reported being stalked by such a partner in the previous 12 months.

    ◆ Women experience more chronic and serious physical assaults at the hands of their partners than men do.

      ❑ The survey found that women who were physically assaulted by an intimate partner averaged 6.9 physical assaults by the same partner.

      ❑ The survey also found that 41.5% of women who were physically assaulted by an intimate partner were injured during their most assault.

  ❖ American Bar Association (2001)

    ◆ Women are much more likely to be victimized than men.

      ❑ Women have a 10 times greater chance of being victimized by an intimate partner than men.

      ❑ Acts committed by women tend to be in self-defense and result in less injury.

      ❑ Males are four times more likely to use a lethal weapon.

   ❖ Estimates of extent of abuse vary by source.
       ◆ Over 1 million women per year suffer nonfatal violence. (Bureau of Justice Statistics)
       ◆ Over 4 million women are seriously assaulted by an intimate partner during an average 12-month period. (American Psychological Association Presidential Task Force on Violence and the Family)
       ◆ Almost one out of every three adult women experience at least one physical assault by a partner.
   ❖ Race and spousal abuse
       ◆ No statistically significant differences exist across ethnic and racial groups.
   ❖ Age and spousal abuse
       ◆ Batterers and victims are from all age groups.
       ◆ Women 19 to 29 report the highest levels of victimization.
       ◆ Women 46 and older had the lowest rates of victimization.
       ◆ Sixty-six percent of the abusers were between 24 and 40.
       ◆ Battering tends to be a pattern of behavior.
       ◆ Forty-seven percent of men who beat their wives do so at least three times a year.
       ◆ Thirty-two percent of battered women are victimized again within six months after an episode.

■ Same-sex partner abuse
   ❖ Domestic violence occurs in same-sex relationships with the same statistical frequency as in heterosexual relationships.
   ❖ Domestic violence occurs in 25% to 33% of gay and lesbian relationships.
   ❖ Limited protections
       ◆ Victims of same-sex battering receive far fewer protections.
       ◆ The number of battered women shelters have increased in the United States, but only a few of these would grant services to victims of same-sex battering.

CHILD ABUSE

Physical, sexual, or psychological abuse of a child. Can include medical, nutritional, or personal neglect.

10.10.2 Child abuse/maltreatment

■ Children and vulnerability
   ❖ Children are probably more vulnerable to abuse than any other societal group because they have little or no power.
   ❖ At younger ages, they are totally or highly dependent on adults for their care and well-being.

- ❖ Children have limited experience upon which to base judgments about right and wrong, normal and abnormal.
- ❖ Children are often trapped in the conflicting emotions of love, fear, anger, and hate.

- Forms of child abuse/maltreatment (Bethea, 1999)
  - ❖ Like other kinds of violence, child abuse can take various forms, including physical, sexual, or psychological abuse, as well as medical, nutritional, or educational neglect.

- Child abuse in the home
  - ❖ Most child abuse occurs in the home. (Bethea, 1999)
  - ❖ Child abuse is closely linked to spousal abuse.
  - ❖ The data indicate that violence within the family tends to follow a pattern.
    - ◆ In as many as 75% of families where there is abuse of the female in the house, there is also abuse of the children.
    - ◆ Children are 15 times more likely to be abused in homes where spousal abuse occurs. (Bethea, 1999; ABA, 2001)
  - ❖ Children can be injured during situations of abuse of the mother by the father during reckless and indiscriminate outbursts of violence.
    - ◆ Many adolescent aged boys are injured trying to protect their mother. (Kruttschnitt and Dornfield, 1992)
  - ❖ While most child abuse occurs at the hands of the father or the primary male in the household, children are also victimized by their mothers, siblings, other relatives, or babysitters.

- Child abuse outside the home
  - ❖ Occurs in any setting where children are being cared for or are supervised by adults, including day care centers, schools, camps, and recreational programs
  - ❖ Although heavily publicized, abuse in settings such as day care and foster homes account for a very small percentage of cases.
    - ◆ Two percent of confirmed cases in 1996 (Bethea, 1999)

- Stress, frustration, and socioeconomic factors
  - ❖ Higher rates of child abuse have been found among members of the lower socioeconomic class.
  - ❖ Such findings are most likely related to the fact that low-income families are subjected to higher levels of stress and have fewer resources for dealing with this stress.
  - ❖ Child abuse also occurs at other socioeconomic levels and affects people at all levels of society.

■ Psychopathology

❖ Various psychological problems may contribute to violence.

❖ Pedophilia is defined as a predisposition to repetitive sexual activity with children who are of prepuberty age.

■ Extent of child abuse

❖ Child abuse is particularly difficult to measure because:

◆ It mostly occurs in the home

◆ Victims rarely report the abuse, especially abuse suffered at the hands of parents.

◆ Most cases of abuse and neglect never come to the attention of authorities.

❖ A prevalent, but underreported problem

◆ From 1985 to 1993, there was a 50% increase in reported cases of child abuse.

◆ About 3 million cases are reported each year.

◆ Each year, approximately 200,000 children suffer severe or life-threatening injuries.

ELDER ABUSE

Abuse of older people, generally over 65, carried out by those who care for them.

10.10.3 Elder abuse

■ With the graying of the U.S. population, abuse of the elderly has become an area of concern.

■ The elderly are generally considered to be individuals 65 and older.

■ Individuals in this age range now constitute 12.4% of the population (approximately 37 million Americans).

■ As people advance in years, they frequently are less able to take care of themselves.

❖ They must be cared for by their families or by extended care centers and are dependent on others for their care.

■ Characteristics of abuse

❖ Elder abuse is underreported for several reasons, such as embarrassment, fear of retaliation, or impaired mental state.

❖ First ever national Elder Abuse Incidence Study was conducted in 1998. (Administration on Aging, 2000)

◆ Found that 551,011 persons over 60 experienced abuse, neglect, and/or self-neglect

◆ Those over 80 had levels of abuse two to three times their proportion in the elder population.

◆ Family members were perpetrators in 90% of the cases.

❏ Sixty-six percent of the perpetrators were adult children or spouses.

❖ Types of abuse (U.S. Department of Justice, 2000)

◆ Physical abuse (15.7%)

◆ Sexual abuse (0.04%)

◆ Emotional abuse (7.3%)

◆ Neglect (58.5%)

◆ Financial exploitation (12.3%)

10.11 Hate crimes are criminal offenses that are committed against person, property, or society motivated by racial or other biases.

■ The crimes can take a variety of forms: destruction of property, verbal harassment, arson, intimidation, assault, battery, or murder.

■ These acts are considered to be hate crimes when they are directed at a person/group because of their race, religious beliefs, sexual orientation, ethnicity, or some other discernible personal characteristic.

10.11.1   Designation of hate crimes

■ FBI began collecting data on hate crimes in 1990 with the passage of the Hate Crime Statistics Act.

■ The Hate Crime Statistics Act has been expanded over the years to broaden coverage beyond race.

10.11.2   Characteristics of hate crimes

■ Levin and McDevitt (1993) identify two basic types of hate crimes:

❖ Thrill seeking

◆ Usually done in groups

◆ Attacking and injuring people or damaging property is seen as fun

❖ Reactive

◆ Motivated by/rationalized as protection against outsiders

◆ Attacks are biased because the offenders perceive others as outsiders and as threats to jobs, ways of life, decency, etc.

■ Hate crimes are different from other kinds of interpersonal violence because they are more vicious, are random and target strangers, and are generally perpetrated by multiple offenders.

❖ Hate groups or gangs

◆ Adopt an ideology that targets racial, ethnic, and other groups

◆ Some of the domestic terrorist groups discussed under terrorism like the Aryan Nations also qualify as hate groups.

- Hate crimes target those who are perceived to be different, including racial or ethnic groups, gays or lesbians, religious groups, or those with disabilities.
  - ❖ These targeted individuals/groups are vulnerable and may be incapable of fighting back.
  - ❖ The specific motives take various forms and may include different factors, alone and in combination.

10.11.3   Hate crime statistics

- A total of 7,722, incidents and 9,080 offenses were reported by participating agencies in 2006.

- Nationwide, 5,449 offenses were classified as crimes against persons:
  - ❖ Intimidation (46%)
  - ❖ Simple assaults (31.9%)
  - ❖ Murder (3 in one year)

- Nationwide, 3,593 hate crimes were perpetrated against property, the overwhelming of which were acts of vandalism or destruction.

- Of the 7,330 known offenders, 58.6% were white, 20.6% were black.

- A total of 9,652 victims were identified.
  - ❖ More than half (52%) were targeted because of their race
    - ◆ Most incidents (31%) took place near or at homes and residences, while 18% occurred on highways or streets.

CHAPTER SUMMARY

➤ Statistics on violent crimes against persons gathered in 2007 indicate that crime is decreasing across the country. In spite of this, violent behavior dominates our culture and is reflected in movies, music, and news media. Fear of violent crime affects many facets of our lives and can profoundly impact individual lifestyles.

➤ According to the FBI, violent crime is defined as four offenses: homicide, rape, robbery, and assault. For the purposes of this chapter, violent crime is defined as homicide, rape and sexual assault, robbery, aggravated assault, kidnapping and terrorism, violent crimes within the family, and hate crimes.

➤ Homicide is defined as the willful killing of one human being by another with malice of forethought. Malice of forethought suggests that the offender knew that murder was wrong but committed it anyway, and that he did so with some degree of reflection or premeditation. First-degree homicide occurs when a person plans the murder before it happens. Second-degree murder occurs in the heat of the moment. The planning to commit murder and the murder itself happen almost simultaneously, such as in a crime of passion. Felony murder is a special category of first-degree murder that involves the murder of an individual during the commission of another felony such as robbery or rape, even if the victim dies accidentally.

➤ The definition of manslaughter varies depending on the jurisdiction, but it generally refers to the unlawful killing of another person without malice. It is commonly referred to as negligent homicide, negligent manslaughter, manslaughter, or involuntary manslaughter. There are two types of manslaughter. Voluntary or non-negligent manslaughter occurs when the killing is intentional, but not with malice, as in a heated argument. Involuntary or negligent manslaughter is unintentional but occurs during the negligent act of taking a life, such as when a drunk driver causes a fatal accident. Vehicular homicide is a special category of involuntary manslaughter, usually a lesser charge that describes manslaughter that occurs due to negligence on the part of the driver.

➤ Serial murder is a criminal homicide that involves the murder of several victims in three or more separate events. Mass murder is the killing of more than three individuals at a single time.

➤ Forcible rape is generally considered nonconsensual intercourse performed by a male on a female, although it has been extended to include rapes that involve a male offender and a male victim. A female can be charged with rape in cases where she was an accomplice to the rape of another female.

➤ Historically, laws restricted the range of eligible rape victims. The rules of evidence also required that the victim prove that the incident was indeed, rape. Rape trials often forced the victim through further trauma rather than focusing on the offender.

➤ Statistics on rape are likely unreliable because rape is often underreported. Individuals may be embarrassed to report the crime or they may not want to endure questioning by the law enforcement officer. Complicating the picture is the fact that a number of myths about rape still exist in our culture. These include the notion that victims may bring false rape charges to get back at men or that women who go out alone are asking to be raped.

➤ Robbery is defined as the taking or attempt to take things of value from a person by threat or violent behavior that puts the victim in fear. Robbery does not necessarily have to be violent; it can involve the illegal appropriation of property, but because it is a committed in a presence of a victim, it is still a crime against a person. Robbery is distinct from burglary in that robbery is a personal crime, whereas burglary happens to homes, cars, etc., when the victim is not present.

➤ Aggravated assault is the unlawful attack by one individual on another with the intent of inflicting severe or aggravated bodily injury and includes offenses that involve deadly weapons. If the assault results in serious injury, the charge is usually aggravated assault even if a weapon is not used. If the assault results in death, the offense then becomes a homicide.

➤ Kidnapping is the taking of a person or persons against their will that often involves transporting the victim to another location. Motives for kidnapping include ransom/reward, selling victims into servitude, and hostage taking.

➤ Terrorism is the commission of violence or the threat of violence by an individual or group that seek to change the political system or the distribution of power and wealth. Terrorist acts include assassinations, bombings, taking of hostages, bioterrorism, and forceful disruption of government, businesses, or transportation.

➤ Domestic violence, or violent crime within a family, is as harmful as other forms of violence, if not more so. Spousal abuse takes a variety of forms, but most commonly involves the wife or female partner as the victim and the husband or male partner as the offender. The abuse can be physical, sexual, or psychological and emotional.

➤ Children are probably more vulnerable than any other social group to abuse. Child abuse can take various forms, including physical, sexual, or psychological abuse, and general medical, nutritional, and educational neglect. Most child abuse occurs at the hands of the father or primary male in the household, but children can also be abused by mothers, siblings, relatives, or babysitters. Child abuse can occur outside the home in schools, day care centers, camps, and other programs that service children, but the occurrence of abuse in these situations accounts for a very small percentage (2%) of all cases. Child abuse is especially difficult to measure because child victims rarely report the abuse.

➤ Elder abuse occurs when older people, those over 65, are abused by those who care for them, either their own families or in extended care facilities. The majority of elder abuse involves neglect. Elder abuse is widely underreported because of embarrassment, fear of retaliation, or the impaired emotional state of the victim.

➤ Hate crimes are also know as bias crimes and are criminal acts against a person, property or society motivated by the offender's bias against a race, religion, disability, sexual orientation, or ethnicity/nationality. Hate crimes can take a variety of forms: destruction of property, verbal harassment, arson, intimidation, assault, or murder.

STUDY QUESTIONS

1. What are the four offenses that the FBI defines as violent crime?
2. What are the distinctions between first-degree and second-degree murders?
3. How have the laws regarding rape changed in the past 30 to 40 years?
4. What are some of the motivations for kidnapping?
5. Name the kinds of crimes that are commonly associated with terrorism.
6. Why is child abuse difficult to measure?
7. What motivates hate crimes?

ONLINE@CRIMINOLOGY INTERACTIVE

Identifying Crimes

Drag and Drop Exercise

Review

Vocabulary Shootout
Section Test

Chapter 11

White-Collar
and Organized Crime

MENU ▲

▲ GLOSSARY

CHAPTER OUTLINE

KEY IDEAS

➤ White-collar crime is crime that is perpetrated by an individual during the course of his employment.

➤ While white-color crime is often not perceived as serious by society or criminologists, it has been estimated that it causes more financial harm than all other crimes combined.

➤ Occupational crime is any employee theft.

➤ Embezzlement occurs when individuals appropriate money from their employer for personal use.

➤ Corporate crime occurs when a group of individuals at a corporation collude to commit a criminal act, such as deceptive advertising or price fixing.

➤ Violence against workers and consumers is another type of corporate crime that occurs when companies commit such acts as creating unsafe working environments, disseminating harmful products in the marketplace, or engaging in practices that contaminate the environment.

➤ Organized crime is the unlawful activity of a highly organized group that supplies illegal goods and services.

➤ Organized crime has a highly defined structure and requires allegiance of all members to the boss, who is in charge of the profit-making activity.

➤ Organized crime groups that are not associated with the Italian mafia exist.

➤ In years past, the criminal justice system has been limited in its ability to fight organized crime, but recent legislation has broadened certain laws and increased punishments.

KEY TERMS

corporate crime
ethnic succession
occupational crime
organized crime
Racketeer Influenced and
    Corrupt Organizations Act
    (RICO)
white-collar crime

11.0   White collar and **organized crime**

11.1   **White-collar crime** (WCC) was defined by Edwin H. Sutherland during his address to the American Sociological Society's as crimes that are committed by one of high social status in the course of their occupation.

- Sutherland (1940, 1949) also stressed several other important points:
    - ❖ Crime is more evenly distributed than most theories indicated.
    - ❖ Official statistics are biased toward those of lower socioeconomic status and do not present the whole picture of crime.
    - ❖ Official/legal definitions of crime are insufficient.
- Many criminologists do not recognize that violations of public and corporate trust by those in authority are as harmful as predatory acts committed by people in a lower social class.
- Sutherland reported on the frequency with which the nation's 70 largest corporations violated the law. (1949)
    - ❖ Each of the corporations had been sanctioned by courts or administrative commissions.
    - ❖ The typical corporation had an average of 14 decisions against it.
    - ❖ Ninety-eight percent of the corporations committed additional corporate crimes after sanctions.
        - ◆ Sutherland said that 90% could be called "habitual criminals."
    - ❖ Types of decisions:
        - ◆ 60 for restraint of trade
        - ◆ 54 for infringements (generally of patents)
        - ◆ 44 for unfair labor practices
        - ◆ 27 for misrepresentation in advertising
        - ◆ 26 for illegal rebates
        - ◆ 43 for miscellaneous offenses
    - ❖ Thirty of the corporations participated in activities that were either illegal in their origin or began illegal activities immediately after their origin.
- Expansion of Sutherland's definition
    - ❖ The original concept defined white-collar crime as criminal acts committed by the rich and powerful, while current definitions include acts committed by people across all socioeconomic levels.

❖ Siegel (2000, p. 386) cites a more recent definition: ". . . illegal or unethical acts that violate fiduciary responsibility or public trust, committed by an individual or organization, usually during the course of legitimate occupational activity by persons of high or respectable social status for personal or organizational gain . . ."

❖ Adler et al. (1998, p. 287) offer this definition: ". . . violation of the law committed by a person or group of persons in the course of an otherwise respected and legitimate occupation or business enterprise . . ."

For more on white-collar crime, visit Criminology Interactive online > White-Collar and Organized Crime > Crime Explained: Definition of White-Collar Crime.

11.1.1 The extent of white-collar crime

■ Since Sutherland's time, it has been argued that the dollar loss from white-collar crime is significant, far exceeding all other crimes combined, because it is so difficult to detect.

■ Economic losses from street crime—specifically robbery, burglary, larceny-theft, and motor vehicle theft—was $17.2 billion in 2001.

  ❖ Select statistics highlight the extent of white-collar crime and the amount of financial damage.

    ◆ During the 1970s, price fixing, pollution, corruption of public officials, and tax evasion cost the American public $200 billion annually. (Kappeler et al., 1996)

    ◆ In 1980, American businesses lost $50 billion to WCC (employee theft).

    ◆ In Florida, the average loss per "street crime" was $35.00 and the average loss per WCC was $621,000. (Long, 2000)

  ❖ U.S. Department of Justice Statistics (USDOJ, 2000)

    ◆ 220,262 fraud arrests (1998)

    ◆ 10,585 embezzlement arrests (1998)

    ◆ 2,613 successful prosecutions of financial institution fraud (1998)

      ❏ $62.4 million in recovered assets

      ❏ $491 million in court ordered restitution

  ❖ In 1997, it was estimated that employee theft totaled $50 billion annually.

    ◆ This represents $110 million per day

    ◆ Twenty percent of all business failures are attributed to losses from employee theft.

❖ NIBRS (2007)
  ◆ 157,749 offenses of fraud (1999)
  ◆ 91,697 offenses of counterfeiting/forgery (1999)
  ◆ 20,694 offenses of embezzlement (1999)

■ Some do not see white-collar crime as harmful or costly as street crime:
  ❖ The economic losses from white-collar are spread over millions of victims.
  ❖ Trauma to the victims is less than that in street crimes.

■ Financial damage is not the only harm done by white-collar crime.
  ❖ Some estimates indicate that corporate crimes account for as many as 20 million serious injuries per year.
    ◆ 110,000 permanent disabilities
    ◆ 30,000 deaths (Siegel, 2000)
  ❖ One hundred thousand workers per year die from job-related diseases. (Friedrichs, 1996)

■ Results of the first National Public Survey on white-collar crime (Rebovich and Layne, 2000):
  ❖ Thirty-seven percent of respondents reported that a member of their household had been the victim of white-collar crime during the previous year.
  ❖ The public considers white-collar crime a serious problem.

For more on the extent of white-collar crime, visit Criminology Interactive online > White-Collar and Organized Crime > Crime Explained: Extent of White-Collar Crime.

To learn about the gender differences in white-collar crime, visit Criminology Interactive online > White-Collar and Organized Crime > Crime Explained: Women vs. Men.

11.1.2   Types of white-collar crime (WCC)

■ Two levels at which WCC occurs
  ❖ Individual crime
    ◆ Committed by individuals for direct personal gain in the course of their occupational duties
    ◆ Acts are usually targeted at the employer, but may be directed at clients
  ❖ **Corporate crime** (Beirne and Messerschmidt, 2000)
    ◆ Committed to further corporate goals rather than personal gain

CORPORATE CRIME

A violation of a criminal statute either by a corporate entity or by its executives, employees, or agents acting on behalf of and for the benefit of the corporation, partnership, or other form of business entity.

- There are a variety of schemes for categorizing white-collar crime.
    - ❖ The following sections are based primarily on the typology used by Beirne and Messerschmidt (2000) and includes:
    - ❖ Occupational crimes
    - ❖ Corporate crimes
    - ❖ Transnational corporate crimes

11.1.3   Focus on violator vs. focus on crime

- In 1967, Presidential Commission on Law Enforcement and the Administration of Justice produced *The Challenge of Crime in a Free Society*, which claimed that the focus of criminal behavior should be the criminal.

- Over the past few decades, concept of white-collar crime has changed and focus has shifted to the crime.
    - ❖ U.S. Department of Justice (1976): "the focus [in cases of white collar crime] . . . has shifted to the nature of the crime instead of persons or occupations involved."
    - ❖ This shift from violator to crime makes for a more effective use of the resources of the appropriate agencies that investigate and prosecute white-collar crimes.

11.1.4   Refinement of conceptual boundaries surrounding white-collar crime

- Herbert Edelhertz in *The Nature, Impact, and Prosecution of White Collar Crime* (1970) defined white-collar crime as any "illegal act or series of illegal acts committed by nonphysical means and by concealment or guile, to obtain money or property, to avoid the payment or loss of money or property, or to obtain business or personal advantages."

- Gilbert Geis in "Upperworld Crime," in Abraham S. Blumberg, ed., *Current Perspectives on Criminal Behavior: Original Essays on Criminology* (1974):
    - ❖ Substituted term "upperworld" for "white collar"
    - ❖ Upperworld crimes are crimes committed by persons who, at the time the crime is committed, are generally not considered to be the "usual" kind of underworld and/or psychological aberrant offenders.

11.1.5   Similarities between white-collar crimes and other crimes

- Similarities
    - ❖ Like other crimes, they involve violence and theft
    - ❖ They result in loss of property and in injury and death

- Two important differences
    - ❖ White-collar crimes involve far more victimization and harm.
    - ❖ Victimization from white-collar crimes is much less apparent. (Beirne and Messerschmidt, 2000)

OCCUPATIONAL CRIME
Any act punishable by law that is
committed through opportunity
created in the course of an
occupation that is legal.

11.1.6   **Occupational crime**

- Any act punishable by law that is committed through opportunity created in the course of an occupation that is legal

- Occupational crimes include job-related law violations of both white- and blue-collar workers.

- Typologies of occupational crime
  - ❖ Gary S. Green in *Occupational Crime* (1990) identified these four categories:
    - ◆ Organizational occupational crime
      - ❏ Crimes committed for the benefit of an employing organization
      - ❏ Individual employees do not benefit
    - ◆ State authority occupational crime
      - ❏ Crimes by officials through the exercise of their state-based authority
      - ❏ Is occupation-specific and only committed by officials in public office or by those working for them
    - ◆ Professional occupational crime
      - ❏ Crimes by professionals in their capacity as professionals, including crimes by physicians, attorneys, and psychologists
    - ◆ Individual occupational crime
      - ❏ Crimes by individuals as individuals, including such crimes as personal income tax evasion, theft of goods and services by employees, and the filing of false expense reports

- General characteristics of occupational crime (adapted from Beirne and Messerschmidt 2000; Adler et al., 1998)
  - ❖ The motive is direct personal gain
  - ❖ Acts are primarily theft and fraud, committed in the course of one's job and are abuses of trust
    - ◆ They may be an abuse of the trust between employer and employee, or between service provider and client/consumer (see Adler et al., 1998)
  - ❖ Both types of abuse ultimately affect consumers.
    - ◆ Directly
      - ❏ When they are the target
    - ◆ Indirectly
      - ❏ When the employer is the target

- Occupational theft
  - ❖ Two major types
    - ◆ Employee theft
      - ❏ Stealing job-related items or merchandise from one's place of employment
      - ❏ One of the most widespread of all crimes
        - Beirne and Messerschmidt (2000) report that 75% of all employees admit to having engaged in some form of workplace theft.
        - In the first national public survey on WCC, 50% of respondents knew someone who had stolen from their employer. (Rebovich and Layne, 2000)
      - ❏ The monetary losses/costs from employee theft are immense.
        - It is now estimated that employee theft costs $200 billion per year. (Beirne and Messerschmidt, 2000)
        - The per-person amount for occupational crime is 8.6 times higher than shoplifting.
        - The per-person amount for dishonest employees is $847.81.
          - It is 8.6 times higher than shoplifting.
        - In 1999, $69,206,754 was recovered from apprehended dishonest employees, a 12.52% increase over 1998. (Hayes, 1999)
          - A 12.52% increase over 1998 (Hayes, 1999)
      - ❏ Workplace theft occurs at all employee levels, including senior staff and management.
    - ◆ Embezzlement (Beirne and Messerschmidt, 2000)
      - ❏ This involves the taking of money (as opposed to merchandise, etc.) for personal use.
      - ❏ Ranges from stealing from the cashbox to adjusting financial records
      - ❏ Employees vary depending upon the opportunities that exist to commit such crimes.
        - Individuals in top business or banking positions have access to large sums of money.
        - Those in the position to embezzle large sums tend to be some of the most important and trusted employees in the company.

- ❐ Computers and embezzlement
  - • Technology has brought less detectable opportunities to embezzle and detection may be as low as 15%.
- ❐ Adler et al. (1998) report that embezzlement costs businesses in excess of $1 billion per year.

- ■ Occupational fraud
  - ❖ Adler et al. (1998) identify eight kinds of occupational fraud
    - ◆ Securities-related fraud
      - ❐ Crimes committed by those who work in the stocks and bonds field and who misuse their position for personal gain
      - ❐ There are several types of securities crimes.
        - • Insider trading
          - • Occurs when a person uses "inside information" (information not available to the general public) to secure a personal advantage over others in buying and selling stock (Beirne and Messerschmidt, 2000)
          - • The information is available to the person in question because of his position.
          - • Example: A corporate executive who has knowledge of an upcoming merger between two companies that will positively affect stock prices may buy stock ahead of the announcement.
    - ◆ Bankruptcy fraud (Adler et al., 1998)
      - ❐ A person or a business that files bankruptcy is not legally responsible for certain financial obligations. Fraud can occur when the person or business develops a scam that relies on loopholes in the bankruptcy laws.
    - ◆ Fraud against the government
      - ❐ Affects all levels of government
      - ❐ Wide range of activities make up this type of fraud such as bid rigging, payoffs and kickbacks for contracts, filing false claims against a budget, when a company/business hires a former government employee or family/friends of government officials to gain influence.
      - ❐ The costs of such fraud are impossible to accurately measure, but they likely total in the hundreds of billions annually.

- Consumer fraud
  - ❏ A consumer is deceived into surrendering money. (Adler et al., 1998)
    - Businesses use deceptive advertising to entice consumers to purchase a product.
      - The classic bait and switch
        - A business advertises a desirable, often top-end item at a low price.
        - As customers try to purchase the item, they are told that the store has sold out and offer a lesser product as a replacement.
        - Fraud may occur when businesses misrepresent products or fail to honor stated warranties.
- Insurance fraud (Adler et al., 1998)
  - ❏ Policyholders/third parties filing false claims
  - ❏ A member of a company is an accomplice to a policyholder filing a false claim.
  - ❏ Insurance companies that sell policies with no intent to ever pay claims
  - ❏ High-ranking managers embezzle and debit the money as claims.
  - ❏ Businesses like auto repair shops defraud insurance companies for services through intentional overcharging and/or charging for work not actually done.
- Tax fraud
  - ❏ Does not refer to an individual cheating on his taxes
  - ❏ This type of fraud occurs when a business attempts to reduce the amount of taxes that are owed through deception, misinformation, etc.
  - ❏ Adler et al. (1998) list three such techniques:
    - Keeping two sets of books
    - Shifting funds continually from account to account to make them hard to detect
    - Faking forms, including invoices and expense accounts
  - ❏ The IRS estimates that the net tax gap for 2001 (the difference between taxes that were paid and those that should have been paid) was $290 billion.

- ◆ Bribery, corruption, and political fraud
  - ❐ Political officials accept payment, favors, etc., in return for favorable decisions or preferential treatment.
  - ❐ This includes a wide range of behaviors: judges who accept bribes, mayors who award contracts for kickbacks, members of Congress voting in certain ways in return for payment.
- ◆ Physician fraud
  - ❐ As one final example of white-collar crime, Beirne and Messerschmidt (2000) provide some disturbing information about the nature and extent of fraud by physicians.
  - ❐ Beirne and Messerschmidt (2000) report:
    - • Twenty-two percent of all antibiotic prescriptions in U.S. hospitals are prescribed unnecessarily.
    - • An estimated 10% of all surgeries annually in the United States are unnecessary.
    - • Physician defrauding of Medicaid/Medicare totals $61 billion annually.
    - • The quality of care provided varies greatly depending on the client and their source of payment.
      - • Medicare clients as compared with individuals who have private insurance receive worse treatment and are subjected to poorly carried out procedures.
    - • Such problems are very widespread, with more than 10% of physicians being "repeatedly guilty of practices unworthy of the profession." (p. 379)

11.1.7 Corporate crime

- ■ It is difficult to identify/define corporate crime.
  - ❖ Corporations are not people; they are legal entities.
  - ❖ The owners of the corporation (shareholders) have limited liability.
  - ❖ The corporation is separate from the people who own and/or run it.
- ■ A "corporate crime is a criminal act committed by one or more employees of a corporation that is attributed to the organization itself." (Adler et al., 1998, p. 292)

- Beirne and Messerschmidt (2000, p. 383) offer a more detailed and broader definition:
  - ❖ "Illegal and/or socially injurious acts of intent or indifference that occur for the purpose of furthering the goals of a corporation and that physically and/or economically abuse individuals in the United States and/or abroad"
  - ❖ This definition includes not only illegal acts, but also socially injurious acts that are not within the jurisdiction of criminal or regulatory law.
  - ❖ This definition includes both acts of commission and of omission, or indifference.
    - ◆ Acts of commission are direct acts that result in harm.
    - ◆ Acts of omission, or indifference, harm others by failing to act.
  - ❖ Beirne and Messerschmidt (2000) identify two general types of corporate crime:
    - ◆ Corporate theft
    - ◆ Corporate violence (including environmental crimes)

For more on corporate crime, visit Criminology Interactive online > White-Collar and Organized Crime > Crime Explained: Corporate Crime.

- The extent and nature of corporate crime
  - ❖ In his seminal work, Sutherland (1949) found that white-collar crime was widespread.
    - ◆ Each of the 70 large corporations that he examined had one or more decisions against them, with the maximum being 50 and the average being 14.
  - ❖ Recent studies indicate corporate crime is still very widespread.
    - ◆ Adler et al. (1998) cite evidence that from 1984 to 1990, an average of 286 corporations were convicted each year of a variety of crimes.
    - ◆ Clinard and Yeager (1980) found that:
      - ❑ Sixty percent of the corporations examined had at least one legal action against them.
      - ❑ Forty-two percent were multiple offenders
      - ❑ Some corporations averaged as many as 23.5 violations.
  - ❖ These figures probably underestimate the true levels.
    - ◆ Detection/prosecution are generally difficult.
    - ◆ Detection/prosecution are not evenly distributed.
      - ❑ Most of the companies prosecuted are small to mid-sized.

- There are three major forms of corporate theft:
    - Deceptive advertising
    - Financial fraud
    - Price fixing
- Deceptive advertising
    - Occurs when "advertisements are misleading in a material respect" (Beirne and Messerschmidt, 2000, p. 391)
    - In this case, misleading is not the same as false
        - In fact, advertisements can be false as long as they are not deceptive, as when advertisements greatly exaggerate the benefits of their product and it is clear that the advertisement is an exaggeration.
        - If an advertisement lies in a way that does not meet the reasonable person test, then it is false and deceptive.
    - Beirne and Messerschmidt (2000) cite several examples of deceptive advertising, such as:
        - Companies claiming that their food products produce results that they cannot
        - Doctoring images in commercials or print ads that make the product look different than it is
- Financial fraud
    - This is when corporate executives engage in fraud that serves/benefits the company, such as money laundering
        - Companies evade reporting cash transactions by converting large amounts of cash into bonds or by secretly shifting money to foreign bank accounts.
        - Companies funnel money that has been obtained through illegal means through legitimate businesses like banks to cover up the illegal activity.
    - Primary link between organized crime and legitimate business
        - Financial institutions benefit by acquiring large sums of money for investments and/or interest-free loans.
        - Organized crime benefits by getting money obtained illegally into the mainstream economy.
- Price fixing
    - A free-market economy is based on the notion of competition keeping prices low and fair. There are laws in place called antitrust laws that were created to stop corporations from fixing prices.

- ◆ Corporations producing the same (competing) products may want to fix prices so that consumers pay higher prices than normal competition might dictate.

- ◆ Keeping prices at a certain level improves everyone's profits.

- ◆ Evidence indicates that this is a very widespread practice that costs consumers a lot of money. (see Kappeler et al., 1996 and Reiman, 1998)

11.1.8   Corporate violence against workers and consumers

- ■ Corporate violence is harm done to workers, consumers, and the general public as a result of corporate actions. (Beirne and Messerschmidt, 2000)

  - ❖ Beirne and Messerschmidt offer three basic types of corporate violence:

    - ◆ Violence against workers

      - ❏ Refers to injury, disease and death to workers, resulting from dangerous/unsafe work conditions

    - ◆ Violence against consumers

      - ❏ Refers to the marketing/distribution of unsafe products and the resultant harms

    - ◆ Violence against the environment

      - ❏ Refers to harm to ecosystems and injury, disease, and death suffered by humans and other animals because of pollutions

- ■ Violence against workers

  - ❖ The numbers of workers who are injured, contract diseases, and die are staggering.

    - ◆ Every year, almost 2 million workers are injured in work-related accidents.

    - ◆ Three hundred ninety thousand workers contract job-related diseases. (Friedrichs, 1996)

    - ◆ One hundred thousand workers die from job-related diseases. (Friedrichs, 1996)

    - ◆ Eleven thousand workers die from work-related accidents. (Friedrichs, 1996)

  - ❖ What can these events be attributed to?

    - ◆ It is often claimed that these accidents and diseases "simply happen." They are actually the result of: (Kappeler et al., 1996):

      - ❏ The pressures of the business world

      - ❏ Worker carelessness

      - ❏ Negligence or oversights

♦ These events are not intended.
  ❏ They are not (cannot be) criminal
  ❏ They should not be treated as such
❖ Some studies, however, have shown that "injuries and deaths caused by corporate violations are not simply a matter of carelessness or neglect; many are the direct result of willful violations of the law." (Kappeler et al., 1996, p. 145)
  ♦ Schraeger and Short (1978)
    ❏ Thirty percent of industrial accidents were attributable to safety violations.
    ❏ Twenty percent of industrial accidents were attributable to unsafe work conditions.
  ♦ Messerschmidt (1986, cited in Kappeler et al., 1996)
    ❏ Thirty five to 57% of the accidents were the result of safety violations by the employer.
  ♦ These estimates are probably low, since the data was drawn from company reports.
❖ There are numerous dramatic examples of companies exposing their workers to extreme dangers and hazards, including cases in which employees have been exposed to asbestos or cyanide.
❖ Criminal sanctions against corporations or corporate executives
  ♦ Various state courts now hold that employers can be criminally prosecuted for exposing workers to unsafe conditions, but such cases are not common.
■ Violence against consumers
❖ Corporations produce and market unsafe/defective merchandise, which results in 20 million serious injuries and 30,000 deaths every year.
❖ Dalkon Shield IUD was marketed despite hundreds of negative reports from physicians about its safety.
  ♦ Around 2.86 million were sold in the United States, and the vast majority of women who used it developed a dangerous infection. (Beirne and Messerschmidt, 2000)
❖ The Ford Explorer was reported to have a high rate of tire-related accidents. The tires were manufactured by Firestone.
  ♦ Such accidents have been linked to 174 deaths (CNN, 2001a) and there have been as many as 200 lawsuits filed.
  ♦ Both companies denied the claim of negligence and blamed the other. (CNN, 2001c)

- ◆ The issue is whether either or both companies are culpable/liable.
  - ❐ It has been claimed that Ford knowingly designed a faulty vehicle and that of four changes proposed by engineers, only two were implemented. (CNN, 2001b)
  - ❐ In spite of this, Firestone recalled a massive number of tires. (CNN, 2001c)
  - ◆ The verdict
    - ❐ Many lawsuits have been settled out of court and no criminal charges have been filed.
- ❖ The Ford Pinto case (adapted from Cullen et al., 1996; Kappeler et al., 1996)
  - ◆ An estimated 900 people were killed over a seven-year period due to the faulty engineering of the Pinto's gas tank, which burst into flames in rear-end collisions.
  - ◆ The situation resulted in numerous civil actions and regulatory and safety investigations.
  - ◆ One prosecutor brought a reckless homicide case based on the charge that Ford took the product to the market despite knowing about the defect.
- ❖ Big tobacco and corporate violence
  - ◆ Since at least the 1960s, tobacco companies' own studies have demonstrated the links between smoking and lung cancer.
  - ◆ There is clear evidence that indicated tobacco companies manipulated nicotine levels to ensure addiction.
  - ◆ Tobacco companies have covertly targeted teens with advertising campaigns.
  - ◆ These cases highlight the problems inherent in holding corporations criminally responsible for their violent actions.

11.1.9   Environmental crimes

- ■ Crimes against the environment is considered corporate violence because corporations have had an immense destructive impact on environment and life.
  - ❖ Pollution, the release of known toxins into air and water supplies, is often motivated by profit margins of large corporations, is an act of violence against the general public, the world community, and the earth itself and is therefore an environmental crime.

**For more on environmental crime, visit Criminology Interactive online >
White-Collar and Organized Crime > Crime Explained: Environmental Crimes.**

11.1.10   The nature and extent of environmental crime

■ The Environmental Protection Agency (EPA) estimates suggest that up to 90% of toxic waste produced by U.S. companies is disposed of improperly and in violation of the law. (Kappeler et al., 1996)

❖ The improper disposal of toxic materials has serious implications to the health of the ecosystem.

❖ When the health of an ecosystem is threatened, the direct health of its inhabitants is in danger.

■ Air pollution may be the most critical environmental problem, since it affects all resources and has a global impact.

❖ Chemical companies in the United States admit to regularly leaking extremely hazardous compounds into the air.

❖ Also of considerable concern is the contamination of our water supplies.

❖ In the 1980s, one out of every five public water systems showed some level of toxic contamination, mostly from seepage from landfills and waste dumps.

❖ A more recent study found that 30,000 different waste sites in the United States create significant health risks because of water system contamination. (Beirne and Messerschmidt, 2000)

■ There are, of course, numerous incidents worldwide that serve to further underscore the problem.

❖ The United States: Love Canal, Three Mile Island, and the Exxon Valdez spill (to name but a few)

❖ Russia: the Chernobyl accident

❖ Bhopal, India: incident at the Union Carbide plant

11.1.11   Victims of environmental crime

■ The levels of victimization from environmental crime are heavily affected by race and socioeconomic status.

■ *Race and the Incidence of Environmental Hazards* (Bryant and Mohai, 1992) explores issues related to environmental equality.

❖ The editors claim that "minority communities were disproportionately exposed to environmental hazards, more so than affluent white communities." (p. 2)

■ Charles Lee (1992) also provides some very disturbing statistics on this inequity.

❖ Communities with at least one hazardous waste facility have twice the percentage of minorities as those without (24% to 12%), with blacks and Hispanics dramatically overrepresented.

- Another component of this problem can be seen in U.S. companies moving their operations to other economically less advantaged countries (e.g., Mexico).
  - ❖ One of the main factors in this movement is the lax environmental laws in these countries.

11.1.12   Environmental laws and their enforcement

- Environmental Protection Agency (EPA)
  - ❖ In 1969, Congress passed the National Environmental Policy Act, which created the EPA as the chief enforcement agency for environmental laws.

- A variety of specific laws have been passed in an attempt to address the broad range of environmental crimes.
  - ❖ The Clean Air Act sets quality standards and provides sanctions for companies that do not meet standards.
  - ❖ The Federal Water Pollution Control Act provides similar standards and sanctions.

- Developing effective laws to protect the environment is a complicated process (Adler et al.1998). Acts of pollution are considerably more varied and harder to define than are crimes like murder and theft.
  - ❖ It is difficult to separate harmful activities from socially useful ones.
  - ❖ When a company is fined for violating laws or regulations, it is unclear if the costs are passed on to the consumer or covered by layoffs that may cause additional harm.

11.1.13   Transnational corporate crimes (Adapted from Beirne and Messerschmidt, 2000)

- Transnational corporate crimes are committed by large corporations that maintain business operations in more than one country.
  - ❖ These crimes are committed by transnational corporations to pursue their own business interests.
  - ❖ There are three types of transnational crimes: bribery, product dumping, and dangerous working conditions.

- The extent/nature of transnational corporate crimes
  - ❖ Oil, pharmaceutical, and motor vehicle companies are the most likely to engage in transnational corporate crimes.

11.1.14   Types of transnational corporate crimes

- Bribery
  - ❖ Occurs when a corporation pays members of a foreign government to gain access to contracts for things like construction, product purchasing, etc.
  - ❖ In one study, 34 U.S. transnationals admitted to paying overseas bribes.

- Product dumping
  - ❖ Occurs when a corporation based in one country "dumps" hazardous products in another country that have been banned or not approved for sale in its own country
  - ❖ U.S. companies with international business interests sell defective devices, drugs, contaminated food, or other dangerous products outside of the United States.
  - ❖ When the Dalkon Shield IUD was found unsafe, the manufacturer dumped over 1 million of these to other countries.
  - ❖ Over 150 million pounds of pesticides banned in the United States are dumped overseas.

- Dangerous working conditions
  - ❖ Companies may relocate operations to other countries because of minimal legal restrictions on worker safety regulations.

11.1.15   High-tech crimes

- "High tech crime involves an attempt to pursue illegal activities through the use of advanced electronic media." (Adler et al, 1998)
  - ❖ High technology is generally considered to be a sophisticated electronic or wireless device such as computers, cellular telephones, or other forms of digital communication.
  - ❖ Siegel (2000) refers to high-tech crime as a "new breed" of white-collar crime.
    - ◆ Crimes can be ongoing or occasional.
    - ◆ Usually involves the theft of "information, resources, or funds" (Siegel, 2000, p. 401)

- The nature/extent of high-tech crime
  - ❖ High-tech crimes generally rely on computers and the Internet.
  - ❖ Such crimes cost billions of dollars per year.
  - ❖ Such crimes will continue to increase as new technology is developed.

11.1.16   Theories on the causes of white-collar crime

- Two formal theories of white-collar crime (as discussed in Siegel, 2000):
  - ❖ Corporate culture theory
  - ❖ Self-control theory

- Corporate culture theory
  - ❖ This theoretical approach is similar to Sutherland's differential association theory.
  - ❖ Claims that some corporations promote white-collar crime by creating a culture that encourages such behavior

- ♦ They may place excessive demands on employees, be intolerant of such behaviors, or offer role models who instill the attitudes of white-collar crime in others
- ♦ Develop a climate tolerant of such behaviors
- ♦ Provide role models for the learning of attitudes and techniques of white-collar crime for new employees

- ■ Self-control theory
  - ❖ This theory is similar to Gottfredson and Hirschi's (1990) theory of self-control that holds that white-collar crime is not caused by the corporate culture, but by low levels of self-control of a few individuals.
  - ❖ Research has shown that:
    - ♦ Individuals with low self-control impulsively commit crime for personal gain or self-interest.

11.2   Organized crime

11.2.1   Organized crime takes diverse forms and is difficult to define.

- ■ The FBI (1999) defines organized crime as "crime committed by any group, having formalized structure whose primary objective is to obtain money through illegal activities."

- ■ The President's Commission on Organized Crime (1986) identified several basic characteristics of organized crime.
  - ❖ It involves conspiracy, usually with a number of individuals who are organized as a hierarchy
  - ❖ Organized crime seeks economic gain by providing illegal goods/services, including gambling, drugs, and prostitution.
  - ❖ Activities are not limited to illegal goods or services; money laundering and fraud are also involved.
  - ❖ Uses a high level of implied and actual violence

- ■ The FBI (1999) categorizes organized crime as "traditional" or "nontraditional."
  - ❖ Traditional organized crime is what is generally referred to as the "Mafia," the "Mob," "La Cosa Nostra," or the "Syndicate."
    - ♦ It consists of 25 crime families based in major cities, including New York, Chicago, Detroit, Boston, and Philadelphia.
  - ❖ Nontraditional organized crime refers to more recent groups, such as Asian, Russian/Eastern European, or Nigerian/West African groups.

For more on organized crime, visit Criminology Interactive online > White-Collar and Organized Crime > Crime Explained: Definition of Organized Crime.

11.2.2   Historical overview of organized crime

- The roots of the Mafia predate organized crime in the United States.

- In Italy, secret societies have flourished for hundreds of years.
  - ❖ The secret societies were the product of extreme poverty, disregard for the law, and national temperament.
  - ❖ Italian Camorra, based in Naples, became infamous for extortion and murder.
    - ◆ The Camorrian code demanded total silence and issued printed licenses to kill.
  - ❖ Fascist ruler Benito Mussolini almost wiped out secret societies in Italy during the 1930s and 1940s.
    - ◆ Those who survived became anti-Fascists, which allowed them to align themselves with American and allied intelligence during World War II.
    - ◆ At the end of World War II, Mafia leaders returned to their positions of power in Italian society.
    - ◆ Relationships began to grow between American and Italian criminal organizations.
  - ❖ The wave of immigration during the late nineteenth and early twentieth centuries brought Italian criminal organizations to the United States.
  - ❖ Two of these organizations were the Mafia and the Black Hand.
  - ❖ The Black Hand intimidated Italian immigrants through extortion and by demanding protection money.
    - ◆ Became especially powerful in Detroit, St. Louis, Kansas City, and New Orleans

- Mafia
  - ❖ Roots are in Sicily
  - ❖ Became a quasi-police organization in the Italian ghettos of large American cities during the industrial era
  - ❖ Enforced its own set of laws or codes

- La Cosa Nostra
  - ❖ A large number of organized criminal groups flourished in cities before the Italians arrived, including the Jewish and the Irish.
  - ❖ The Italians made their impact through what is known as **ethnic succession**, the ongoing process of one immigrant or ethnic group succeeding another and assuming a particular position in society.
    - ◆ Throughout the late 1800s and early 1900s, Jewish gangsters ran many of the rackets in New York City.

ETHNIC SUCCESSION

The continuing process whereby one immigrant or ethnic group succeeds another through assumption of a particular position in society.

- ❖ Italian-American organizations began to take control of the rackets around 1915.
- ❖ Today, Italian-American organized criminal groups are also affected by ethnic succession.
  - ❏ African-American, Hispanic, and Asian-American gangs now run much of the drug trade.

- ■ Prohibition and official corruption
  - ❖ Mafia influence could be seen in most American cities by the 1920s.
  - ❖ Prohibition provided organized crime with a new business and income stream.
    - ◆ Prior to Prohibition, the Mafia focused on gambling, protection rackets, and loan-sharking.
    - ◆ Many also belonged to an organization called Unione Siciliana, whose members had expertise in the manufacture of low-cost, high-proof, untaxed alcohol that they had brought from their homeland.
    - ◆ The selling of liquor and related activities gave Mafia families the opportunity to accumulate great wealth during the Great Depression.
  - ❖ The success of the illegal liquor industry led to bribery of government officials and the corruption of many law enforcement officers.
    - ◆ The Twenty-first Amendment repealed the Eighteenth Amendment, ending Prohibition in 1933.
  - ❖ By the time the Twenty-first Amendment eliminated Prohibition in 1933, official corruption had become part of American life in some parts of the country.

- ■ The centralization of organized crime
  - ❖ During Prohibition, there were struggles between Mafia groups, while at the same time attempting to consolidate power.
    - ◆ Gang warfare dominated these struggles.
    - ◆ Following a number of spectacular crimes, Alphonse "Al" Capone forged a crime syndicate in Chicago in the mid-1920s.
      - ❏ George "Bugs" Moran, a local gang leader, disputed Capone's claim as the leader of Chicago's organized crime families.
      - ❏ Capone lured Moran's men to a garage on Chicago's East Side claiming that liquor was to be delivered.
      - ❏ Once inside the garage, Moran's men were surprised by five of Capone's men.

- ❏ Moran's men were executed in what has become known as the St. Valentine's Day massacre.
- ❏ Capone became the undisputed ruler of organized crime in Chicago.

- ❖ 1931
  - ◆ New York City crime figure Giuseppe "Joe the Boss" Masseria was gunned down in a Brooklyn restaurant.
  - ◆ The killing appears to have been ordered by Salvatore Maranzano, who then declared himself "boss of bosses" over all New York crime families.
  - ◆ Maranzano soon lost favor and was killed.
  - ◆ Within the next two days, 30 Mafia leaders had died in similar gang-ordered executions.
  - ◆ When the smoke cleared and the killings had stopped, the Mafia had become an integrated, coordinated criminal organization.
  - ◆ Following 1931, Mafia activity went underground.
- ❖ In 1951, U.S. Attorney General convened the Kefauver Committee, a federal special committee, to investigate organized crime.
  - ◆ The committee concluded that:
    - ❏ A nationwide crime syndicate exists, known as the Mafia.
    - ❏ The Mafia has international connections that can leverage narcotics traffic.
    - ❏ Mafia leaders are usually found in control of the most lucrative rackets in their cities.
    - ❏ Leadership is centralized, but appears be in a group rather than in a single individual.
- ❖ Years of federal investigation into Italian-American organized criminal groups developed this profile:
  - ◆ Twenty-four families or groups of varying sizes (20 to 700) operating in the United States under direction of a commission
  - ◆ Bosses of nation's most powerful families directed the commission.
  - ◆ All exclusively Italian
  - ◆ The wealthiest and most powerful groups were in New York, New Jersey, Illinois, Florida, Louisiana, Nevada, Michigan, and Rhode Island.
  - ◆ Organization
    - ❏ The boss maintains order and directs the profit-making activities.
    - ❏ An underboss collects information for the boss and acts as a messenger.

       ❑ Counselor (consigliere) serves as an advisor.

       ❑ Lieutenants (caporegime) serve as chiefs for operating units.

       ❑ Soldiers (soldati), lowest member of the family, operate such illicit enterprises as loan-sharking, lottery, and smuggling.

       ❑ Large number of employees and agents are not members of the family or of Italian descent. These members carry out most of the work and are not protected from law enforcement.

    ◆ Members swear allegiance to a code of conduct.

       ❑ Lower levels should not interfere with leaders' interests and should not seek protection from the police.

       ❑ Members will go to prison so that the bosses may gain wealth.

       ❑ Leaders have authoritarian power over everyone in the organization.

       ❑ Family members are expected to be loyal, honorable, respectful, and absolutely obedient.

11.2.3 Types of organized crime

- The FBI (1999) list a wide variety of activities that organized crime groups engage in.
  - ❖ Historically, these have been gambling, prostitution, drug trafficking, loan-sharking, labor racketeering, and murder for hire.
  - ❖ More recently, these include financial institution fraud, health-care fraud, fraud against the government, money laundering, and securities fraud.

- Beirne and Messerschmidt (2000) break organized crime into three groups:
  - ❖ Illegal sale and distribution of goods/services: gambling, drugs, loan-sharking
  - ❖ Involvement in legitimate businesses: direct investment, racketeering, money laundering
  - ❖ Involvement with the state: corruption of government officials, performing political favors

- Money is the primary motivation for all organized criminal activities.

- Throughout the past 50 years, Sicilian-American criminal cartels have continued to be involved in the establishment and control of both legalized and illicit forms of gambling, including:
  - ❖ Lotteries
  - ❖ Bookmaking

- ❖ Horse-race wagering
- ❖ Bets on athletic contests
- ❖ Loan-sharking
- ❖ Large-scale drug trafficking
- ❖ Fencing of stolen goods

- ■ Infiltration of legitimate businesses, including labor unions that can be used as legitimate fronts for money laundering and other activities

- ■ Labor union racketeering via which legitimate businesses are intimidated through threats of strikes, walkouts, and sabotage

- ■ As states have begun to operate their own lotteries, revenue in this area for organized crime has decreased.
  - ❖ Sicilian-Americans have moved into legitimate gambling, buying stakes in casinos in Nevada and New Jersey.

- ■ Today, some evidence suggests that organized crime is becoming involved in the illegal copying and distribution of copyrighted software, music, and other forms of recorded media.

11.2.4   Other organized crime groups

- ■ Examples of other organized crime groups in the United States:
  - ❖ Black Mafia
  - ❖ Cuban Mafia
  - ❖ Haitian Mafia
  - ❖ Columbian cartels
  - ❖ Russian Mafia
  - ❖ Asian criminals
    - ◆ Chinese Tongs
    - ◆ Japanese Yakuza
    - ◆ Vietnamese gangs
    - ◆ Taiwan's Triads
  - ❖ Inner-city gangs
    - ◆ Los Angeles Crips
    - ◆ Los Angeles Bloods
    - ◆ Chicago Vice Lords
  - ❖ International drug rings
  - ❖ Outlaw motorcycle gangs
    - ◆ Hell's Angels
    - ◆ Pagans

11.2.5   The costs of organized crime

- Organized crime is lucrative. In 1927, Al Capone was listed in the *Guinness Book of World Records* as having the highest individual income of anyone in the world.

- Citing United Nations data from the early 1990s, Adler et al. (1998) report that the combined annual sales of illicit goods and services by organized crime groups is over $700 billion.

- Narcotics trafficking alone yields $300 billion per year.

- Organized crime activities inhibit legitimate competition in various kinds of business.
    - ❖ It has been estimated that this results in an annual loss of 400,000 jobs.
    - ❖ Costs $18 billion in productivity
    - ❖ It also costs the general public an extra $6.5 billion in taxes each year since organized crime profits are not reported.

11.2.6   Combating organized crime

- For many years, American law enforcement was limited in their ability to fight organized crime.

- They could only prosecute solitary organized crime offenders using laws against robbery, assault, gambling, prostitution, etc.

- In 1946, the Hobbs Act was enacted, the first federal legislation directed at organized crime.
    - ❖ The Act made engaging in any type of criminal behavior that interferes with interstate commerce a federal crime.
    - ❖ It criminalized foreign and interstate travel for the purpose of furthering criminal activity.
    - ❖ It made illegal the actual or attempted use of telephones, mail, or highways to support criminal activity. (Schmalleger, 2000)

- **Racketeer Influenced and Corrupt Organizations Act (RICO)**
    - ❖ In 1970, Congress passed the Organized Crime Control Act, defining organized crime as a highly organized and disciplined group of individuals that supply illegal goods and services, including gambling, prostitution, loan-sharking, narcotics, labor racketeering, and other unlawful activities. (Schmalleger, 2000, p. 419)
        - ◆ Title IX of this Act is the Racketeer Influenced and Corrupt Organizations Act (RICO).
            - ❏ This is considered to be the most effective aspect of the Act for dealing with organized crime. (Siegel, 2000)

RACKETEER INFLUENCED AND CORRUPT ORGANIZATIONS ACT (RICO)

A statue that was part of the Federal Organized Crime Control Act of 1970, which developed broader definitions of racketeering and made punishments harsher.

❖ RICO does not make racketeering itself illegal; it makes it unlawful for any person to gain income or benefit from racketeering.

❖ Punishment under RICO

◆ Those convicted under RICO may receive up to 20 years in prison, as well as a $25,000 fine. (Siegel, 2000)

◆ Punishments can also include asset forfeiture.

11.2.7   Transnational organized crime

■ Unlawful activity undertaken and supported by criminal groups operating across national boundaries

■ Transnational crime is now a major force in world finance, able to affect countries at critical stages of their economic development.

❖ Examples of world's major crime clans:

◆ Hong Kong-based Triads

◆ South American cocaine cartels

◆ Italian Mafia

◆ Japanese Yakuza

◆ Russian Mafiya

◆ West African crime groups

■ Russian organized crime has grown quickly since the collapse of the Soviet Union and has taken root in the United States and other countries.

For more on organized crime, visit Criminology Interactive online > White-Collar and Organized Crime > Crime Explained: Organized Crime Today.

CHAPTER SUMMARY

➤ White-collar crime is crime that is perpetrated by an individual of high social status during the course of his professional occupation. While-white collar crime is every bit as predatory and deviant as crime committed by those of lower socioeconomic status. Criminologists and society as a whole do not always recognize its seriousness. It has been estimated that the dollar loss from white-collar crime is far more significant than all other crimes combined.

➤ White-collar crime falls into several general categories. Occupational crime involves employee theft that causes immense monetary loss to employers. Embezzlement involves taking money, as opposed to merchandise for personal use, and can range from stealing from the cashbox to high-level manipulating of financial records.

➤ Occupational fraud includes a variety of criminal activities. Securities-related crimes are generally committed by those who work in a brokerage-related business who misuse their position for financial gain. Bankruptcy fraud, the practice of defrauding the government by developing a scam that takes advantages of loopholes in the bankruptcy laws, is another form of occupational fraud. Consumer fraud occurs when a consumer is deceived into surrendering money because of false claims. Insurance fraud happens when policyholders or third parties file false claims. In tax fraud, a company, rather than an individual, attempts to reduce their taxes by manipulating their books or shifting funds. Bribery occurs primarily at the bureaucratic level when officials or politicians accept payment in return for preferential treatment. Physician fraud includes physicians performing unnecessary surgery or prescribing unnecessary medications, and is a particularly disturbing area of occupational fraud.

➤ Corporate crime is a criminal act that is committed by a small number of employees at a corporation. Corporate crime occurs through corporate theft, such as when a corporation practices deceptive advertising or price fixing. Another major category of corporate crime is corporate violence against workers and consumers. This can take the form of creating an unsafe working environment, knowingly disseminating harmful products to consumers in the marketplace, or engaging in practices that knowingly pollute and contaminate our environment. Transnational crime is another form of corporate crime that involves large corporations that maintain businesses in more than one country, and may involve bribery, product dumping, or unsafe working conditions, across international lines. High-tech crimes are a new breed of corporate crime accomplished through the use of advanced electronic media, which usually involve the theft of resources, proprietary information, or monetary funds.

➤ Organized crime refers to the unlawful activities of a highly organized group that is in engaged in supplying illegal goods and services such as gambling, prostitution, etc. Organized crime existed in Italy for hundreds of years and its influence could be felt in the United States in most cities by the 1920s. Prohibition created a growth opportunity for organized crime through participation in providing low-cost, high-proof alcohol.

➤ Studies of organized crime indicate that they have a highly defined structure, headed by a boss who maintains order and directs the profit-making activities. All members of the organized crime group, or family, swear total allegiance to the boss and follow a strict code of conduct.

➤ Today, organized crime can be organized into three groups of activities: illegal sale and distribution of goods and services such as gambling, drugs, and loan-sharking; involvement in legitimate businesses such as money laundering and direct investment; and involvement with the state, including corruption of government officials.

➤ There are other organized crime groups besides those associated with the original Italian mafia. Haitian Mafia, Columbian cartels, inner-city gangs, and international drug rings are just some examples.

➤ High crime is a lucrative business that inhibits the efforts of legitimate businesses. For many years, the criminal justice system was limited in its ability to fight organized crime, but recent legislation has redefined certain laws to make them broader and to increase their penalties.

STUDY QUESTIONS

1. How is white-collar crime harmful to society as a whole?
2. What are the distinctions between occupational crime and corporate crime?
3. How are white-collar crimes similar to other crimes? How are they different?
4. What are some of factors that constitute violence against workers?
5. What are environmental crimes? What are some of the major environmental crimes that have occurred in the last 100 years?
6. What were the factors that led to the development of organized crime in the United States?
7. Name some of the illegal activities that organized crime is involved in.
8. What other organized crime groups exist beyond the Italian Mafia?

 ONLINE@CRIMINOLOGY INTERACTIVE

Identifying Crimes

Drag and Drop Exercise

Review

Vocabulary Shootout
Section Test

Chapter 12

Public Order Crimes

CHAPTER OUTLINE

KEY IDEAS

➤ Public order crimes are criminal acts that are ambiguous in terms of the victim and how much harm the crime actually causes.

➤ Prostitution is a public order crime that involves the unlawful engagement of sexual activity for profit. There has been much debate over whether prostitution causes substantial harm to its victims or to society.

➤ Pornography, the sale of sexually explicit material, is protected by the First Amendment, but obscenity, which is the measure of whether material is offensive to morality, is not. Pornography becomes illegal when a community or society determines that the material is obscene.

➤ The most extensive debate about public order crimes surrounds the use of illegal and legal drugs. The cost of drug enforcement, incarceration of those who sell and use drugs, and the "drug war" are often cited as key reasons for seeking new, more effective ways of dealing with drug abuse, including rehabilitation and decriminalization of certain less harmful drugs.

KEY TERMS

drug decriminalization
drug legalization
pornography
prostitution
public order crime

12.0 Public order crimes

PUBLIC ORDER CRIME
A crime that does not clearly create harm to society and that does not have a clear victim.

PROSTITUTION
The act of engaging in sexual behavior for money or its equivalent.

PORNOGRAPHY
The sale of sexually explicitly material.

12.1 **Public order crimes** are criminal acts that have considerable amount of ambiguity about the existence of a victim and harm to society.

    12.1.1 Public order crimes are crimes that many consider do not harm society, and include drug use, **prostitution**, **pornography**, homosexuality, gambling, and abortion.

12.2 Harm, morality, and crime

    12.2.1 Edwin Schur (1974) argued that when goods and services are exchanged between willing partners, no crime has been committed.

- When laws are passed against such behaviors, they create victimless crimes.

    12.2.2 Victimless crimes

- Many claim that victimless crimes should not be seen as criminal.

- Opponents to this view feel that they should remain criminal because the purpose of law is to maintain order and to protect shared moral responsibility.

- The link between morality and criminal is not clear.
  - ❖ There are acts that many find seriously immoral that are not illegal. Examples:
    - ◆ Not assisting a person in need
    - ◆ Not showing love to our children
  - ❖ Many violations of conventional morality are tolerated. Examples:
    - ◆ People gamble on office football pools or at their local tavern.
    - ◆ People from many walks of life watch sexually explicit movies.
  - ❖ Some well-intentioned acts are still identified as criminal. Examples:
    - ◆ Assisted suicide for the terminally ill
    - ◆ Theft to feed one's hungry family

12.3 Prostitution

    12.3.1 Morality, sexuality, and crime

- Social control of sexual morality/behavior
  - ❖ All societies attempt to exert control over sexual behavior.
  - ❖ The kinds of behaviors that are criminalized vary across societies and across time.

- ◆ The United States is no exception.
  - ❏ Until 1962, sexual intercourse between unmarried persons and all forms of unnatural sexual relations were illegal.
  - ❏ In 1962, Model Penal Code made significant changes in how sex was viewed under the law.
    - Sexual relations between consenting adults were said to be beyond the control of law.
    - Did not extend this to activities involving children, which continue to be strongly prohibited
    - There are some sexual behaviors between consenting adults that are still criminalized.

12.3.2 Definition of prostitution: the unlawful engagement of sexual activity for profit

- Assisting or promoting prostitution is illegal.
- Sexual significance
  - ❖ The act has sexual significance to the customer.
- Economic transaction
  - ❖ Something of value is exchanged.
- Emotional indifference
  - ❖ The activity is not based in affection.
- Prostitution is a misdemeanor in 49 states.
  - ❖ It is legal in some, but not all counties in Nevada
- Crime to be a prostitute
  - ❖ At one time in history, a woman was considered to be a prostitute, under law, by having intercourse with more than one man.
  - ❖ In 1962, the U.S. Supreme Court ruled that criminal liability relates only to committing an act in violation of the law.
    - ◆ One can only be penalized for engaging in solicitation of sex for economic exchange.
    - ◆ The act of solicitation is called prostitution.

12.3.3 Nature and extent of prostitution

- Types of prostitutes
  - ❖ Siegel (2000) identifies several different types of prostitutes/prostitution:
    - ◆ Streetwalkers/hookers
      - ❏ Work the streets to meet clients, whose slang term is "john."

❑ Lowest paid individuals in the profession

❑ Most vulnerable to violence, drug addiction, and other abuse

◆ Bar girls (b-girls)

❑ Work bars to meet clients

◆ Brothel prostitutes

❑ Work out of business establishments usually run by a madam

◆ Call girls

❑ Arrange dates via the telephone, usually from a client list and/or by referral

❑ Most highly paid

◆ Escort services/call houses

❑ A combination of the brothel and call girl approach

❑ Call a service to arrange the date

◆ Circuit travelers

❑ Small groups of prostitutes who follow migrant work camps

◆ Skeezers

❑ These individuals exchange sex for drugs.

❑ They are often linked to the rise in popularity of crack cocaine

■ Extent of prostitution

❖ The full extent of prostitution is very difficult to assess.

❖ Official statistics show steady declines in arrests for prostitution, yet other research suggests that prostitution is thriving.

❖ There are approximately 250,000 full-time female prostitutes in the United States.

◆ These women service approximately 1.5 million customers each week. (Miethe and Mccorkle, 1998)

◆ Female prostitutes gross about $7 to $9 billion annually.

❖ There is no way to estimate the number of part-time and occasional prostitutes.

■ Males are more involved in prostitution as clients than females.

❖ Males are almost always the clients of female prostitutes.

❖ Female prostitutes often work for a male pimp who is their business manager and protector.

❖ There are estimated to be as many male prostitutes as there are female.

- Characteristics associated with prostitution

  - ❖ Prostitutes often come from troubled homes/family backgrounds.

  - ❖ Many prostitutes have been victims of sexual abuse by family members, beginning at a young age. (Siegel, 2000)

  - ❖ Drug abuse/addiction is often a factor. (Chesney-Lind, 1997)

- Motives for becoming involved in prostitution

  - ❖ Overriding motive is economic.

    - ◆ One study reports that most prostitutes engage in prostitution when they are short of money. (Bierne and Messerschmidt, 2000)

    - ◆ Prostitutes come to view their bodies as commodities.

      - ❑ Prostitution may offer the most lucrative option for employment, especially when one has limited education/opportunities.

    - ◆ Desperation and other coercive factors also play a role in becoming a prostitute.

  - ❖ Some people are forced into a life of prostitution, but they are the exception.

- The debate about prostitution

  - ❖ Adler et al. (1998, p. 331) observe that "popular, political, and scientific opinions on prostitution have changed" because of its changing nature.

    - ◆ Unlike in the past, most people who enter into prostitution are not forced into doing so; they do so because it offers financial rewards that they do not have access to through legitimate opportunities.

  - ❖ Two opposing views of prostitution

    - ◆ Sexual equality view

      - ❑ Advocates that women must become emancipated from male oppression to reach sexual equality

      - ❑ Argues that prostitutes are victims of male domination and oppression (Siegel, 2000) and that women will not reach sexual equality until they are emancipated from this oppression

    - ◆ Free choice view

      - ❑ This view proposes that women need to control all attempts at domination by men.

      - ❑ If freely chosen, prostitution is seen as an expression of women's equality and allows women to control attempts of domination by men.

    ❖   The debate about whether adult prostitutes are victims does not apply to children, who are clearly victimized.

        ◆   Their vulnerability makes them far different than consenting adults who engage in prostitution

12.4   Pornography is the violation of laws that prohibit the sale of sexually explicit material.

- Like prostitution, pornography has a sexual component.
    - ❖ Unlike prostitution, there is no contact between individuals.
- Pornography is illegal.
    - ❖ All states have statutes making it criminal to produce, offer for sale or sell, distribute, or exhibit pornographic material.
    - ❖ There are federal laws relating to transportation and dissemination of such materials. (Adler et al., 1998)
    - ❖ What constitutes pornography is not clearly defined.
- Material depicting nudity and sex is protected under the First Amendment.
- Obscene material is not protected.
    - ❖ The definition/identification of pornography rests on our ability to define/identify what is obscene.
    - ❖ Obscene is defined as material that is offensive to one's sense of modesty or propriety, intended to provoke lust and is licentious, lewd, disgusting, or foul. (Landau, 1997)
- The interpretation about what is obscene affects whether or not the material is illegal.
    - ❖ Such decisions raise serious concerns about First Amendment protections of free speech.
    - ❖ It also raises questions as to whether anti-obscenity statutes could be used to control social and political dissent. (Siegel, 2000)

12.4.1   Pornography and harm

- While definitions of pornography do not concern themselves with the harm and danger of pornographic materials, there has been debate about whether pornographic material is harmful.
- Kinds of harm associated with pornography
    - ❖ Pornography is seen to have a negative impact on public morals, especially among the young.
- Pornography may play a role in violent behavior.
- Pornography and violence
    - ❖ Two government commissions investigated the relationship of pornography and violence.

- Commission on Obscenity and Pornography (1970)
  - ❑ "Found no evidence that exposure to explicit sexual materials plays a significant role in the causation of delinquent or criminal behavior among youths or adults" (p. 27)
- Attorney General's Commission on Pornography (1986)
  - ❑ The findings of the Attorney General's Commission on Pornography are less clear.

12.5 Drug use and the war on drugs

12.5.1 Historical overview

- As far back as there are written records, there are accounts of humans using drugs for religious, medical, and social/recreational purposes.
  - ❖ The Egyptians used opium for religious rituals in 3500 B.C.E.
  - ❖ The Incas used cocaine at least 5,000 years ago.
  - ❖ Hemp (the plant from which marijuana comes) has been in use for 5,000 years. (Adler et al., 1998)
- Contemporary views of drug use and our attempts to control it are very complex, and involve:
  - ❖ Individual/personal issues
  - ❖ Health concerns (both mental and physical)
  - ❖ Social and economic issues
  - ❖ Political implications (domestic and international)
  - ❖ Ethical standards
  - ❖ Various types of drugs (licit and illicit)
  - ❖ Control, treatment, and education

12.5.2 Official reaction to drugs in the United States

- During the 1800s, opiate products were readily available and widely used (Beirne and Messerschmidt, 2000) and prescribed as tranquilizers for pain relief, even for babies.
- Beginning in the late 1800s, laws began to restrict the use opiates.
  - ❖ These views may have been brought about by concern about the growing number of addicts. (see Adler et al., 1998)
  - ❖ Some have implicated other social factors, including those involving race. (see Beirne and Messerschmidt, 2000)
    - In 1875, San Francisco made opium dens illegal.
      - ❑ This law is said to have targeted Chinese laborers who were perceived as heavy opium users.

♦ A similar situation arose involving cocaine.

◻ During the late 1800s and early 1900s, cocaine was widely used for medicinal purposes.

◻ In 1914, Congress passed the Harrison Act, which regulated the use, sale, and transfer of opiate and cocoa-derived products.

- There is evidence that strong racist beliefs about the susceptibility of African-Americans to cocaine motivated laws like the Harrison Act, although most of those addicted were actually white.

■ Criminalization of drugs

❖ Following the Harrison Act (1919–1922), the Supreme Court issued a series of decisions making it illegal for physicians to prescribe narcotics.

❖ This made it impossible for addicts to get drugs to which they had become addicted.

❖ An illicit drug trade quickly developed to fill the void, and prices increased 50 times. (Beirne and Messerschmidt, 2000)

❖ Goode (1984) claims that these legal actions produced a new criminal class of addicts.

♦ These new criminals were mainly lower-/working-class individuals.

♦ Middle-class addicts began to use drugs like tranquilizers to feed their addictions.

■ Late 1920s and early 1930s

❖ Efforts were made to bring some uniformity to drug laws across states.

♦ By 1937, 35 states had enacted the Uniform Drug Act. (Abadinsky, 2001)

❖ Marijuana

♦ This time period saw marijuana attract serious attention.

■ 1950 to 1951

❖ News stories began to appear about heroin use spilling out of the ghetto and into middle-class America.

❖ Boggs Amendment was passed as an amendment to the Harrison Act in 1951.

♦ It substantially increased penalties for the possession and trafficking of marijuana and other substances (Abadinsky, 2001) and ushered in a new stance on illegal drugs that included harsher penalties.

♦ It ushered in the law-and-order stance on illegal drugs

- 1970s
  - ❖ Comprehensive Drug Abuse, Prevention, and Control Act replaced all previous laws that dealt with dangerous substances.
    - ◆ All drugs controlled by the Act came under federal jurisdiction.
    - ◆ The original intent was to target all dangerous drugs.
      - ❏ Pharmaceutical companies succeeded in keeping many drugs that they produced off the list.
- 1980s
  - ❖ Comprehensive Crime Control Act (1984) was passed to address the growing crime problem.
  - ❖ Anti-Drug Abuse Act (1986) further strengthened the drug laws and penalties.
    - ◆ Created position of Drug Czar
      - ❏ Position is a presidential appointment
      - ❏ Oversees policies/enforcement relating to heroin, cocaine, and marijuana

12.5.3 Marijuana and the law

- Hemp
  - ❖ Marijuana has long been cultivated as a crop with a wide range of uses.
  - ❖ From 1000 B.C.E. until after the American Civil War, it was the most widely grown agricultural crop in the world.
  - ❖ Hemp was widely and heavily grown in the United States until the 1930s.
    - ◆ From 1901 to 1937, the U.S. Department of Agriculture predicted that it would become the number one farm crop in the United States.
    - ◆ By 1937, technology had reached the point where hemp could be economically processed.
      - ❏ Hemp-based paper could be produced for half the cost of wood-based paper.
      - ❏ Warmer and more water resistant hemp fabric could compete with cotton.
      - ❏ Science was exploring the medicinal uses of hemp.
  - ❖ Two economic/political fronts pushed for the criminalization of hemp/marijuana.
  - ❖ During the 1930s, Mexicans were seen as a threat to white survival because they worked for low pay.
    - ◆ White citizens, criminal justice officials, and politicians from the Southwest pushed the federal government to intervene (Beirne and Messerschmidt, 200, p. 310) and the Marijuana Tax Act of 1937 was passed.

- Power and the criminalization of marijuana (adapted from Parascope, 2001)
  - ❖ Hemp posed a serious threat to key American industrialists in the 1930s, such as William Randolph Hearst and the du Pont family, because it offered cheaper alternatives and produced superior products to theirs.
  - ❖ William Randolph Hearst and the du Pont family set into motion a two-pronged attack to destroy the hemp industry (and thereby eliminate their competition).
    - ◆ Using Hearst's newspaper empire, they launched a massive propaganda campaign.
    - ◆ The power of government was also used to cripple and ultimately destroy the hemp industry.
  - ❖ The Hearst news machine
    - ◆ A story about a car wreck in which a marijuana cigarette was found remained on the front page for weeks.
    - ◆ Stories in Hearst's newspaper warned of Negro men raping white women while under the influence of marijuana.
    - ◆ Racial prejudices were further inflamed by claims that "Negroes and Mexicans," once under marijuana's devil influence, dared to look white people in the eye and to look at white women twice.
    - ◆ Hearst actually published in his paper that "if the hideous monster Frankenstein came face-to-face with the monster marijuana he would drop dead of fright." (Parascope, 2001, part 2, p. 2)
    - ◆ These stories created mass panic about the evils of marijuana.
  - ❖ Politics and power
    - ◆ Harry Anslinger was the first director of the Federal Bureau of Narcotics (FBN) and was instrumental in getting the Marijuana Tax Act of 1937 enacted by Congress.
    - ◆ Anslinger was a key player in the criminalization of marijuana, using statistics that traced the use of marijuana in "Latinos, Negroes, and Greeks" to 50% of all violent crimes.
- The fate of marijuana/hemp
  - ❖ Possession of marijuana became a crime.
    - ◆ To a large extent, the criminalization of marijuana was based on fear, racism, and the misuse of power and wealth rather than health issues.

- ◆ The criminalization of marijuana created a whole new class of criminals.
    - ❐ Tens of billions of dollars are spent in prosecuting and incarcerating marijuana offenders.

12.6   Drug use in America

12.6.1   Many of the facts and statistics provided in this section come from *Drug War Facts* (updated 2007), compiled by Common Sense for Drug Policy (DWF) and is available at www.drugwarfacts.org.

- ■ The extent and nature of drug use:
    - ❖ "An estimated 112,085,000 Americans, aged 12 or over (46.1% of the U.S. population aged 12 and over) report having used an illicit drug at least once in their lifetime." (DWF)
    - ❖ A 2005 National Survey on Drug Use & Health reports estimates that for those 12 and over:
        - ◆ 82.9% reported they had used alcohol
        - ◆ 70.8% reported they had used tobacco
        - ◆ 40.1% reported they had used marijuana
        - ◆ 13.8% reported they had used cocaine
        - ◆ 3.3% reported they had used crack
        - ◆ 1.5% reported they had used heroin
    - ❖ The total number of drug users in the world is now estimated at some 2 billion people, equivalent to about 5% of the global population age 15 to 64. (United Nations Office on Drugs and Crime, *World Drug Report 2006*, Vol. 1: Analysis, p. 9)
    - ❖ In 2006, 43.9% of the 1,889,810 arrests for drug violation were for marijuana (a total of 829,627). Of those, 738,916 were arrested for marijuana possession alone." (DWF)
    - ❖ According to the 2007 National Survey on Drug Use & Health (2008), an estimated 19.9 million (8.3%) Americans age 12 and older are current users of an illicit drug.
    - ❖ From 2002 to 2007, there were declines in the rate of current drug use in nearly every category. (2007 National Survey on Drug Use & Health, 2008)

12.6.2   Drugs and crime

- ■ Drugs as crime
    - ❖ Arrest for drug offenses
        - ◆ According to the UCR for 2007, there were 1,841,182 arrests for drug abuse violations.
        - ◆ Law enforcement made more arrests for drug abuse violations (13% of the total number of arrests) than for any other offense in 2007.

♦ Sale/manufacturing represented 17% of all drug abuse violations in 2007.

♦ Possession represented 82.5% of all drug abuse violations.

♦ Arrests by race for drug abuse violations
  ❏ White—880,742 arrests (63.7%)
  ❏ Black—485,054 arrests (35.1%)
  ❏ American Indian or Alaskan Native—8,872 arrests (0.6%)
  ❏ Asian or Pacific Islander—8,115 arrests (0.6%)

■ Drug use as a factor in other crimes
  ❖ Advocates of strict drug laws and harsh punishments often base their position on the relationship between drugs and other crime.
  ❖ Drugs affect crime when individuals engage in criminal activities such as theft, burglary, or robbery to obtain money to purchase drugs.
    ♦ Addiction and crime
      ❏ Substances like heroin are very expensive because of their illegal status.
      ❏ This economic strain can push individuals toward crime to support their habit. (Beirne and Messerschmidt, 2000)
  ❖ Use and violence
    ♦ There is concern that drug use can make people more prone to violent behavior.
    ♦ According to the National Center for Addiction and Substance Abuse (1998), alcohol is associated with more violent crimes than any other drug.
      ❏ Twenty-one percent of violent felons in state prisons were under the influence of alcohol alone when they committed their crime.
      ❏ Three percent were under the influence of crack/powder cocaine alone when they committed their crime
      ❏ One percent was under the influence of heroin alone when they committed their crime
    ♦ According to federal statistics, the largest overall percentage of offenders (36.3%) were under the influence of alcohol alone at the time of their offense. (DOJ, 1998)
  ❖ Drugs as a cause of crime
    ♦ The existence of a high correlation between drug use and crime is well established. (Abadinsky, 2001)

❐ Correlation does not imply that drugs cause crime.

❐ The relationship between crimes that are committed because of drugs and those that are not is difficult to untangle.

◆ Given the confusing nature of the connection between drugs and nondrug crimes, NIJ (1993) concluded that "it is impossible to say quantitatively how much drugs influence the occurrence of crime." (cited in Abadinsky, 2001, p. 16)

◆ Beirne and Messerschmidt (2000, p. 313) cite several studies that conclude that "drugs do not cause criminality."

❐ These studies lead to the conclusion that both drug abuse and crime are the result of the "same set of unfavorable social circumstances." (p. 313)

❐ The interaction is more complex than what the "addiction-leads-to-crime view" proposes. (p. 313)

❐ Beirne and Messerschmidt cite evidence that addiction does not escalate involvement in criminal behavior; rather, the expense of the drug and the fact that it is illegal escalates criminal involvement.

◆ Kappeler et al. (1996, p. 173) were more extreme, stating that "it is a myth that drugs cause crime."

❐ They claim that a review of the evidence indicates that alcohol is the only drug that is clearly linked to crime.

❐ By extension, then, laws that prohibit drugs cause the criminality.

◆ Menard, Mihalic, and Huizinga (2001, p. 295) conclude that:

❐ The "drug use equals crime" hypothesis does not hold up.

❐ More serious forms of both behaviors usually follow more minor forms; they rarely occur in the absence of minor forms.

❐ Once crime and drug use are initiated, each seems to increase the likelihood/continuity of the other.

❐ Crime and drug use are more closely related in adolescence than in adulthood.

❐ In looking at the transition from adolescence to adulthood, the most likely conclusion is crime affects drug use and drug use affects crime.

12.6.3   Drugs and harm

- Research clearly indicates that the abuse of alcohol, tobacco, and legal and illegal drugs is our nation's most serious health problem.

    ❖ More deaths, illnesses, and disabilities are attributable to substance abuse than any other preventable health condition. (Ericson, 2001)

- Every year, 8,000 to 14,000 people die from illegal drugs; 500,000 or more die from alcohol, tobacco, and prescription drugs. (Califano, 1998)

- Causes of death (CDC and other sources)

    ❖ Tobacco-induced causes

        ◆ Average number of cigarette smoking related deaths per year (1997 to 2001) is 438,000. (Center for Disease Control, 2005)

    ❖ Alcohol-induced causes

        ◆ In 2005, a total of 21,634 persons died of alcohol-induced causes in the United States. (CDC, 2008)

    ❖ Drug-induced causes

        ◆ A total of 33,541 persons died of drug-induced causes in the United States in 2005. (CDC, 2008)

    ❖ Suicide (National Institute of Mental Health, 2007)

        ◆ Suicide was the eighth leading cause of death for males, and 16th leading cause of death for females in 2004.

        ◆ Almost four times as many males as females die by suicide.

        ◆ Firearms, suffocation, and poison are by far the most common methods of suicide.

    ❖ Homicide (UCR, 2008)

        ◆ Nationwide, in 2007, an estimated 16,929 persons were murdered.

    ❖ Marijuana

        ◆ None ever recorded as causes of death in the United States

12.7   The war on drugs: By the numbers

12.7.1   George Bush, Sr.'s war on drugs (Donziger, 1996)

- Only 3% of Americans named drugs as the biggest problem in the United States.

- The Bush Administration's emphasis on drugs in the media caused 40 to 45% of Americans to see drugs as our biggest problem. (Chomsky, 2001)

- President Bush unveiled his antidrug strategy in 1989, a strategy that called for:
  - ❖ The deployment of military assistance to several South American countries to fight the war at the source
  - ❖ The allocation of federal dollars to state and local law enforcement to combat street-level use and dealing
  - ❖ The rigorous application of seizure and forfeiture laws (Adler et al., 1998)

12.7.2   Cost of the war on drugs

- During the 1990s, the United States spent $150 billion fighting the war on drugs. (Media Awareness Project, 2000)

- During 2001, the federal government spent $19.2 billion on the "war on drugs."
  - ❖ This amounts to $609 per second

- Federal spending on the war on drugs increased from $1.65 billion in 1982 to $19.2 billion in 2001 (Drug Sense, 2001), an increase of 11.5 times.
  - ❖ By contrast, the federal budget for education increased by 43% from 1985 to 1999. (U.S. Department of Education, 2000)

- Incarceration, the war on drugs, and dollars and cents
  - ❖ Incarceration rates
    - ◆ In 1985, the incarceration rate in the United States was 313 per 100,000.
    - ◆ In 2000, the incarceration rate had risen to 645 per 100,000. (DOJ, 2000)
    - ◆ This increase is 3 to 10 times higher than other modern democratic societies. (DOJ, 2000)
  - ❖ The largest single contributing factor to the increase is drug arrests.
    - ◆ Drug arrests increased eight-fold from 1985 to 2000.
    - ◆ Drug offenders were the largest group in federal prisons in 1998 (58%), up from 53% in 1990. (DOJ, 2000)
  - ❖ In 1986, BJS estimated that it was costing $8.6 billion to keep drug law violators behind bars and federal prisons requested substantial additional monies to construct prisons to house drug offenders.
    - ◆ It costs up to $450,000 to put a single drug dealer in prison. (Schaffer, 2001)
  - ❖ It is estimated that putting a person in prison generates approximately $15 in related welfare costs for every $1 spent on incarceration. (Schaffer, 2001)
    - ◆ Using conservative figures cited earlier ($450,000), this raises the cost of incarcerating one dealer to $525 million.

❖ In 1997, states spent $32.5 billion on corrections and $22.2 billion on assistance to the poor. (National Association of State Budget Offices, 2000)

❖ Since the enactment of mandatory minimum sentencing for drug users, the FBI's budget has increased by 1,350%. (BJS, 1997)

◆ The FBI budget was $220 million in 1986.

◆ The FBI budget was $3.19billion in 1997.

12.7.3   Collateral damage

■ When a person goes to prison, he is not the only one affected. The families left behind suffer serious negative consequences.

■ According to the Bureau of Justice Statistics (2008):

❖ An estimated 809,800 prisoners of the 1,518,535 held in the nation's prisons at midyear 2007 were parents of minor children. (BJS, 2008)

❖ Between 1991 and midyear 2007, parents held in state and federal prisons increased by 79% (357,300 parents). (BJS, 2008)

❖ The number of children under 18 with a mother in prison more than doubled since 1991.

◆ The nation's prisons, by midyear 2007, held approximately:

❑ 744,200 fathers with 1,559,200 children

❑ 65,500 mothers with 147,400 children

❖ Black children (6.7%) were seven-and-a-half times as likely to have a parent in prison than white children (0.9%), while Hispanic children (2.4%) were two-and-a-half times more likely than white children to have a parent in prison.

❖ About half of parents in state prisons provided the primary financial support for their minor children prior to incarceration.

■ The war on drugs and racial bias

❖ Domestic efforts on drug enforcement have focused "almost exclusively on low-level dealers in minority neighborhoods." (Donziger, 1996, p. 115)

❖ At the height of the drug war, African-American arrest rates were five times higher than whites based on equal rates of drug use.

◆ The evidence indicates equal rates of drug use.

❖ Crack vs. powder cocaine

◆ The penalties for crack cocaine are much more severe than those for powder cocaine.

☐ Five grams of crack is a felony punishable by a mandatory minimum sentence of five years in many jurisdictions.

☐ Five grams of powder cocaine is a misde-meanor that carries a one-year sentence in many jurisdictions.

◆ About 90% of arrestees for crack are African-American. Fifty-five percent of users are white. (Monk, 1996)

◆ Seventy-five percent of arrestees for powder cocaine are white. (Donziger, 1996)

12.8   The legalization/decriminalization debate

12.8.1   Drugs as the root of all evil

■ Drugs are seen as causing a wide range of social problems.

❖ Family breakdown

❖ Crime

❖ A widening generation gap

■ The perception has become that if we could reduce the avail-ability of drugs, things would improve.

❖ Traditional families would be restored.

❖ Crime would be eliminated.

❖ Children would do better in school and get along with their parents.

■ The primary strategy for improving this problem has been to wage a war on drugs (and on those who use them) with the criminal justice system as the main weapon.

■ There are those who seriously question the real roles that drugs play in such social problems.

❖ From this perspective, drug use should be either **legalized** or at least **decriminalized**.

◆ Legalization suggests that all legal prohibitions on drugs be removed.

◆ Decriminalization is "the minimization, or actual removal of, criminal prohibitions for illegal drugs while still *regulating* their use." (Beirne and Messerschmidt, 2000, p. 314)

❖ This approach also contends that our efforts and resources should target treatment and education.

DRUG LEGALIZATION

The removal of legal prohibitions for all drugs.

DRUG DECRIMINALIZATION

The minimization of criminal prohibitions with accompanying regulation of their use.

12.8.2   Prolegalization/decriminalization arguments

■ Controlling drugs is beyond the capabilities of law enforcement.

❖ Less than 1% of all crimes committed result in arrest.

❖ Current policies overwhelm and distort the criminal justice system; they crowd court dockets, overwhelm jails and prisons, and prevent efforts to deal with more serious crimes.

■ Current policies have not served to minimize social harm.

❖ Drug prohibition is even more dangerous than drug use and accounts for over 7,000 deaths each year through drug-related crimes, AIDS, and poisoned drugs.

❖ If current laws are not causing harm, then these laws are expressions of moral disapproval and an infringement on individual rights.

■ Arnold S. Trebach offers the following points in support of legislation in *Taking Sides* (1996):

❖ There is no scientific basis for distinguishing between legal and illegal drugs.

❖ Drugs affect people only within the context of how they are used; either category of drugs can be abused.

❖ Drug prohibition generates crime and violence, not drugs themselves.

❖ The drug war represents a huge cost with little return and diverts attention away from real social problems, including racial division, criminal violence, and health issues such as AIDS.

❖ Legal drugs have not historically produced significant crime.

◆ Trebach cites as an example the fact that crime rates before Prohibition were a small fraction of what they became afterwards.

❖ Trebach advocates heightened education and other steps to reduce harm as part of a legalization strategy.

12.8.3   Antilegalization arguments

■ James A. Inciardi offers the following points in opposition to legalization:

❖ Drug prohibition policies have been problematic, but they have kept drugs away from most people.

❖ Despite arguments to the contrary, marijuana, heroin, cocaine, and other such substances are not benign.

❖ Crack cocaine is especially problematic.

◆ It has unique pharmacological and sociocultural effects.

◆ These effects create a situation where "use rapidly becomes compulsive use . . ." (p. 269)

❖ The research on heroin and other drug use shows that drug use tends to intensify and perpetuate criminal behavior once it is in place.

❖ Shift the focus of the war on drugs away from enforcement and into treatment.

❖ Drug control should remain in the criminal justice system.

◆ It provides the best vehicle for getting compulsory treatment to those most in need of it

◆ These compulsory programs should be expanded.

❖ The war on drugs will continue, but a more humane use of the criminal justice system should be implemented.

◆ Treatment in lieu of incarceration

◆ Correction-based treatment for those who are incarcerated

■ Inciardi concludes that our drug policies are not likely to undergo drastic change in the near future.

❖ "There is far too much suffering as the result of drug abuse that is not being addressed." (p. 270)

CHAPTER SUMMARY

➤ Public order crimes are criminal acts that have considerable amount of ambiguity about the existence of a victim and how much harm the crime actually causes. They include such activities as drug use, pornography, homosexuality, gambling, and abortion.

➤ Edwin Schur in 1974 argued that when goods and services are exchanged between willing parties, there is no harm and no crime. When these activities are made illegal, Schur contends, they create victimless crimes. Opponents to this view claim that the purpose of law is to maintain order and morality, and that many victimless crimes actually have society as their victims.

➤ Prostitution is a public order crime that is defined as the unlawful engagement of sexual activity for profit. It is a misdemeanor in 49 states and legal in some counties in Nevada. The definition of a prostitute has changed over time from a woman who simply had sex with more than one man, to a woman who actively solicits sex and is paid for it. The debate about prostitution has two opposing views. The sexual equality view argues that women are the victims of male domination and oppression, and that prostitution is a form of female sexual slavery. The free choice view argues that prostitution, if chosen freely, is an expression of women's equality as it allows them to control domination by men.

➤ Pornography, which is the sale of sexually explicit material, is another controversial public order crime. While material depicting nudity and sex is protected under the First Amendment, obscene material is not offered such protection. Obscene material is defined as material that is offensive to one's sense of modesty or propriety, especially as it applies to sexuality. The determination of whether material is obscene is essential to determining what kind of pornography is considered unlawful. There is considerable debate about whether pornography has harmful effects, although some studies have found that pornography is related to violent behavior.

➤ The most extensive debate about public order crimes centers on the use of illegal and legal drugs. The historical background of drug use in the United States indicates that antidrug laws that have been passed over the last 150 years are based on racist misconceptions about drug use among minorities, most notably Mexicans and blacks. Early industrialists such as William Randolph Hearst waged a media battle against marijuana in order to eliminate the marijuana industry as a competitor in the production of paper and other goods.

➤ Drug abuse, particularly abuse of marijuana, cocaine and crack cocaine, heroin, and methamphetamine, is at the heart of a controversy that concerns the relationship of drugs to other crimes, the negative health impact of drug use, and the cost/benefit ratio of enforcing drug laws. The specific connection of drugs to other crimes is complex. Offenders may engage in burglary to support a drug habit, for instance, but that may be caused by the high price of drugs because of their illegal status. What is clear, however, is that research clearly indicates that the abuse of alcohol, tobacco, and illegal drugs is the nation's most serious health problem and is a cost to society. The war on drugs includes efforts to eradicate drug abuse through various methods, including increased penalties, which result in higher rates of incarceration. Many claim that the war on drugs represents a huge cost with little return. Money used in the war on drugs would be better used to support diversion, treatment, and education programs. Opponents to this view claim that while drug prohibition laws are problematic, they do keep drugs away from most people.

STUDY QUESTIONS

1. What are some examples of public order crimes?

2. What are the distinctions between the two views of prostitution—the sexual equality view and the free choice view?

3. What is the definition of obscenity? How does it affect whether material is considered pornographic?

4. What are some of the complexities that surround the relationship of drug abuse to other crimes?

5. What are some of the arguments for and against decriminalization of certain drugs?

Glossary

access to opportunities   Ability to work, earn money, promote, and succeed in traditional middle-class ways.

administrative law   Regulates many daily business activities, and violations of such regulations generally result in warnings or fines, depending upon their adjudged severity.

Age of Reason   A social movement which arose during the eighteenth century, and built upon ideas such as empiricism, rationality, free will, humanism, and natural law.

aggravated assault (UCR)   The unlawful attack by one person upon another for the purpose of inflicting severe or aggravated bodily injury. See also **simple assault**.

alloplastic adaptation   A form of adjustment that results from changes in the environment surrounding an individual.

analogous behavior   Behavior similar to and in the same class with actions of interest, such as criminal acts found in Gottfredson & Hirschi's low self-control theory.

anarchist criminology   Seeks to demythologize the concepts behind the criminal justice system and the legal order on which it is based.

androcentric   Male-centered; part of the feminist critique of traditional criminology theories.

anger   An element in general strain theory that enhances level of stress and increases chances of deviance.

anomie   A breakdown in the rules or the moral norms of society thought to be related to suicide and crime. A social condition in which norms are uncertain or lacking.

antisocial (asocial) personality   Refers to individuals who are basically unsocialized and whose behavior pattern brings them repeatedly into conflict with society.

applied research   Scientific inquiry that is designed and carried out with practical application in mind.

arson   Any willful or malicious burning or attempt to burn, with or without intent to defraud, a dwelling house, public building, motor vehicle or aircraft, personal property of another, and so on.

assault   The unlawful attack by one person upon another for the purpose of inflicting severe or aggravated bodily injury.

asset forfeiture   The authorized seizure of money, negotiable instruments, securities, or other things of value. In federal antidrug laws, the authorization of judicial representatives to seize all monies, negotiable instruments, securities, or other things of value furnished or intended to be furnished by any person in exchange for a controlled substance, and all proceeds traceable to such an exchange.

atavism   Subhuman or primitive trait used by Lombroso to describe the characteristics of criminals. The term "atavism" is derived from the Latin term *atavus*, which means "ancestor."

attachment   This is important for creating conformity, even when those being conformed to are deviant.

attachment theory   The theory that a child's attachment to their parents is important for creating conformity even when those others are deviant themselves.

audit trail   A sequential record of computer system activities that enables auditors to reconstruct, review, and examine the sequence of states and activities surrounding each event in one or more related transactions from inception to output of final results back to inception.

autoplastic adaptation   A form of adjustment that results from changes within an individual.

bank fraud   Fraud or embezzlement that occurs within or against financial institutions that are insured or regulated by the U.S. government. Financial institution fraud may include commercial loan fraud, check fraud, counterfeit negotiable instruments, mortgage fraud, check kiting, and false credit applications.

behavior theory   An approach to understanding human activity, which holds that behavior is determined by the consequences it produces for the individual.

belief   Constitutes the acknowledgment of society's rules as being fair.

biological theories   Theory that maintains that the basic determinants of human behavior, including criminality, are constitutionally or physiologically based and often inherited.

biosociology   Biological characteristics of an individual arc only one part in the equation of behavior—other parts are the physical and social environment.

body types   Used in some theories; certain physical features are believed to indicate a propensity to crime.

bond to the moral order   Part of Hirschi's theory of social control that describes the ties that exist between individuals and the dominant, middle-class values of society.

born criminals   Individuals who are born with a genetic predilection toward criminality.

bourgeoisie   In Marxian theory, the class of people who own the means of production.

bridging theories   These theories attempt to tell us how social structure comes about and how people become criminal.

broken windows thesis   A perspective on crime causation that holds that physical deterioration in an area leads to increased concerns for personal safety among area residents and to higher crime rates in that area.

bulletin board system (BBS)   A computer accessible by telephone; used like a bulletin board to leave messages and files for other users. Also called *computer bulletin board*.

burglary (UCR)   The unlawful entry of a structure to commit a felony or a theft.

capable guardian   A person, who if present, could prevent the occurrence of the crime.

capital punishment   The legal imposition of a sentence of death upon a convicted offender. Also called *death penalty*.

carjacking   The stealing of a car while it is occupied.

Cesare Beccaria   One of the best-known theorist of the Classical School; opposed the arbitrary and capricious nature of the criminal justice systems of his time.

Chicago School   A type of sociological approach that emphasizes demographics (the characteristics of population groups) and geographics (the mapped location of such groups relative to one another). Sees the social disorganization that characterizes delinquency areas as a major cause of criminality and victimization. Also called the *ecological theory of criminology*.

child abuse   Physical, sexual, or psychological abuse of a child. Can include medical, nutritional, or personal neglect.

chivalry hypothesis   Old conception of men doing things for women and perhaps showing leniency toward female offenders. Some argue that this may explain differences in arrest and incarceration rates for women.

civil law   The body of laws that regulates arrangements between individuals, such as contracts and claims to property.

Classical School   A criminological perspective operative in the late 1700s and early 1800s that had its roots in the Enlightenment and held that men and women are rational beings, that crime is the result of the exercise of free will, and that punishment can be effective in reducing the incidence of crime since it negates the pleasure to be derived from crime commission.

clearance rate   The proportion of reported or discovered crimes within a given offense category that are solved.

Code of Hammurabi   An early set of laws established by the Babylonian King Hammurabi around the year 2000 B.C.

cohort   A group of individuals who have certain significant social characteristics in common, such as gender, time, and place of birth.

cohort analysis   A social scientific technique that studies a population with common characteristics, over time. Cohort analysis usually begins at birth and traces the development of cohort members until they reach a certain age.

collective solution   This solution requires a change in the way status is attained by jointly establishing new norms.

commitment   Hirschi's idea that the emotional investment one builds up in conventional activities and pursuits of achievement will bond them to nondelinquent behavior.

common law   A body of unwritten judicial opinion originally based upon customary social practices of Anglo-Saxon society during the Middle Ages.

complexity   A view of reality as being very complex and incorporating that view into an understanding of human behavior.

computer abuse   Any incident associated with computer technology in which a victim suffered or could have suffered loss and/or a perpetrator by intention made or could have made gain.

computer bulletin board (CBB)   A computer accessible by telephone used like a bulletin board to leave messages and files for other users. Also called *bulletin board system*.

computer crime   Any violation of a computer crime statute. Also called *cybercrime*.

computer-related crime   Any illegal act for which knowledge of computer technology is involved for its investigation, perpetration, or prosecution.

computer virus   A set of computer instructions that propagates copies or versions of itself into computer programs or data when it is executed.

concentric zones   A conception of the city (Chicago) as a series of distinctive circles radiating from the central business district used to describe differences in crime rates.

conceptual scheme   A set of concepts used to build a theory.

conditioning   A psychological principle that holds that the frequency of any behavior can be increased or decreased through reward, punishment, or association with other stimuli.

conduct norms   The shared expectations of a social group relative to personal conduct.

confidence games   Crimes in which the offender gains a victim's confidence and then cheats them.

confidentiality   An ethical requirement of social scientific research, which stipulates that research data not be shared outside of the research environment.

conflict perspective   An analytical perspective on social organization that holds that conflict is a fundamental aspect of social life itself and can never be fully resolved.

conflict subculture   In this subculture, gangs would cause trouble equally for the community's criminal and noncriminal adults in an effort to gain "respect."

conflict theories   Based on the assumption that disagreement among people over values and laws is common and their differences are primarily about power and economics.

conformity   Striving for socially approved goals and following normal means of achieving them. Most people adapt this way; if not, according to Merton, the very existence of society would be threatened.

confounding effects   Rival explanations that are threats to the internal or external validity of any research design. Also called *competing hypotheses*.

consensus model   An analytical perspective on social organization that holds that most members of society agree as to what is right and what is wrong, and that the various elements of society work together in unison toward a common and shared vision of the greater good. Also called *consensus perspective*.

consensus theories Based on the assumption that there is agreement among people in a society over morals, values, and law.

conservatism A recent movement toward a more punitive treatment of crime and offenders, often involving religious fundamentalism, even to the extent of political involvement.

constitutional theories Theories that explain criminality by reference to offenders' body types, inheritance, genetics, or external observable physical characteristics.

constitutive criminology The study of the process by which human beings create an ideology of crime that sustains the notion of crime as a concrete reality.

containment The aspects of the social bond that act to prevent individuals from committing crimes and keep them from engaging in deviance.

containment theory A form of control theory that suggests that a series of both internal and external factors contribute to law-abiding behavior.

control-balance theory This theory combines ideas from control and deterrence theories, some "propensity" theories, and subjective theories.

control group A group of experimental subjects that, although the subject of measurement and observation, are not exposed to the experimental intervention.

controlled experiments Those which attempt to hold conditions (other than the intentionally introduced experimental intervention) constant.

control theory A perspective that predicts that when social constraints on antisocial behavior are weakened or absent, delinquent behavior emerges. Rather than stressing causative factors in criminal behavior, control theory asks why people actually obey rules instead of breaking them.

corporate crime A violation of a criminal statute either by a corporate entity or by its executives, employees, or agents acting on behalf of and for the benefit of the corporation, partnership, or other form of business entity.

correctional psychology Aspect of forensic psychology that is concerned with the diagnosis and classification of offenders, the treatment of correctional populations, and the rehabilitation of inmates and other law violators.

correlation A causal, complementary, or reciprocal relationship between two measurable variables. See also **statistical correlation**.

Cosa Nostra Literally, "our thing." A term signifying organized crime, and one of a variety of names for the "Mafia," the "Outfit," the "Mob," the "syndicate," or "the organization."

crime Human conduct in violation of the criminal laws of a state, federal government, or a local jurisdiction that has the power to make such laws.

crime-event The rationalist perspective of the theory proposes that this must be capable of gratifying the offender.

criminal anthropology The scientific study of the relationship between human physical characteristics and criminality.

criminal homicide (UCR) The causing of the death of another person without legal justification or excuse; the illegal killing of one human being by another.

criminal behavior Behavior that violates the laws that society has mandated.

criminal justice The scientific study of crime, the criminal law, and components of the criminal justice system, including the police, courts, and corrections.

criminal justice system The various agencies of justice, especially the police, courts, and corrections, whose goal it is to apprehend, convict, punish, and rehabilitate law violators.

criminal law The body of law that regulates those actions that have the potential to harm the interests of the state or the federal government.

criminal personality A psychological approach to explaining criminality based on traits, thinking, and behavior.

criminal subculture   The primary focus is on profit-making activities and violence is minimal; criminal trades would be practiced under the loose supervision of organized crime.

criminality   A behavioral predisposition that disproportionately favors criminal activity.

criminalization   The process by which behavior is classified a crime.

criminalize   To make illegal.

criminaloids   A term used by Cesare Lombroso to describe occasional criminals who were pulled into criminality primarily by environmental influences.

criminologist   One who is trained in the field of criminology. Also, one who studies crime, criminals, and criminal behavior.

criminology   An interdisciplinary profession built around the scientific study of crime and criminal behavior, including their form, causes, legal aspects, and control.

criminology of place   An emerging perspective that emphasizes the importance of geographic location and architectural features as they are associated with the prevalence of criminal victimization. (*Note:* As the term has been understood to date, environmental criminology is not the study of environmental crime, but rather a perspective that stresses how crime varies from place to place.)

critical criminology   A perspective that holds that the causes of crime are rooted in social conditions that empower the wealthy and the politically well organized, but disenfranchise those less fortunate. Also called *Marxist criminology*.

critical-incident metatheory   A theory by Williams that proposes a way to view and structure reality, thus a way to "understand" the existing evidence on crime and criminals.

cultural transmission   According to this theory, juveniles who live in socially disorganized areas have greater opportunities for exposure to those who espouse delinquent and criminal values.

culture conflict theory   A theory that sees conflict as a major social process, set in motion by the differences in values and cultures among groups of people.

cybercrime   Crime committed with the use of computers or via the manipulation of digital forms of data. Also called *computer crime*.

cyberspace   The computer-created matrix of virtual possibilities, including on-line services, wherein human beings interact with each other and with technology itself.

cyberterrorism   A form of terrorism that makes use of high technology, especially computers and the Internet, in the planning and carrying out of terrorist attacks.

cycloid   A term developed by Ernst Kretschmer to describe a particular relationship between body build and personality type.

cycloid personality   Individuals with a heavy-set, soft type of body, was said to vacillate between normality and abnormality; commits mostly nonviolent property crimes.

cynical deviants   These people exhibit an awareness of the deviant nature of their behavior, but do not care and exhibit no remorse.

dangerous drugs   A term used by the Drug Enforcement Administration (DEA) to refer to "broad categories or classes of controlled substances other than cocaine, opiates, and cannabis products." Amphetamines, methamphetamines, PCP (phencyclidine), LSD, methcathinone, and "designer drugs" are all considered "dangerous drugs."

dangerousness   The likelihood that a given individual will later harm society or others. Dangerousness is often measured in terms of recidivism, or as the likelihood of additional crime commission within a five-year period following arrest or release from confinement.

data confidentiality   The ethical requirement of social scientific research, which stipulates that research data not be shared outside of the research environment.

data encryption   The process by which information is encoded, making it unreadable to all but its intended recipients.

date rape　Unlawful forced sexual intercourse with a female against her will that occurs within the context of a dating relationship.

***Daubert* standard**　A test of scientific acceptability applicable to the gathering of evidence in criminal cases.

deconstructionist theories　Approaches that challenge existing criminological perspectives to debunk them, and that work toward replacing them with concepts more applicable to the postmodern era. Deconstructionist theories are generally postmodernist approaches, none of which have yet developed fully enough to actually deserve the name "theory."

decriminalization (of drugs)　Reduces criminal penalties associated with the personal possession of a controlled substance.

deductive framework　Moving from the general to the specific.

deductive reasoning　Reasoning that moves from given statements toward conclusions.

defensible space　Any physical area that would be better insulated against crime if those who live there recognize it as their territory and keep careful watch over the area.

definitions　Way of perceiving or interpreting a situation. Also known as *values*.

degree of integration　The form of delinquent subculture depends on the presence of this in the community.

demographics　The characteristics of groups usually expressed in statistical fashion.

demography　The study of the characteristics of population groups.

deprivation　The lack of some critical need that provides the motivation to commit deviant behavior to gain satisfaction.

deregulation　Describes a condition where the general procedural rules of a society have broken down and people do not know what to expect from each other.

descriptive statistics　Describe, summarize, or highlight the relationships within data that have been gathered.

designer drugs　New substances designed by slightly altering the chemical makeup of other illegal or tightly controlled drugs.

deterrence　The prevention of crime. According to the Classical School, this is the only justification for punishment.

deterrence strategy　A crime-control strategy that attempts "to diminish motivation for crime by increasing the perceived certainty, severity, or celerity of penalties."

deviance　Behavior that violates social norms or that is statistically different from the "average."

differential anticipation　In this theory, Glaser incorporated social learning concepts and said expectations determine conduct.

differential association　The sociological thesis that criminality, like any other form of behavior, is learned through a process of association with others who communicate criminal values.

differential identification　In this approach by Glaser, the stronger the identification with another person, the more likely an individual is to accept the other's values.

differential reinforcement　Key to Jeffery's learning theory that says people have different conditioning histories, and therefore, learn differently.

differential shaming　Posited as the "tipping point" that occurs when the direction the individual takes is not explained.

discrediting information　Information that is inconsistent with the managed impressions being communicated in a given situation.

discriminative stimuli　Do not occur after behavior, but are present either before or as the behavior occurs.

disengagement　A process of constructing rationalizations that overcomes internal inhibitions.

disintegrative shaming　The process of destroying the moral connection between the offender and the community without the intention of reconnecting the two.

disjunction   A discrepancy between goals and means that leads to strain that may result in crime or deviance.

displacement   A shift of criminal activity from one spatial location to another.

diplastic personality   Individuals who are highly emotional.

distributive justice   The notion that rightful rewards for those in society are based on cultural expectations.

DNA fingerprinting (or profiling)   The use of biological residue found at the scene of a crime for genetic comparisons in aiding the identification of criminal suspects.

domestic terrorism   The unlawful use of force or violence by a group or an individual who is based and operates entirely within the United States and its territories without foreign direction and whose acts are directed at elements of the U.S. government or population.

domestic violence   Violence that occurs within the context of the family.

dramaturgical perspective (also *dramaturgy*)   A theoretical point of view that depicts human behavior as centered around the purposeful management of interpersonal impressions.

drift   A state of limbo that makes deviant acts possible.

drug decriminalization   The minimization of criminal prohibitions with accompanying regulation of their use.

drug-defined crimes   Violations of laws prohibiting or regulating the possession, use, or distribution of illegal drugs.

drug legalization   The removal of legal prohibitions for all drugs.

drug-related crimes   Crimes in which drugs contribute to the offense (excluding violations of drug laws).

drug trafficking   Includes manufacturing, distributing, dispensing, importing, and exporting (or possession with intent to do the same) a controlled substance or a counterfeit substance.

due process   This had to be followed, according to the thought of the Classical School, to maintain that all individuals were equal before the law.

duration   In differential association, the measure of the length of time one spends exposed to the values of an influential other time.

***Durham* rule**   A standard for judging legal insanity that holds that "an accused is not criminally responsible if his unlawful act was the product of mental disease or mental defect."

early child-rearing practices   A major influence on the formation of certain propensities for some criminologists.

ecological school   Borrows from ideas of studying plants and animals in their natural environment or surroundings.

ecological theory   A type of sociological approach that emphasizes demographics (the characteristics of population groups) and geographics (the mapped location of such groups relative to one another) and sees the social disorganization that characterizes delinquency areas as a major cause of criminality and victimization. Also called *the Chicago School of criminology*.

economic marginalization   This theory states that it is the absence of real, meaningful opportunities for women that leads to increases in crime.

ectomorph   A body type originally described as thin and fragile, with long, slender, poorly muscled extremities, and delicate bones.

ego   The reality-testing part of the personality; also referred to as the reality principle. More formally, the personality component that is conscious, most immediately controls behavior, and is most in touch with external reality.

elder abuse   Abuse of older people, generally over 65, carried out by those who care for them.

electroencephalogram (EEG)   Electrical measurements of brain wave activity.

encryption   The process by which information is encoded, making it unreadable to all but its intended recipients.

endomorph A body type originally described as soft and round, or overweight.

end-to-end integrative models A structural, macro-level theory that precedes a middle-level theory; microtheory might conclude the process.

Enlightenment A social movement that arose during the eighteenth century, and built upon ideas such as empiricism, rationality, free will, humanism, and natural law. Also called the *Age of Reason*.

environmental crimes Violations of the criminal law that, although typically committed by businesses or by business officials, may also be committed by other persons or organizational entities, and that damage some protected or otherwise significant aspect of the natural environment.

environmental criminology An emerging perspective that emphasizes the importance of geographic location and architectural features as they are associated with the prevalence of criminal victimization. (*Note:* As the term has been understood to date, environmental criminology is not the study of environmental crime, but rather a perspective that stresses how crime varies from place to place.)

environmental design The idea that crime prevention should focus on changing the physical environment rather than on changing the offender.

environmental scanning A systematic effort to identify in an elemental way future developments (trends or events) that could plausibly occur over the time horizon of interest, and that might impact one's area of concern.

eros Survival instinct.

ethnic succession The continuing process whereby one immigrant or ethnic group succeeds another through assumption of a particular position in society.

etiology The branch of knowledge that studies the cause or origin of various phenomena.

eugenic criminology Theory that claimed that the root causes of criminal behavior were passed genetically from generation to generation.

eugenics The study of hereditary improvement by genetic control.

event decisions Decisions in which the tactics of carrying out an offense are determined.

evolutionary ecology An approach to understanding crime that draws attention to the ways people develop over the course of their lives.

experiential foreground What is happening at the moment is crucial to the choice to engage in criminal action.

experiment See **controlled experiments** or **quasi-experimental design**.

expert systems Computer hardware and software that attempt to duplicate the decision-making processes used by skilled investigators in the analysis of evidence and in the recognition of patterns that such evidence might represent.

external validity The ability to generalize research findings to other settings.

false consciousness Marx's theory that a group's position in society shaped its consciousness of that society; the working class was led to believe the capitalist structure of society was in their interest.

federal interest computers Those that are the property of the federal government, belong to financial institutions, or are accessed across state lines without authorization.

felony A serious criminal offense; specifically one punishable by death or by incarceration in a prison facility for a year or more.

felony murder A special class of criminal homicide whereby an offender may be charged with first-degree murder whenever his or her criminal activity results in another person's death.

feminist criminology A developing intellectual approach that emphasizes gender issues in criminology.

fencing Buying, selling, and distributing stolen goods, usually by an individual who has not been directly involved in the burglary itself.

first-degree murder Criminal homicide that is planned or involves premeditation.

focal concerns The key values of any culture, and especially the key values of a delinquent subculture.

folkways Time-honored ways of doing things. While they carry the force of tradition, their violation is unlikely to threaten the survival of the group. See also **mores**.

forcible rape (UCR) The carnal knowledge of a female forcibly and against her will. Assaults or attempts to commit rape by force or threat of force are also included in the UCR definition; however, statutory rape (without force) and other sex offenses are excluded.

foreign terrorist organization (FTO) A foreign organization that engages in terrorist activity that threatens the security of U.S. nationals or the national security of the United States and that is so designated by the U.S. secretary of state.

forensic psychiatry The branch of psychiatry having to do with the study of crime and criminality.

forfeiture The authorized seizure of money, negotiable instruments, securities, or other things of value. In federal antidrug laws, the authorization of judicial representatives to seize all monies, negotiable instruments, securities, or other things of value furnished or intended to be furnished by any person in exchange for a controlled substance, and all proceeds traceable to such an exchange.

fraud The use of trickery and deception to coerce something of value from another.

frequency In differential association, the measure of how often one is regularly exposed to the values of someone influential.

frustration-aggression theory Holds that frustration, which is a natural consequence of living, is a root cause of crime. Criminal behavior can be a form of adaptation when it results in stress reduction.

full-integrated models To borrow concepts from several theories without regard to either the assumptions or the general thrust of the theories; these concepts are then put together in a new fashion.

future criminology The study of likely futures as they impinge on crime and its control.

futures research A multidisciplinary branch of operations research whose principle aim "is to facilitate long-range planning based on (1) forecasting from the past supported by mathematical models, (2) cross-disciplinary treatment of its subject matter, (3) systematic use of expert judgment, and (4) a systems-analytical approach to its problems."

futurist One who studies the future.

general deterrence A goal of criminal sentencing that seeks to prevent others from committing crimes similar to the one for which a particular offender is being sentenced.

general strain Agnew's theory that strain exists at the individual level, primarily in unavoidable, undesirable, and stressful situations.

general theory Attempts to explain all (or at least most) forms of criminal conduct through a single, overarching approach.

goals Things people strive for, which for Merton were success and middle-class values that might not be accessible to all equally in our current society.

grounded labeling theory Melossi's suggestion that critical theorists return to their roots in labeling.

guilty but mentally ill (GBMI) A finding that an offender is guilty of the criminal offense with which they are charged, but because of their prevailing mental condition, they are generally sent to psychiatric hospitals for treatment rather than to prison. Once they have been declared "cured," however, such offenders can be transferred to correctional facilities to serve out their sentences.

habitual offender statutes Laws intended to keep repeat criminal offenders behind bars. These laws sometimes come under the rubric of "three strikes and you're out."

hacker A person who views and uses computers as objects for exploration and exploitation.

hate crimes Crimes that are motivated by a bias against a person, property, or society.

hedonism The major explanation for human behavior during the eighteenth century; the concept that people would automatically attempt to maximize pleasure and minimize pain.

hedonistic calculus   The belief, first proposed by Jeremy Bentham, that behavior holds value to any individual undertaking it according to the amount of pleasure or pain that it can be expected to produce for that person.

heroin signature program   A DEA program that identifies the geographic source area of a heroin sample through the detection of specific chemical characteristics in the sample peculiar to the source area.

homicide   The causing of the death of another person without legal justification or excuse. Also, the illegal killing of one human being by another.

hot spots   The most crime-ridden places in a city.

hypoglycemia   A condition characterized by low blood sugar.

hypothesis   (1) [A]n explanation that accounts for a set of facts and that can be tested by further investigation. (2) [S]omething that is taken to be true for the purpose of argument or investigation.

id   The aspect of the personality from which drives, wishes, urges, and desires emanate. More formally, the division of the psyche associated with instinctual impulses and demands for immediate satisfaction of primitive needs.

identity fraud   The unauthorized use of another individual's identity to gain money or goods to avoid the payment of a debt of criminal prosecution.

illegitimate opportunity   Standard illegitimate avenues used to reach cultural goals.

illegitimate opportunity structures   Subcultural pathways to success that are disapproved of by the wider society.

imitation   The notion that those who are socially inferior copy the behaviors of those who are superior.

impression management   The intentional enactment of practiced behavior that is intended to convey to others one's desirable personal characteristics and social qualities.

incapacitation   The use of imprisonment or other means to reduce the likelihood that an offender will be capable of committing future offenses.

individual rights advocates   Those who seek to protect personal freedoms in the face of criminal prosecution.

inductive reasoning   Reasoning moves from an observation to arrive at a hypothesis, and then a theory.

inferential statistics   Specify how likely findings are to be true for other populations, or in other locales.

informed consent   An ethical requirement of social scientific research, which specifies that research subjects will be informed as to the nature of the research about to be conducted, their anticipated role in it, and the uses to which the data they provide will be put.

infrastructure   The basic facilities, services, and installations needed for the functioning of a community or society, such as transportation and communications systems, water and power lines, and public institutions, including schools, post offices, and prisons.

innovation   A case of adaptation in which the emphasis on the approved goals of society is maintained while legitimate means are replaced by other, nonapproved means.

insanity (legal)   A legally established inability to understand right from wrong, or to conform one's behavior to the requirements of the law.

insanity (psychological)   Persistent mental disorder or derangement.

insider trading   Equity trading based on confidential information about important events that may affect the price of the issue being traded.

institutional strain   Anomie produced by the weakening of social institutions such as family, schools, religion, and law.

integrated theory   An explanatory perspective that merges (or attempts to merge) concepts drawn from different sources.

integrative theory   Blending existing mainstream theories with criminological truisms.

intensity   In differential association, the measure of the impact or meaningfulness of the time one spends exposed to influential individuals.

interactional theory   Thornberry's idea that social control and learning mechanisms are two-way relationships; thus, involvement in delinquency is self-reinforcing.

interactionist perspectives   Emphasize the give-and-take that occurs between offender, victim, and society, specifically between the offender and agents of formal social control such as the police, courts, and correctional organizations. Also known as *social process theories*.

interdiction   An international drug control policy that aims to stop drugs from entering the country illegally.

internal validity   The certainty that experimental interventions did indeed cause the changes observed in the study group; also the control over confounding factors, which tend to invalidate the results of an experiment.

international terrorism   The unlawful use of force or violence by a group or an individual who has some connection to a foreign power or whose activities transcend national boundaries, against people or property to intimidate or coerce a government, the civilian population, or any segment thereof, in furtherance of political or social objectives.

Internet   The world's largest computer network.

intersubjectivity   A scientific principle that requires that independent observers see the same thing under the same circumstances for observations to be regarded as valid.

involvement   Hirschi's bond of social control that measures the degree of activity available for conventional or unconventional behavior.

involvement decisions   Decisions in which the choice is made to become involved in an offense, continue with an offense, or withdraw from an offense.

irresistible-impulse test   A standard for judging legal insanity that holds that a defendant is not guilty of a criminal offense if the person, by virtue of their mental state or psychological condition, was not able to resist committing the action in question.

Jeremy Bentham   One of the best-known theorists of the Classical School, opposed the arbitrary and capricious nature of the criminal justice systems of the time.

jockeys   Professional car thieves who have an organized and consistent pattern of car theft.

joyriding   The opportunistic theft of a car for the purpose of a short-term ride, often by teenagers seeking fun and thrills.

Juke family   A well-known "criminal family" studied by Richard L. Dugdale.

just deserts   The notion that criminal offenders deserve the punishment they receive at the hands of the law, and that punishments should be appropriate to the type and severity of crime committed.

Kallikak family   A well-known "criminal family" studied by Henry H. Goddard.

kidnapping   The taking of a person against his will, usually involving the transport of that person to another location.

Kriminalpolitik   The political handling of crime, or a criminology-based social policy.

labeling theory   An interactionist perspective that sees continued crime as a consequence of limited opportunities for acceptable behavior that follow from the negative responses of society to those defined as offenders.

larceny   The unlawful taking or attempted taking of property other than a motor vehicle from the possession of another by stealth, without force or without deceit, with intent to permanently deprive the owner of the property.

larceny-theft (UCR)   The unlawful taking, carrying, leading, or riding away by stealth of property, other than a motor vehicle, from the possession or constructive possession of another, including attempts.

law and order advocates   Those who suggest that, under certain circumstances involving criminal threats to public safety, the interests of society should take precedence over individual rights.

Law Enforcement Assistance Administration (LEAA) Established under Title I of the Omnibus Crime Control and Safe Streets Act of 1967.

learning This takes place in social settings and through what the people in those settings communicate.

learning theory The general notion that crime is an acquired form of behavior.

left realism The basic notion represents a deviation from the Marxist view that all crime is a product of the capitalist system.

legal images Turk's concept that the law itself can come to be seen as something that is more important than people.

legalization (of drugs) Eliminates the laws and associated criminal penalties that prohibit the production, sale, distribution, and possession of a controlled substance.

legitimate opportunity Standard legitimate avenues used to reach cultural goals.

liberal feminism This perspective in criminology focuses on gender discrimination and women's liberation.

life course Developmental theory concept that individuals and their influencing factors change over time, usually in patterned ways

life course theories Explanations for criminality that recognize that criminogenic influences have their greatest impact during the early stages of life, and hold that childhood experiences shape individuals for the rest of their lives.

life-course persistent offenders Offenders, frequently with neurological problems, who begin antisocial behaviors in childhood and continue offending into adulthood

life history A form of folk psychology, this type of study shifted away from theoretical abstracts to the more intimate aspects of the real world.

lifestyle offender Individual's faulty thinking patterns characterized by irresponsibility, self-indulgence, interpersonal intrusiveness, and social rule breaking.

lifestyle theory A brand of rational choice theory that suggests that lifestyles contribute significantly to both the volume and type of crime found in any society.

living time Turk's concept that as time goes on, the generation of people who were a part of the old society will die out; the remaining people will be less likely to compare the new social order to the old one.

macrotheories Abstract theory that looks at whole of society and explains effects of social structure, particularly economics on crime rates.

Mafia A term signifying organized crime. Also referred to as the "Outfit," the "Mob," the "syndicate," or "the organization."

mala in se Acts that are thought to be wrong in and of themselves.

mala prohibita Acts that are wrong only because society says they are.

Marxist criminology A perspective that holds that the causes of crime are rooted in social conditions that empower the wealthy and the politically well organized, but disenfranchise those less fortunate. Also called *critical criminology*.

Marxist feminism This group of feminists see the capitalist system as exploiting subordinate groups for capital production.

mass murder The illegal killing of three or more victims at one location, within one event.

master status Conveys the notion that there are central traits to people's identities binding us to their other characteristics.

means Appropriate ways to achieve goals, which by middle-class standards, are working hard and following the rules and laws of our society.

mechanical solidarity Primitive society where all work toward group needs performing simple, nonspecialized labor.

mesomorph A body type described as athletic and muscular.

meta-analysis A study of other studies about a particular topic of interest.

metatheories   Theories about theories that are best viewed as ways of looking at and interpreting reality.

metatheory   This theory tells us how to put unit theories together, or they specify the things that should be included in unit theories about a particular subject.

microtheories   More concrete theories that explain why crime occurs at the individual level, and why this type or group of people and not others.

middle-class measuring rod   A set of standards that are difficult for the lower-class child to attain, which include sharing, delaying gratification, and respecting others' property.

misdemeanor   A criminal offense that is less serious than a felony. One is punishable by incarceration, usually in a local confinement facility, typically for a year or less.

M'Naughten **rule**   A standard for judging legal insanity that requires that either an offender did not know what he was doing, or that, if he did, that he did not know it was wrong.

Mobilization for Youth Project   A subcultural project in New York City designed to increase educational and job opportunities for youths in deprived communities.

modeling theory   This involves the process of learning by observing the behavior of others.

modes of adaptation   Merton's five ways of adapting to strain caused by restricted access to the socially approved goals and means.

money laundering   The process of converting illegally earned assets, originating as cash, to one or more alternative forms to conceal such incriminating factors as illegal origin and true ownership.

monozyotic (MZ) twins   Twins that develop from the same egg and carry virtually the same genetic material.

moral enterprise   A term that encompasses all the efforts a particular interest group makes to have its sense of propriety enacted into law.

mores   Behavioral proscriptions covering potentially serious violations of a group's values, and include strictures against murder, rape, and robbery. See also **folkways**.

motivated offender   Cohen and Felson's theory states that this must be present first in a predatory criminal event.

motor vehicle theft (UCR)   The theft or attempted theft of a motor vehicle. This offense category includes the stealing of automobiles, trucks, buses, motorcycles, motorscooters, snowmobiles, and so on.

National Crime Victimization Survey (NCVS)   Conducted annually by the Bureau of Justice Statistics (BJS) and provides data on surveyed households that report they were affected by crime.

National Incident-Based Reporting System (NIBRS)   A new form of the UCR that collects data on each single incident and arrest within 22 crime categories.

natural law   The philosophical perspective that certain immutable laws are fundamental to human nature and can be readily ascertained through reason. Man-made laws, in contrast, are said to derive from human experience and history—both of which are subject to continual change.

natural rights   The rights that, according to natural law theorists, individuals retain in the face of government action and interests.

near groups   Loosely formed gangs.

negative avoidance   Not being able to avoid an undesirable outcome or painful situation.

negligent homicide (UCR)   Causing death of another by recklessness or gross negligence.

neoclassical criminology   A contemporary version of classical criminology, which emphasizes deterrence and retribution with reduced emphasis on rehabilitation. Also known as *neoclassical perspective*.

neuroendocrinolgy   The study of the way the nervous system interacts with the endocrine system.

neurophysiology   The study of brain activity and the nervous system.

neurosis   Functional disorders of the mind or of the emotions involving anxiety, phobia, or other abnormal behavior.

neutralizations A series of rationalizations to overcome conventional values.

nurturant strategy A crime control strategy that attempts "to forestall development of criminality by improving early life experiences and channeling child and adolescent development" into desirable directions.

occupational crime Any act punishable by law that is committed through opportunity created in the course of an occupation that is legal.

offense (1) A violation of the criminal law, or in some jurisdictions, (2) a minor crime, such as jaywalking, sometimes described as "ticketable."

Office of Juvenile Justice and Delinquency Prevention (OJJDP) A part of the U.S. Department of Justice that develops and implements programs for juveniles.

operant behavior Behavior that affects the environment in such a way as to produce responses or further behavioral cues.

operationalization The process by which concepts are made measurable.

opportunity structure A path to success. Opportunity structures may be of two types: legitimate and illegitimate.

organic society Characterized by highly interactive sets of relationships, specialized labor, and individual goals.

organized crime The unlawful activities of the members of a highly organized, disciplined association engaged in supplying illegal goods and services, including but not limited to gambling, prostitution, loan-sharking, narcotics, and labor racketeering.

Panopticon House A prison designed by Jeremy Bentham, which was to be a circular building with cells along the circumference, each clearly visible from a central location staffed by guards.

paradigm An example, model, or theory.

paranoid schizophrenics Schizophrenic individuals who suffer from delusions and hallucinations.

Part I offenses Group of offenses, also called "major offenses" or "index offenses," for which the UCR publishes counts of reported instances, and which consist of murder, rape, robbery, aggravated assault, burglary, larceny, auto theft, and arson.

participant observation A variety of strategies in data gathering in which the researcher observes a group by participating, to varying degrees, in the activities of the group.

participatory justice A relatively informal type of criminal justice case processing that makes use of local community resources rather than requiring traditional forms of official intervention.

paternalism Idea that females need to be protected for their own good, which some feel may explain why women may receive differential treatment within the criminal justice system.

peace model An approach to crime control that focuses on effective ways for developing a shared consensus on critical issues that have the potential to seriously affect the quality of life.

peacemaking This perspective looks at the entire enterprise of criminal justice and argues that we are going about things the wrong way.

peacemaking criminology A perspective that holds that crime-control agencies and the citizens they serve should work together to alleviate social problems and human suffering and thus reduce crime.

penal couple A term that describes the relationship between victim and criminal. Also, the two individuals most involved in the criminal act—the offender and the victim.

penology The study of the techniques of crime control, the punishment of criminals, and the management of prisons.

personality An individual's unique set of characteristics determines his temperament, motivation, and behavior.

pharmaceutical diversion The process by which legitimately manufactured controlled substances are diverted for illicit use.

phenomenological criminology   The study of crime as a social phenomenon that is created through a process of social interaction.

phenomenology   The emphasis on understanding the motives and intents of the people involved in committing crime. The study of the contents of human consciousness without regard to external conventions or prior assumptions.

phone phreak   A person who uses switched, dialed-access telephone services as objects for exploration and exploitation.

phrenology   The study of the shape of the head to determine anatomical correlates of human behavior. The chief practitioners of this believed that the characteristics of the brain are mirrored in bumps in the skull.

pink-collar ghetto   Where pay is low and work is unrewarding for women.

piracy   The unauthorized and illegal copying of software programs.

pluralism   Oriented toward multiple groups.

pluralistic perspective   An analytical approach to social organization that holds that a multiplicity of values and beliefs exist in any complex society, but that most social actors agree on the usefulness of law as a formal means of dispute resolution.

pornography   The sale of sexually explicit material.

position in the social structure   The higher one's position, the lower the risk of victimization.

positive blockage   The imposition of specific forces that stop progress toward a desired goal or outcome.

positivism   A product of eighteenth century Enlightenment philosophy, emphasizing the importance of reason and experience.

postcrime victimization or secondary victimization   Refers to problems in living, which tend to follow from initial victimization.

postmodern criminology   A brand of criminology that developed following World War II, and that builds upon the tenants inherent in postmodern social thought.

postmodernism   Theories that developed as a reaction to and a critique of modern positivistic approaches.

power   The central concept of pluralist conflict theories.

power-control theory   A perspective that holds that the distribution of crime and delinquency within society is to some degree founded upon the consequences that power relationships within the wider society hold for domestic settings, and for the everyday relationships between men, women, and children within the context of family life.

primary conflict   Occurs when individual is caught between two different cultures governing behavior.

Primary data   Data gathered for a distinct purpose.

primary deviance   Initial deviance often undertaken to deal with transient problems in living.

primary research   Research characterized by original and direct investigation.

priority   In differential association, the value and emphasis that one places on certain relationships and associations over others.

process theories   Attempt to explain how people become criminal, usually in steps as critical events occur.

proletariat   In Marxian theory, the working class.

propensity to crime   Gottfredson & Hirschi's idea that some people are predisposed with low self-control that entices individuals and promises pleasure from crime and deviance.

proposition   A statement that indicates a relationship between at least two properties.

prostitution   The act of engaging in sexual behavior for money or its equivalent.

protection/avoidance strategy   A crime-control strategy that attempts to reduce criminal opportunities by changing people's routine activities, increasing guardianship, or by incapacitating convicted offenders.

psychiatric criminology   The branch of psychiatry having to do with the study of crime and criminality.

psychiatric theories Derived from the medical sciences, including neurology, and that, like other psychological theories, focus on the individual as the unit of analysis.

psychoactive substances That which affect the mind, mental processes, or emotions.

psychoanalysis The theory of human psychology founded by Freud on the concepts of the unconscious, resistance, repression, sexuality, and the Oedipus complex.

psychoanalytic criminology A psychiatric approach developed by Freud that emphasizes the role of personality in human behavior, and that sees deviant behavior as the result of dysfunctional personalities.

psychological profiling The attempt to categorize, understand, and predict the behavior of certain types of offenders based upon behavioral clues they provide.

psychological theories Derived from the behavioral sciences and focus on the individual as the unit of analysis. Psychological theories place the locus of crime causation within the personality of the individual offender. Also known as *psychological perspective*.

psychopath (psychopathy) A person with a personality disorder, especially one manifested in aggressively antisocial behavior, which is often said to be the result of a poorly developed superego.

psychopathology The study of pathological mental conditions; that is, mental illness.

psychosis A form of mental illness in which sufferers are said to be out of touch with reality.

psychotherapy A form of psychiatric treatment based upon psychoanalytical principles and techniques.

public order crime A crime that does not clearly create harm to society and that does not have a clear victim.

public policy A course of action that government takes in an effort to solve a problem or to achieve an end.

punishment Undesirable behavioral consequences likely to decrease the frequency of occurrence of that behavior.

pure research Research undertaken simply for the sake of advancing scientific knowledge.

qualitative methods Research techniques that produce results that are difficult to quantify.

quantitative[Au: Missing word here?] The development of research skills and techniques, incorporating statistical tests of theory usually using large aggregate data sets.

quantitative methods Research techniques that produce measurable results.

quasi-experimental designs Approaches to research that, although less powerful than experimental designs, are deemed worthy of use where better designs are not feasible.

Racketeer Influenced and Corrupt Organizations (RICO) A statute that was part of the Federal Organized Crime Control Act of 1970, which developed broader definitions of racketeering and made punishments harsher.

radical criminology A perspective that holds that the causes of crime are rooted in social conditions that empower the wealthy and the politically well organized, but disenfranchise those who are less fortunate. Also called *Marxist criminology* or *critical criminology*.

radical feminism Its primary focus is on the way in which power is constructed and dominated by males in society.

randomization The process whereby individuals are assigned to study groups without biases or differences resulting from selection.

rape (NCVS) Carnal knowledge through the use of force or the threat of force, including attempts. Statutory rape (without force) is excluded. Both heterosexual and homosexual rapes are included.

rational choice theory A perspective that holds that criminality is the result of conscious choice, and that predicts that individuals choose to commit crime when the benefits outweigh the costs of disobeying the law.

rationality The decision-making process of determining the opportunities for meeting needs, the potential costs of action, and the anticipated benefits.

reaction formation   The process in which a person openly rejects that which he or she wants, or aspires to, but cannot obtain or achieve.

realist criminology   An emerging perspective that insists upon a pragmatic assessment of crime and associated problems.

rebellion   This mode of adaptation focuses on the substitution of new goals and means for the original ones.

recidivism   The repetition of criminal behavior.

recidivism rate   The percentage of convicted offenders who have been released from prison and who are later rearrested for a new crime, generally within five years following release.

reinforcement   Any event that follows the occurrence of behavior and that alters and increases the frequency of the behavior.

reintegrative shaming   The process of humiliating or condemning the offender publicly in order to prepare him to re-enter the community with better awareness and sensitivity toward the need for conforming behavior

relative deprivation   The feeling that because of social inequality, they are not offered equal opportunities to achieve legitimate success.

replicability (experimental)   A scientific principle that holds that the same observations made at one time can be made again at a later time if all other conditions are the same.

research   The use of standardized, systematic procedures in the search for knowledge.

research design   The logic and structure inherent in an approach to data gathering.

research methods   The various methods that structure and offer logic to data gathering.

restitution   A criminal sanction, in particular the payment of compensation by the offender to the victim.

restorative justice   A postmodern perspective that stresses "remedies and restoration rather than prison, punishment and victim neglect."

retreatism   This mode of adaptation involves a rejection of both the goals and means.

retreatist subculture   Their primary focus is on drugs, and their gang-related activities are designed to bring them the money for their drug use.

retribution   The act of taking revenge upon a criminal perpetrator.

retrospective interpretation   Provides us with an idea of how identities can be reconstructed to fit a new label.

reward   Desirable behavioral consequences likely to increase the frequency of occurrence of that behavior.

ritualism   A mode of adaptation where the goals themselves are rejected and the focus in shifted to the means.

robbery (UCR)   The unlawful taking or attempted taking of property that is in the immediate possession of another by force or threat of force or violence and/or by putting the victim in fear.

routine activities theory or lifestyle theory   A brand of rational choice theory that suggests that lifestyles contribute significantly to both the volume and type of crime found in any society.

satiation   No longer experiencing a need or drive; to be fulfilled in a way that curtails further motivations.

scenario writing   A technique intended to predict future outcomes, and that builds upon environmental scanning by attempting to assess the likelihood of a variety of possible outcomes once important trends have been identified.

schedule of consequences   Refers to the frequency and probability with which a particular consequence will occur, as well as to the length of time it will occur after the behavior.

schizoid personality   Individuals with athletic, muscular bodies, deemed more likely to be schizophrenic.

schizophrenics   Mentally ill individuals who suffer from disjointed thinking and, possibly, delusions and hallucinations.

scientific method   A methodology that relies on observable, empirical, and measurable evidence to prove a hypothesis.

secondary analysis   The reanalysis of existing data.

secondary conflict   Smaller cultures existing within a larger culture begin, over a period of time, to create their own set of values where there are enough differences to cause conflict.

secondary data   Data collected for reasons other than a specific research project, usually by government agencies, private foundations, or private businesses.

secondary deviance   This concept suggests that, in addition to audience reaction, there is the possibility an individual will react to the label.

secondary research   New evaluations of existing information that has already been collected by other researchers.

second-degree murder   Criminal homicide that is unplanned, and that is often described as a "crime of passion."

securities fraud   The theft of money resulting from intentional manipulation of the value of equities, including stocks and bonds. Securities fraud may also include theft from securities accounts and wire fraud.

selective incapacitation   A social policy that seeks to protect society by incarcerating those individuals deemed to be the most dangerous.

self-control theory   Focused on the individual rather than on external sources of control.

self-interest   Human behavior tends to revolve around this, as self-preservation and gratification are characteristic of human nature.

self-interested behavior   Behavior serving to provide pleasure to an individual; basis for impulsivity in Gottfredson & Hirschi's low self-control theory.

self-report surveys   Surveys in which individuals report on their own criminal activity.

serial murder   Criminal homicide that involves the killing of several victims in three or more separate events.

sexism   Refers to attitudes or practices having the effect of producing inequality between the sexes.

simple assault (NCVs)   An attack without a weapon resulting either in minor injury or in undetermined injury requiring less than two days of hospitalization.

situational choice theory   A brand of rational choice theory that views criminal behavior "as a function of choices and decisions made within a context of situational constraints and opportunities."

situational crime prevention   A social policy approach that looks to develop greater understanding of crime and more effective crime prevention strategies through concern with the physical, organizational, and social environments that make crime possible.

social bond   The rather intangible link between individuals and the society of which they are a part. The social bond is created through the process of socialization.

social bond theory   A theory that looks at the rather intangible link between individuals and the society of which they are a part and the role socialization plays in that link.

social capital   The degree of positive relationships with other persons and with social institutions that individuals build up over the course of their lives.

social class   Distinctions made between individuals on the basis of important defining social characteristics.

social contract   The Enlightenment-era concept that human beings abandon their natural state of individual freedom to join together and form society. Although, in the process of forming a social contract, individuals surrender some freedoms to society as a whole, government, once formed, is obligated to assume responsibilities toward its citizens and to provide for their protection and welfare.

social control theory   A perspective that predicts that when social constraints on antisocial behavior are weakened or absent, delinquent behavior emerges. Rather than stressing causative factors in criminal behavior, control theory asks why people actually obey rules instead of breaking them.

social development perspective   A perspective that looks at how an individual's rate of crime fluctuates over time.

social disorganization theory   A condition said to exist when a group is faced with social change, uneven development of culture, maladaptiveness, disharmony, conflict, and lack of consensus.

social dynamite   According to Spitzer, these groups include political activists, criminals, and revolutionaries.

social ecology theory   An approach to criminological theorizing that attempts to link the structure and organization of human community to interactions with its localized environment.

social epidemiology   The study of social epidemics and diseases of the social order.

social junk   According to Spitzer, as long as the problem group is relatively quiet and poses no immediate threat to the ruling class, there is little need to expend scarce resources on their control.

social learning theory   A psychological perspective that says people learn how to behave by modeling themselves after others whom they have the opportunity to observe.

social pathology   A concept that compares society to a physical organism and sees criminality as an illness.

social policies   Government initiatives, programs, and plans intended to address problems in society. The "war on crime," for example, is a kind of generic (large-scale) social policy—one consisting of many smaller programs.

social problems perspective   The belief that crime is a manifestation of underlying social problems such as poverty, discrimination, pervasive family violence, inadequate socialization practices, and the breakdown of traditional social institutions.

social process theories   Emphasize the give-and-take that occurs between offender, victim, and society—and specifically between the offender and agents of formal social control such as the police, courts, and correctional organizations. Also known as *interactionist perspectives*.

social reality   Six propositions from theorist Richard Quinney, whose theory incorporated concepts from differential association, social learning, and labeling.

social relativity   The notion that social events are differently interpreted according to the cultural experiences and personal interests of the initiator, the observer, or the recipient of that behavior.

social responsibility perspective   A viewpoint that holds that individuals are fundamentally responsible for their own behavior, and that they choose crime over other, more law-abiding courses of action.

social roles   Based on the expectations of others, people conduct themselves in certain ways and construct lifestyles more or less conducive to victimization.

social structure   The pattern of social organization and the interrelationships between institutions characteristic of a society.

social structure approach   Theories that attempt to explain crime by reference to various aspects of the social fabric. Specifically, they look at the relationships among social institutions and describe the types of behavior that tend to characterize groups of people as opposed to individuals.

socialist feminism   Uniting radical and Marxist principles, this group identifies the oppression of women as a symptom of the patriarchal capitalist system.

socialization   The lifelong process of social experience whereby individuals acquire the cultural patterns of their society.

social structural theories   Explain crime by reference to various aspects of the social fabric. They emphasize relationships between social institutions, and describe the types of behavior that tend to characterize groups of people as opposed to individuals.

societal reaction school   A position in which those associated with labeling argued that earlier theories had placed too great a reliance on the individual deviant and neglected the variety of ways people could react to deviance.

society at large audience   These people are primarily important as a group with the ability to define good and bad, and to stir the authorities into action.

society of saints   Durkheim's example illustrating that crime serves a boundary maintenance function.

sociobiology   The systematic study of the biological basis of all social behavior.

sociopath   A person with a personality disorder, especially one manifested in aggressively antisocial behavior, which is often said to be the result of a poorly developed superego.

soft free will   Matza's drift concept used in rational theories built on the classical perspective that although behavior is deterministic there is some limited degree of individual choice in actions of deviance.

software piracy   The unauthorized and illegal copying of software programs.

somatotypes   Explanation of categories of a combination of body types and personality temperaments that may be associated with delinquency.

somatotyping   The classification of human beings into types according to body build and other physical characteristics.

Sourcebook of Criminal Statistics   An annual report on crime statistics organized in tables, which provides characteristics of the criminal justice system, attitudes toward crime, and the distribution of offenses.

Southerness hypothesis   This theory attempts to explain why the southern region of the United States has a higher homicide rate than other regions.

specific deterrence   A goal of criminal sentencing that seeks to prevent a particular offender from engaging in repeat criminality.

state-organized crime   Acts defined by law as criminal and committed by state officials in the pursuit of their job as representatives of the state.

statistical correlation   The simultaneous increase or decrease in value of two numerically valued random variables. Also called *correlation*.

statistical school   A criminological perspective with roots in the early 1800s that seeks to uncover correlations between crime rates and other types of demographic data.

status frustration   Lower-class children lose ground in the search for status and suffer from this.

statute   A formal written enactment of a legislative body.

statutory law   Law in the form of statutes or formal written strictures, made by a legislature or governing body with the power to make law.

stigmatic shaming   Form of shaming, imposed as a sanction by the criminal justice system that is thought to destroy the moral bond between the offender and the community.

strain   These theories require that people be motivated to commit criminal and delinquent acts.

strain theory   A sociological approach which posits a disjuncture between socially and subculturally sanctioned means and goals as the cause of criminal behavior. Also known as *anomie theory*.

strategic assessment   A technique that assesses the risks and opportunities facing those who plan for the future.

structure theories   Focus on the way society is organized, the distribution of power, and its effect on behavior.

subcultural theory   A sociological perspective that emphasizes the contribution made by variously socialized cultural groups to the phenomenon of crime.

subculture   A collection of values and preferences that is communicated to subcultural participants through a process of socialization.

subculture of violence   Those in this subculture learn a willingness to resort to violence and share a favorable attitude toward the use of violence.

subjective theory   Shuns statistics and focuses on describing the essence of behavior or why people do certain things.

sublimation   The psychological process whereby one aspect of consciousness comes to be symbolically substituted for another.

substantial-capacity test   A standard for judging legal insanity that requires that a person lack "the mental capacity needed to understand the wrongfulness of his act, or to conform his behavior to the requirements of the law."

subterranean values Respectable values that are present in the larger culture.

suitable target Something worth stealing or taking, or that has the appearance of worth.

superego The moral aspect of the personality; much like the conscience. More formally, the division of the psyche that develops by the incorporation of the perceived moral standards of the community, is mainly unconscious, and includes the conscience.

supermale A human male displaying the XYY chromosome structure.

superpredators A new generation of juveniles "who are coming of age in actual and 'moral poverty' without the benefits of parents, teachers, coaches, and clergy to teach them right from wrong and show them 'unconditional love.'" The term is often applied to inner-city youths who meet the criteria it sets forth.

surplus value The capitalist exploitation of the difference between the cost of production and the value of the product.

survey research A social science data-gathering technique that involves the use of questionnaires.

symbolic interaction Developed from a belief that human behavior is the product of purely social symbols communicated between individuals.

tagging Like labeling, the process whereby an individual is negatively defined by agencies of justice.

target hardening The reduction in criminal opportunity, generally through the use of physical barriers, architectural design, and enhanced security measures, of a particular location.

techniques of crime The specific skills and abilities one needs to learn from more experienced associates.

techniques of neutralization These techniques allow individuals to neutralize and temporarily suspend their commitment to societal values, thus providing the freedom to commit delinquent acts.

TEMPEST A standard developed by the U.S. government that requires that electromagnetic emanations from computers designated as "secure" be below levels that would allow radio receiving equipment to "read" the data being computed.

terrorism Premeditated, politically motivated violence perpetrated against noncombatant targets by subnational groups or clandestine agents, usually intended to influence an audience.

testability of theory To be able to apply the principles of a theory in an empirical or experimental setting to see if there is evidence of support.

testosterone The primary male sex hormone, produced in the testes and functioning to control secondary sex characteristics and sexual drive.

tests of significance Statistical techniques intended to provide researchers with confidence that their results are in fact true, and not the result of sampling error.

Thanatos A death wish.

theory A series of interrelated propositions that attempt to describe, explain, predict, and ultimately control some class of events. A theory gains explanatory power from inherent logical consistency, and is "tested" by how well it describes and predicts reality.

threat analysis Involves a complete and thorough assessment of the kinds of perils facing an organization. Also known as *risk analysis*.

three-strikes A provision of some criminal statutes that mandates life imprisonment for criminals convicted of three violent felonies or serious drug offenses.

total institutions Facilities from which individuals can rarely come and go, and in which communal life is intense and circumscribed. Individuals in total institutions tend to eat, sleep, play, learn, and worship (if at all) together.

trafficking Includes manufacturing, distributing, dispensing, importing, and exporting (or possession with intent to do the same) a controlled substance or a counterfeit substance.

traits The general theory of crime declares individuals have certain characteristics such as impulsivity, insensitivity, self-centeredness, and lower than average intelligence.

trephination A form of surgery, typically involving bone, especially the skull. Early instances of cranial trephination have been taken as evidence for primitive beliefs in spirit possession.

turning points Events at various stages during life, affecting cohorts of people that strengthen or weaken social bonds and chances of engaging in criminal activity.

Twelve Tables Early Roman laws written around 450 B.C., which regulated family, religious, and economic life.

unicausal Having one cause. Theories that are unicausal posit only one source for all that they attempt to explain.

Uniform Crime Reports (UCR) A summation of crime statistics tallied annually by the Federal Bureau of Investigation (FBI) and consisting primarily of data on crimes and arrests reported to the police.

unit theories Emphasize a particular problem and make testable assertions about that problem.

utilitarianism The belief, first proposed by Jeremy Bentham, that behavior holds value to any individual undertaking according to the amount of pleasure or pain that it can be expected to produce for that person. Also known as *hedonistic calculus*.

variable A concept that can undergo measurable changes.

verstehen The kind of subjective understanding that can be achieved by criminologists who immerse themselves into the everyday world of the criminals they study.

victim-impact statement A written document that describes the losses, suffering, and trauma experienced by the crime victim or by the victim's survivors. In jurisdictions where victim-impact statements are used, judges are expected to consider them in arriving at an appropriate sentence for the offender.

victim lifestyles Examining the associations, environment, and activities of individuals for indicators of high risk for victimization.

victimization rate (NCVS) A measure of the occurrence of victimizations among a specified population group. For personal crimes, this is based on the number of victimizations per 1,000 residents age 12 or older. For household crimes, the victimization rates are calculated using the number of incidents per 1,000 households.

victimogenesis The contributory background of a victim as a result of which he or she becomes prone to victimization.

victimology The study of victims and their contributory role, if any, in crime causation.

victim-precipitated homicides Killings in which the "victim" was the first to commence the interaction or was the first to resort to physical violence.

victim proneness The degree of an individual's likelihood of victimization.

Victims of Crime Act (VOCA) Passed by the U.S. Congress in 1984. Regulates the Crime Victim Fund, which assists with various programs that benefit the victims of crime.

victim-witness assistance programs Counsel victims, orient them to the justice process, and provide a variety of other services such as transportation to court, child care during court appearances, and referrals to social service agencies.

virus (computer) A set of computer instructions that propagates copies or versions of itself into computer programs or data when it is executed.

white-collar crime Violations of the criminal law committed by a person of respectability and high social status in the course of his or her occupation.

women's liberation This 1970s movement was instrumental in bringing feminist issues to the surface.